Embassy Kid

Embassy Kid

An American Foreign Service Family Memoir

Kid

J.K. Amerson López

Illustrations by Camila Acosta Sánchez

Westphalia Press
An Imprint of the Policy Studies Organization
Washington, DC

ADST MEMOIRS AND OCCASIONAL PAPERS SERIES
Series Editors: LISA TERRY & MARGERY THOMPSON

In 2003, the Association for Diplomatic Studies and Training (ADST), a non-profit organization founded in 1986, created the Memoirs and Occasional Papers Series to preserve firsthand accounts and other informed observations on foreign affairs for scholars, journalists, and the general public. Through its book series, its Foreign Affairs Oral History program, and its support for the training of foreign affairs personnel at the State Department's Foreign Service Institute, ADST seeks to promote understanding of American diplomacy and those who conduct it. In this compelling memoir, J.K. Amerson López vividly recounts the extraordinary journey of an American foreign service family, capturing the unique challenges and profound experiences of growing up across different continents during pivotal moments in history.

RELATED TITLES FROM ADST SERIES

THOMPSON BUCHANAN, *Mossy Memoir of a Rolling Stone*

CHARLES T. CROSS, *Born a Foreigner: A Memoir of the American Presence in Asia*

JOHN GUNTHER DEAN, *Danger Zones: A Diplomat's Fight for America's Interests*

PETER D. EICHER, *Raising the Flag: Adventures of America's First Envoys in Faraway Lands*

BRANDON GROVE, *Behind Embassy Walls: The Life and Times of an American Diplomat*

DONALD P. GREGG, *Pot Shards: Fragments of a Life Lived in CIA, the White House, and the Two Koreas*

ALLEN C. HANSEN, *Nine Lives: A Foreign Service Odyssey*

CAMERON R. HUME, *Mission to Algiers: Diplomacy by Engagement*

DENNIS JETT, *American Ambassadors: The Past, Present, and Future of America's Diplomats*

WILLIAM MORGAN and CHARLES STUART KENNEDY, eds., *American Diplomats: The Foreign Service at Work*

DAVID D. NEWSOM, *Witness to a Changing World*

*For a complete list of series titles, visit **adst.org/publications***

*To Mom and Dad, who gave us the world,
to Susie, who shared it with me,
and to all the other American foreign service families
before and since.*

A Call and Farewell

(1964)

I cannot leave this place
This town
Or any land
But must look back
And then I see
One beckoning
And gently waving hand.

James T. Robb, Sr., my grandfather,
upon leaving Bogotá, Colombia

Laboring in the vineyards of cross-cultural communication, winning over the hearts and minds of international audiences, helping build global peace and freedom: I tingled with excitement. Nancy was willing to try it out for a year or two.

My father, Robert Clayton Amerson

I was such a homebody that I didn't even go to sleepovers as a kid. This was supposed to be Bob's two-year adventure. The baby might learn some Spanish, and the year-round springtime weather of Caracas would be a welcomed break from Minnesota winters. I didn't realize that Uncle Sam would also require something from me. How naïve that all sounds now.

My mother, Nancy Robb Amerson

We grew up like everyone else.

My sister, Susan Robb Amerson Hartnett

Don't worry, Mommy. This is pretend. I'm an American.

Jane Kelly Amerson López

TABLE OF CONTENTS

PREFACE

"Where are you from?"

It's a very American question. Our country's melting pot character makes our individual origins a critical part of the United States' cultural identity. Ancestry tracing has become big business.

For many years, however, I struggled to answer the question. I was born in Minnesota, but my father's diplomatic work took our family to eight cities in six countries on three continents before I was eighteen. My blue eyes and blond hair show my Norwegian ancestry, but Spanish was my first language. Overseas, my father's embassy employment made my identity as an American crystal clear, but I felt like a foreign girl when we moved stateside.

When I was in second grade in the ancient city of Rome, I was sure that I'd grow up to be an archaeologist. That goal evaporated when we moved to another part of the world, but I now realize that I have spent the better part of my adult life sifting through the detritus of my childhood, looking for the evidence of where I am from.

My memories, family lore, and my parents' books, journals, letters, and interviews, revealed this story of an ordinary American family living through extraordinary times in the service of their country—when America was the undisputed leader of the Free World, and the tenets of democracy were the bedrock of American patriotism.

This, then, is where I am from. I am an Embassy Kid.

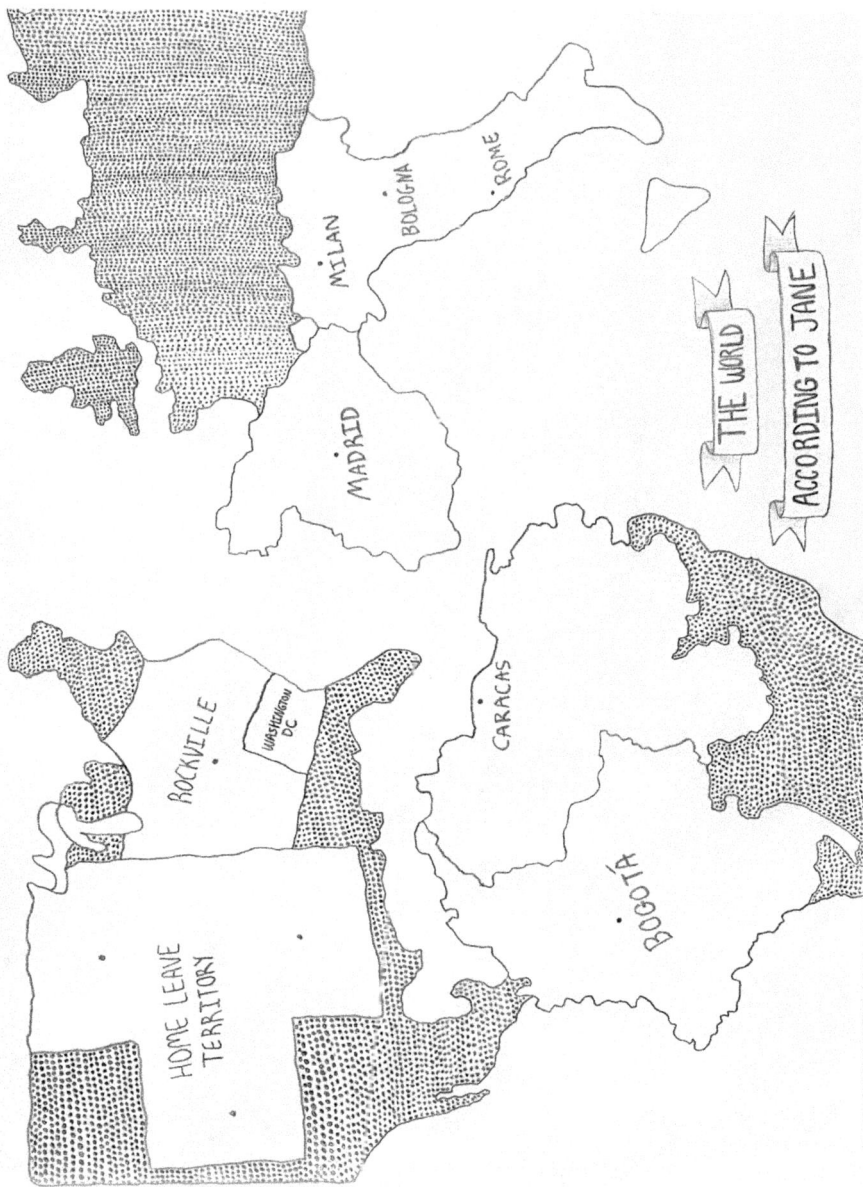

THE WORLD

ACCORDING TO JANE

MILAN
BOLOGNA
ROME

MADRID

ROCKVILLE
WASHINGTON DC

HOME LEAVE
TERRITORY

CARACAS

BOGOTÁ

Part I

Caracas

(1955-59)

*We were two little girls, spouting Fina-taught Spanish
as our first language, singing, counting, imitating.*

1

1. REVOLUTION

The telephone rang, sharp and insistent, shocking my mother upright in bed. It was January 23, 1958. The clock glowed 3:00 a.m. Family, it must be family. Caracas was so far from home.

The phone trilled again.

My father's long legs had propelled him into the living room. He picked up the receiver before the telephone could sound the alarm again. "Bob Amerson here."

My mother's feet sought out her slippers, an instinct informed by the dangers lurking in Venezuela's tropical soil. No need to aggravate the hepatitis. She pulled on her robe and hurried to my father's side.

"Roger that." My father hung up and adjusted his tortoise-shell glasses. "That was Harry." Harry Casler, Dad's boss at the US Embassy, was covering the telephone lines this week.

Mom exhaled as she plopped down on the sofa. So, it wasn't bad news from home.

Dad continued. "It's happened, Nan. PJ is out."

The three words dropped like lead.

The ruthless Venezuelan dictator Marcos Pérez Jiménez—PJ, as they called him at the embassy—had ruled with an iron fist since 1952.

"Out?"

"Harry said he's flying into exile, just took off from La Carlota near the palace." My father spoke over his shoulder as he went into the bedroom for his slippers and bathrobe.

As press attaché, my father's network of contacts within the underground resistance had kept the embassy abreast of the highly combustible situation for months now. Clandestine political movements and dissidents within the military had pushed against the repressive regime's widespread corruption in oil-rich Venezuela. The dreaded Seguridad Nacional, Pérez Jiménez' political police, suppressed criticism and imprisoned those who opposed the dictator. Civil rights violations and the torture of political prisoners were well known.

"We knew things were about to break loose," my father said as he returned to the living room. "The strike got all that rioting going on downtown, and they've finally succeeded."

A general strike had spiked the revolutionary pressure, with mobs roving the downtown area to express their anger. People had been killed near the American Embassy. But that was miles from our quiet, tree-lined residential *barrio*.

My father sat back down in the easy chair by the telephone. "The flight path from La Carlota will take the plane right over us. We should be hearing it in a minute."

The night was going to get a lot louder. "I'll go see to the girls," my mother said as she stood and tightened her bathrobe belt.

She walked down the short hallway to the second bedroom and swung open the door. I didn't stir and Susie was sound asleep, curled around her baby blanket.

"*¿Señora?*"

My mother jumped. Josefina's quiet slippers hadn't given her away as the maid approached from her room behind the kitchen.

My mother gave my sleeping baby sister and me one more look, then silently shut the bedroom door. She straightened her shoulders, assuming the authoritative role that she had grown into over nearly four years. *La señora de la casa,* the lady of the house, couldn't betray her nerves, even though it still felt pretty unreal to this modest Minnesotan to have a maid. Even one that felt like a member of the family.

My mother turned to face our maid. "Josefina," she said in a voice just above a whisper, *"Pérez Jiménez se va."* Pérez Jiménez is leaving.

"*¡Ay Dios mio!*" Oh, my God. Josefina had survived Spain's brutal civil war. Government transitions were bloody affairs.

"*Cálmese.*" Calm down, my mother said. She put a steadying hand on Josefina's sturdy shoulder.

"*Las niñas.*" The girls. Josefina made a move toward the bedroom door.

My mother tightened her grip. The last thing they needed right now was two kids worrying about why they were awake in the middle of the night.

My mother looked Josefina in the eye. "Fina," she said, using the familiar form of the maid's name, *"Cálmese."* Calm down. It was as if she were telling one of us girls to settle down. She could do more with a quiet tone and a look than an excitable mother could do with a yell.

My mother steered Fina down the hall and into the living room.

My father looked up from the open briefcase on his lap, his index finger marking a line on the paperwork. "Fina." He nodded and then returned to scanning the papers.

My mother settled herself and Fina on the pheasant-print sofa. It had been a wedding gift from her in-laws on the farm in South Dakota. The contrast between the prairie images and the bright colors of Caracas normally coaxed a smile. Tonight, the distance between the Midwest and Venezuela felt much farther than three thousand miles. Sitting and waiting didn't help.

She stood up. "How about some coffee? *¿Fina, nos haces un café?*" The maid got to her feet, ready.

My father lifted his finger off the page. "Harry said we'd hear the plane." He looked up at the ceiling. "And here it comes."

The two women followed his gaze. A fat cockroach crawled across the ceiling toward the corner over the bookcase. The faint rumble of a propeller airplane sounded in the distance, growing louder as it approached. It built to a roar, shaking the house. As the airplane thundered overhead, the bug dropped to the linoleum, and the glass ashtray on the coffee table trembled. The sound slowly diminished into nothing.

My father broke the spell with a small salute. "*Adiós, señor presidente.*" Goodbye, Mr. President.

Fina let out a short cry, and my mother said, "*¿Fina, el café, por favor?*" The coffee please?

The maid headed to the kitchen, mumbling rosary incantations under her breath. My mother followed to check on Susie and me. We were still curled under our sheets. The resiliency of kids. She walked back into the living room.

"Thank goodness the girls slept through that," she said. She sat at the edge of the couch.

"So, should we be doing something? What's the plan?"

"We're to sit tight. Hard to tell what's going to happen, but better to be here together than to get caught up by a crowd in the street." My father held up the telephone tree paperwork that the embassy team had prepared. "This is how we're staying connected."

"Do you think we should call my parents?" my mother asked.

"Well, no need to alarm your folks, I think. Let them keep the Caracas of their visit."

"I suppose." She sighed. Tonight, Caracas was a different place from the easygoing, eternally springtime city she had shared with my grandparents two years before. "So, Bob, if PJ is out, who's in charge?"

"That's what makes this moment so interesting," my father said, his voice barely containing his excitement. "There might even be a chance for democracy. And what a front-row seat. Just think, this might have happened while we were on home leave last year back in the States."

"Yes, that would have been ..." My mother's words trailed off. It would have been so much better to be safe in the Midwest while this crazy country figured itself out. But that wasn't the deal they had signed up for with Washington. The short-term embassy assignment had felt like a brief tropical interlude. Now, nearly four years in, it had become a full-fledged adventure.

My father turned on Radio Caracas. Sporadic news bulletins interrupted the familiar rhythms of Venezuelan folk tunes on the nightly program, *Música Criolla.* Each announcement reflected a scenario that was still evolving—that the completely united army had overthrown the regime; that some army rebels, along with other armed forces and civilians, were the heroes; that there was violence downtown. Excited voices urged citizens to stay home, to remain calm, to refrain from harming foreigners.

When the staff at the Canadian Embassy had approached their American counterparts several months before about consolidating evacuations, the chances of needing such a plan seemed remote. Maybe not anymore. Dad turned down the radio.

"Let me give Russ a call." His embassy colleague lived in our Zucatarate neighborhood. My father spoke quietly into the receiver as Fina arrived with the coffee.

"*¿Algo más?*" Will there be anything else?

My mother forced her lips into a smile. "*No, gracias,* Fina." No, thank you.

The maid nodded. "*Pues, buenas noches.*" Good night, then. Fina returned to her room.

My mother took a sip of the strong coffee. None of that wimpy American brew down here. There was so much they truly loved about this place. She took another sip, allowing the liquid heat to relax her back into the sofa.

My father hung up the phone and turned the radio back up a bit. "Okay, so maybe there's something."

My mother snapped to high alert.

"We may want to hide the car," he said.

"Hide the car?"

"They're looking for PJ's head honchos. A mob mistook Russ's diplomatic plates for Venezuelan regime issue. Lucky for them, the men headed down the block before Russ shot his gun."

"His gun?" My mother sat up straighter. "We don't have a gun." She paused. "Dad's hunting gun."

"Well, yes, we have your father's gun, but no, I don't think it's going to come to that."

The radio crackled as an enthusiastic announcer broke in. "*¡Periodistas!*" Journalists! He continued in Spanish, "You are finally free. Tell the public that the dictator is gone!"

"Imagine that," my father said. "An uncensored newspaper."

"The car?" my mother prompted. The diplomatic plates on the Oldsmobile sitting in our driveway a few feet from the street could easily be confused with those issued for the Venezuelan government. "Do you think maybe we should put out the American flag?

I mean, we're the good guys, right?"

My father considered the suggestion. "Well, *we* know we're the good guys, but I'm not so sure everyone agrees. Better play it safe. Got some Crisco?"

My mother retrieved the blue tub of shortening from the refrigerator. My father scooped out a slick handful. He opened the front door slowly, paused, and stepped out. The air was still. The pop-pop-pop of fireworks echoed from downtown, or was that gunfire?

My mother huddled in the doorway as my father took three long strides across the little yard to the Oldsmobile. He crouched down, mixed dirt into the grease, and smeared the goop onto the license plate. Satisfied, he hurried back inside. My mother shut the door and secured the lock.

Dad turned off the radio. "Let's try to get some sleep."

The words were barely out of his mouth when a car careened around our corner, brakes screeching, horn blaring in defiance of Pérez Jiménez's edict against honking. My mother froze, her eyes wide. Would the camouflage work? Would my grandfather's shotgun be necessary? But the driver and his euphoric passengers flew by cheering and continued toward downtown.

"Like winning the big game," my father said with a shrug. Another car swept loudly past. "I think all the action's downtown. Nothing more to do except get that rest. It's going to be a long day."

My mother looked in on us girls again. Susie and I were still fast asleep, untroubled by the noise and innocent of the drama unfolding around us. Routine would keep us safe, at home in a city that was in chaos.

She climbed back into bed.

"Everyone okay?" Dad said.

"So far."

They lay still, eyes closed and ears open. A car gunned past. And another. In the distance, car horns blared off-key against the unmistakable staccato rhythms of gunfire. The night wore on.

As dawn made its tentative advance, they heard a whispering from the street, like prairie grass in the summer wind. It grew steadily louder. They crept to the living room window and peered through the glass slats and metal bars. Out of the fading night emerged a parade of men and women, their passage marked by the soft whoosh-whoosh of the *alpargata* slippers worn by the people that lived in the shacks up the hill. It was like an Easter processional—only instead of the statue of a saint, each person carried a chair or a television or a file cabinet.

"Looters," my father said. "They've broken into the police station."

2. DEMOCRACY

F ree of the tyrant and with the police in hiding, Caracas exploded.

An enraged crowd surrounded the fortress of the Seguridad Nacional, a stronghold into which hundreds of Venezuelans had disappeared. The National Guard, a military force sent in to control the crowd, fired on the fortress instead when the trapped secret police began shooting from inside. After the military smoked out the police, political prisoners, some barely able to walk, emerged into the arms of their families. Looters sacked and set fire to the building.

Our little family sheltered in place. My father worked the embassy phones while my mother and Fina kept Susie and me entertained. A morning of pretend shopping wearing Mom's dress-up shoes, the high heels tapping against the green Formica floors. At noon, *almuerzo,* lunch, in the kitchen while Mom's typewriter chattered out the weekly letter to America, its cheery dings announcing the end of another line. An afternoon of splashing in the tin washtub, Fina's strong fingers in our daisy-yellow hair. The springtime-fresh everyday sun perfuming the air with the sticky-sweet scent of overripe mangos as Mom buffed us dry in our terry cloth robes. A dinner of slick green slices of smooth avocado on golden warm *arepas,* corn cakes. My father and his guitar singing us to sleep with "Goodnight Ladies."

Her weekly letter home revealed my mother's emotions. "To be honest, I was rather frightened," she wrote. "There was quite a mess in the downtown sections, many mobs and a great deal of trouble between the police and the people."

A group of military men and civilians from the underground movement asserted some control. Slowly, looting ebbed.

Caraqueños began to manage themselves. In a poignant bit of civil service, the Boy Scouts stepped in to direct traffic. Speaking to an audience on Cape Cod many years later, Mom recalled the valiant youth. "They were shorter than the cars. If you looked over your hood, you'd see this little person wearing a cap. It was absolutely thrilling to see after such a tough period in the country."

As the Caracas she loved began to re-emerge, my mother's letter home ended on a positive note: "We keep saying how lucky we were to have been able to see all this."

* * *

A fragile democracy took shape. The leaders of the three dominant political parties created a governing body, the Junta Patriótica, which the United States formally recognized. Previously clandestine revolutionaries took positions of leadership in the government, media, and business communities.

With the demise of the Seguridad Nacional, Mom and Dad could be assured that their mail had not been intercepted or their telephone tapped. My mother's routine afternoon call to my father at the embassy was once interrupted by a harsh, Spanish-speaking male voice: "This is the Seguridad Nacional. You do not have anything to tell your husband."

Ambassador Edward J. Sparks, a soft-spoken career diplomat, arrived in March to assume leadership at the embassy, a position left vacant at the end of 1957 by Ambassador Dempster McIntosh. Washington became more confident in the strength of the new governing junta and its control over fringe elements.

As the Junta Patriótica settled into the business of governing, the pool of Venezuelans willing to make public their support of democracy swelled my father's talking-head roster on the television program he produced as press attaché. Pro-American propaganda like *Venezuela Mira a Su Futuro*—Venezuela Looks to Its Future—

was the bread and butter of the United States Information Agency, my father's foreign service employer.

A positive press was the daily fare, while sharing American culture was USIA's long game. Washington beefed up the cultural envoy trips. The great Nat King Cole arrived for a series of concerts, fresh from the Tropicana in Havana. When Mom took Mrs. Cole shopping, she later recalled, "Nat invited me in for his favorite drink, a banana daiquiri. Wow!" Louis Armstrong, Woody Herman, and composer Aaron Copeland brought music and conversation to greater and more relaxed audiences at the binational Centro Cultural. The USIS lending library saw English-language books fly off the shelves.

Leonard Bernstein and the New York Philharmonic flew down for a May 1 concert at Central University, where they played the Venezuelan national anthem with appropriate emotion in counterpoint to the May Day labor union march downtown. At the press conference before the event, my father got a kick out of helping Lennie work his renowned charm on the local press. The headlines in the newspapers the next day spoke of "international understanding."

As Ambassador Samuel R. Gannon III would later recount in the Association for Diplomatic Studies and Training's oral history collection: "You make all your mileage out of culture—the long-term, slow moving crafty exploitation of the parts of your culture that have made you worthy of respect and admiration."

There was a very real concern about the anti-American sentiment simmering just beneath the surface, and the opportunity it represented for communist forces to get a foothold in Venezuela. A big part of quelling the potential for trouble was up to my father and USIA.

"You have no idea how busy Bob is," Mom wrote home. "It is such an important time now that it is almost too much to ask of one person. All I want is for things to get back to normal so that Bob can have dinner on time and play a few games of tennis. Anyway ... we are fine!"

Before normal could be guaranteed, however, an American vice president almost lost his life.

3. Nixon

Things were going well enough in mid-May to include Venezuela as the final stop on Vice President Richard Nixon's eight-nation goodwill tour of South America. The trip symbolized the high priority the United States assigned to the Western Hemisphere, and it was an opportunity for the vice president to gather foreign policy experience in preparation, it was said, for the 1960 election. Mrs. Nixon was traveling with the vice president, as were Tad Szulc from *The New York Times* and reporters from *Time-Life*, *Newsweek*, and the AP, some twenty in all.

It was a bumpy trip. In Buenos Aires, traffic caused the Nixon motorcade to be late for the inauguration of President Arturo Frondizi, which some Argentines considered an affront to their dignity. In Uruguay, the VP successfully engaged leftist students in dialogue, but a similar effort in Peru ended with the Nixons being pelted with stones and fruit by communist extremists.

Things went more smoothly in Ecuador, where there were no negative episodes worthy of press reporting. Colombia gave the Nixons a rousing welcome. If things stayed calm in Caracas, the overall impression of the vice president's trip would be positive.

However, the post-revolutionary calm in Caracas had begun to bubble. A communist newspaper ran a photo of Nixon with his teeth crudely altered to make him look like Dracula. The same newspaper disclosed a letter from a previous ambassador, Fletcher Warren, congratulating dictator Pérez Jiménez for the Seguridad Nacional's quelling of an attempted coup the prior year. Things could get ugly. There was a rumor of a possible Nixon assassination.

Still, most newspapers urged Venezuelans to respond to the vice president's visit with dignity and maturity. The junta assured the embassy that they did not foresee any unmanageable security problems. The embassy conveyed the message to Washington, and Washington conferred with the vice president before he departed Bogotá. He refused to be frightened away. Air Force Two and the press plane would come to Caracas.

"There would be some negative notes sounded," my father would later write. "But we had to trust that such negative emotionalism would prove ephemeral while the more significant values symbolized by the vice president's visit dominated in the long run."

The May 13 itinerary following the Nixons' mid-morning arrival included visiting Simon Bolivar's tomb to lay a wreath; lunch at the ambassador's residence; meeting with the government junta at the presidential palace; and dinner and accommodations at the Círculo Militar, the luxurious military officers' club in which Dad had organized a large press center.

* * *

A little after 9:00 that morning, Dad and his boss, Harry Casler, drove down the hill to Maiquetía Airport in the black Ford station wagon that would be the press-pool car in the motorcade back to Caracas. A flatbed truck for photographers would be in the lead behind the police escorts.

Dad parked the station wagon in its assigned location behind Ambassador Sparks's Cadillac. Mrs. Sparks would ride back to Caracas with Mrs. Nixon in the Caddy, while the ambassador and the vice president took the handsome open-air convertible that was parked in the lead. A placard on its windshield read "*Número 1.*"

Out on the tarmac, Ambassador Sparks, Mrs. Sparks, and the Venezuelan foreign minister stood by a formal honor guard and military band ready to greet the American vice president when he descended to the red carpet. Nixon's orders were no military presence.

As Dad scanned the road outside the airport, buses began disgorging what soon became a loud crowd. This could be trouble. The crowd flowed into the terminal and onto the balcony overlooking the tarmac. Now, Dad could read their signs, some in English and some in Spanish—*Fuera Nixon*. Nixon, Out. He hoped the Nixons would interpret the shouting as a welcome, though the spectators were beginning to look like a mob.

Air Force Two landed right on schedule. The Nixons emerged from the airplane, smiling and waving, and stood at the top of the stairs as the military band played "The Star-Spangled Banner" and the Venezuelan national anthem. Dad hoped the music would cover the shouting, but it came back in full force as the Nixons descended to shake hands with the foreign minister and the ambassador. The vice president said a few words to the foreign minister, and then continued toward the motorcade, bypassing the microphones set up for the formal welcome. He had been in politics long enough to know when to abandon a plan.

The crowd on the balcony stood between the Nixons and the exit. As the VP approached, the military band inexplicably started to play the Venezuelan anthem again. A master of protocol, Nixon stood still out of respect to his host country.

The waiting crowd on the balcony saw their quarry trapped. White specks of spit began to rain down on the Nixons, staining Mrs. Nixon's red hat and marking up the blue shoulders of the vice president's suit. The screaming protest nearly drowned out the music. Still, the Nixons stood their ground. Dad wondered aloud why they didn't get into the waiting cars.

"Dignity," Casler replied, his eyes narrowed. "He's showing these bastards real *dignidad*."

The anthem ended. The Secret Service detail forged a path through the crowd now descending from the balcony. The convertible was a no-go. Nixon saw his wife into the second car in the motorcade, then commandeered the ambassador's Cadillac, waving off Sparks in favor of the foreign minister. The interpreter and Nixon's security detail scrambled in with the VP, leaving the ambassador to join his wife and Mrs. Nixon. Dad and Casler quickly herded the press into the media car and nosed in behind the ambassador and Mrs. Nixon. Somewhere behind Dad and Casler was the car carrying the embassy military attachés.

The motorcade began its climb up the mountain toward Caracas, following a police escort and the open truck carrying the press photographers and *The New York Times'* reporter Tad Szulc, who had leapt in at the last moment for a closer view.

But more trouble lay ahead. Small, fast cars cut in and out of the motorcade on the highway. At the edge of the city, people leapt out from hiding places, shouting obscenities and hurling stones at the vice president's car. A large rock lodged itself in the Cadillac's rear window.

As the motorcade entered Caracas, truck blockades slowed the vehicles to a crawl and then stopped progress altogether. The chants of "*Fuera Nixon,*" Nixon Out, became "*Muera Nixon,*" May Nixon Die. Demonstrators surrounded Nixon's car, ripping off the American and Venezuelan flags, kicking at the doors, beating on the roof.

"God damn it!" Dad said. "They're trying to flip the car! This is getting serious."

"Serious?" Casler said. "Life-threatening."

They watched as four Secret Service agents, holstered guns visible, pressed their way out of the Caddy and surrounded the vehicle. Slowly, they pushed the crowd back, but the motorcade made little progress. What should have been a pleasant drive to the Bolivar monument had turned into a nightmare.

The agents jumped back in the car as the police escort made room for the motorcade to proceed, but instead of following the police, the Caddy veered into a side street. Mrs. Nixon's car followed suit, with my father and Casler close behind.

Later, Dad learned that it had been Nixon who ordered the car off the planned route, much to the objection of the foreign minister.

"But we cannot leave our protection!"

"If that's the kind of protection we are going to get," the VP said, "we're better off going it alone."

Nixon's instincts and quick decision no doubt saved lives. Five thousand agitated Venezuelans awaited the vice president at the Bolivar memorial, having already ripped to shreds the ceremonial wreath and attacking the car that delivered it. While most of the motorcade followed the Cadillac safely off into the side streets, the car carrying the embassy military attachés missed the turn and had to be rescued from the mob by the Venezuelan Army. The police discovered a cache of homemade bombs at the memorial that undoubtedly would have been used if the ceremony had taken place as scheduled.

The rest of the motorcade passed through the guarded gate of the ambassador's residence, and the Caddy pulled to a stop in front of the house. The car's black metal surface was scarred and dented in a hundred places, the windows splintered and smeared with dried sputum.

They were an hour early. The Nixons stood at the door waiting to be let in, the foreign minister at attention just behind them, despite a bloody handkerchief covering an eye cut by a sliver of glass from the rear window. A flustered maid answered the door just as Ambassador and Mrs. Sparks arrived and ushered the Nixons upstairs. There was a hurried conversation as arrangements were made for the Nixons to remain at the residence—the Círculo Militar was out.

My father went looking for my mother who, along with the other embassy wives, had been working all morning to prepare the luncheon. Any residence event was a command performance for both the staffer and his wife. Their understood dual role was to establish personal relationships with people who counted—make conversation, create goodwill. My mother made up for her lack of experience in foreign countries with a personal grace that put people at ease, and the cocktail dresses she had bought during Dad's training in Washington fit beautifully around her toned dancer's body.

Dad found Mom organizing the *hors d'oeuvres*. He took her by the elbow to talk privately in a corner of the buffet room.

"What happened?" she said, glancing at her watch. "You weren't supposed to get here for another hour."

"Things got ugly. You know that nice quiet ride in from the airport, uphill through the palms, the blue ocean in the background? Turned into a mob scene. Could barely get the cars through." My father shook his head. "And even before we got on the road, the Nixons got spit on at the airport."

"What?"

"And attacked along the road most of the way."

"Oh, my gosh."

"So, Nixon pulled the plug on laying the wreath at the Bolivar monument," Dad continued. "He is one cool customer, never raised his voice, and even wanted the Caddy to be left out front. 'Let 'em see what communists are really like.' And here we are. The Nixons are staying here, changing now." He spread his arms out with a resigned shrug. "And the *junta*, which they were going to meet at the palace, is on its way here instead to apologize."

"Got it," Mom said.

As the wife of the press attaché, she was presumed to know who was who. It would be her job to whisper the name of each person to Mrs. Nixon just before he or she faced the vice president's wife in the reception line. My father would do the same for Mr. Nixon. They both knew the shortlist—the newspaper publishers, the intellectuals, the political figures. Now, Mom also needed to be prepared to introduce the three leaders of the junta.

She took a final glance at the food table and then ducked into the kitchen to deposit her apron before assuming her position by in the residence foyer.

* * *

The Nixons descended, looking fresh. Before the front doors opened, the vice president gave a press conference as scheduled—translated by my father—and my mother sat with Mrs. Nixon while she was interviewed by two female journalists.

My mother's letter to her parents contained this behind-the-scenes look at the front-page story. "Of course, both the Nixons were in a terrible state of shock, and it was some time before they came out of their room, but they showed real poise when they sat down to talk with officials. The Venezuelans were terribly embarrassed. The Nixons both really charmed the Venezuelans with their graciousness, and the press conferences were very well received."

Nixon was never higher in Dad's esteem than he was at that moment, statesmanlike, speaking with such reserve and calm about it not being easy to see one's wife spit upon.

Speaking on Cape Cod years later, my father said, "Nixon earned our respect that day. He conducted himself without anger, without rancor, and put the events in excellent perspective. He really did a great job for his country that day."

My mother recalled both Nixons' grace under fire. "The vice president told me how good everything looked on the buffet table, and that he'd have a little of this and a little of that. I don't know how he did that so calmly. And I sat with Mrs. Nixon while she did a press conference. I wrote home to my mother, 'She's a lot prettier than her pictures.'"

As the day unfolded, the news wires reported that President Eisenhower had ordered the Marines to US bases in the Caribbean in case they were needed in Venezuela. The Venezuelan newspapers reported that the Marines had been deployed to rescue Nixon. The images of American soldiers in battle dress flying toward Caracas screamed Yankee imperialism.

The Marines stood down when word filtered back to the White House that the Nixons were safe. After a quiet night, the vice-presidential party flew to Puerto Rico before returning to a hero's welcome in Washington.

4. LEAVING

The Junta Patriótica led Venezuela forward to "fair and free" elections at the end of 1958, with the three junta leaders on the ballot. Rómulo Betancourt emerged the victor. Venezuela, at long last, had a democratically elected president.

As Betancourt prepared to take office, Fidel Castro and his guerillas in Cuba succeeded in overthrowing the American-backed dictator, Fulgencio Batista, a former soldier who'd seized power in a 1952 coup. The parallels between the ousters of Pérez Jiménez and Batista made it inevitable that Venezuela would celebrate the one-year anniversary of its revolution by inviting Fidel to Caracas.

"It was almost a family affair, an extension of their own experience," my father later wrote. "The valiant band of brothers, in a country similarly warmed by the tropical sun and lapped by Caribbean waters, had ousted the despot through bold action and underground support, opening the way for freedom and democratic self-determination."

The tall, bearded, and virile legend arrived at Maiquetía Airport to the cheers of fifty thousand enthusiasts on January 23, 1959. Clad in a fatigue cap and uniform and carrying a rifle slung over his shoulder, Castro dominated the next three days, giving hours-long speeches that drew roars of approval from the Venezuelans.

Castro did not address, nor was he asked about, reports of communists among his followers and of Marxist ideology behind his plans for Cuba. Charismatic and cocky in triumph, he seemed to insist that the Cuban revolution revolved around him personally.

Venezuelan democracy marched forward, and Betancourt was inaugurated on February 13. President Eisenhower sent New York Governor Thomas E. Dewey, a highly respected Republican figure, to lead the American delegation. Dad was at the airport to meet

Dewey, and he flew back to Caracas with the delegation via military plane. There was no way the embassy would risk a repeat of Nixon's near-fatal motorcade.

* * *

My parents marked the fourth anniversary of our arrival in Caracas by working the 1959 Independence Day reception at the ambassador's residence, playing their supporting roles to Ambassador and Mrs. Sparks with the grace that comes from experience.

Four years was a long time in a foreign service post. When my father's first two years in Caracas were up in 1957, USIA had offered him the choice of returning to civilian life in America, or—after "home leave," a trip to South Dakota and back on the State Department's dime—extending the assignment for another two years. My parents opted for staying. My mother later recalled that flying back to Caracas after visiting the American Midwest felt like returning home.

For my sister and me, Caracas was not a foreign service post. It *was* home. Approaching my fifth birthday, I was a regular at Kinder Mickey, a school run by German immigrants out of a nearby garage. Susie, nearly three, had Fina to herself most mornings. In the afternoon, Mom took us swimming at the Círculo Militar, the country club—and abandoned Nixon quarters—to which our diplomatic status deemed us to belong. The eternal springtime of Caracas was our magical kingdom, and Spanish was our most intimate language.

In fact, Dad had been offered the opportunity to stay on in Caracas with the vaunted Rockefeller family, whose work in Latin America dated back to FDR's State Department.

Venezuela was a kind of second home to Nelson Rockefeller. Rocky served on the board of Creole Petroleum, the Rockefeller-founded Standard Oil affiliate, and he was a frequent visitor to his three farms and hilltop *hacienda* ranch outside Caracas. When

Rockefeller won the governorship of New York State in November 1958, he flew down to Venezuela for a ten-day rest, and my father was tapped to handle the media.

Over that weekend, Dad joined Rocky on a drive out to the family *hacienda,* while my mother entertained Mrs. Rockefeller—Mary Todd Hunter Clark, a flinty Philadelphia society girl. Rockefeller's multiple affairs were public knowledge, and his next wife was already in the wings—Margarette Fitler "Happy" Murphy, whom Rockefeller would marry after his 1962 divorce, had volunteered during the 1958 gubernatorial campaign. I imagine that the frustration of the first Mrs. Rockefeller might have made it a challenging day for my mother.

However, Rocky and my dad got along very well, so much so that the conversation turned into a job offer to stay on in Caracas as a Rockefeller employee. Dad was tempted—"Being next to Nelson really made you feel like you were his buddy," he said years later—but the global possibilities afforded by his embassy work were more of a pull. He declined the offer.

The USIA public and cultural relations angle had proved a surprisingly good fit for both my parents. Dad was grounded in the work ethic of South Dakota farm life, inspired by a passion for languages and travel, and schooled in corporate public relations at General Mills. Mom's small-town, middle-class Minnesotan values and the grace imparted by her brief dance career in New York City made her a natural at public diplomacy. Their experience in Caracas had revealed to my parents that they had a role to play in America's emerging role as the democratic global power.

So, the foreign service it would be for the Amerson family. But where? Dad was working on his Italian with the immigrant *barbiere,* barber, down the street from the embassy, toying with the idea of returning to Italy. He had fallen in love with the country in 1951 on a three-month motorcycle adventure. As he completed the annual "April Fool Sheet"—a routine preference form due each

April to guide personnel in making changes in assignments—he checked off Italy. No harm in aiming high.

My mother's mind was not quite so settled. Another Latin American country would be the logical next post. She didn't take to other languages as readily as Dad, but she had bridged the language gap with Fina and with shop merchants by sheer effort. From early attempts at direct translation—asking for *Siete Arriba* only to find 7-Up being called *Seve Oop* —she had developed a fine conversational Spanish, which coupled with her innate graciousness was a huge asset to the work.

She tried to make light of the hepatitis she had contracted in early 1956—the virus lurked in contaminated food and water—and which resurged periodically, making her feel sick and exhausted. "I surely don't want this to reappear every year as it is no darned fun," she wrote home. "Maybe living in a different climate will do the trick." She brushed off her worries—at least publicly—with this "silver lining" comment: "Do you know that I've lost three gorgeous inches off my fanny? I recommend hepatitis."

In the back of her mind, perhaps she hoped my father would be disappointed in whatever offer USIA sent back, and that we would head home to our families and friends in Minnesota, where Susie and I could grow up with our American cousins. This had been a great adventure, but Mom missed the comfort of being a permanent part of a community.

However, America was not to be our home. In September, Dad got the country he wanted—Italy—and a job he was ready for—assistant branch public affairs officer in Milan. If, of course, he wanted a career in the foreign service. "Bob announced our move from Caracas to Milan by calling to say I should 'put the pasta on,'" Mom later wrote.

She saw my father's delight and remembered how oddly lonely she felt when we visited her hometown on home leave. She was no longer as connected to Winona as she was to her husband and children, and, yes, to foreign service life. We had become a part of a new community—embassy people.

Perhaps over-idealistically, my parents felt that their efforts at the Caracas Embassy had significance, for our family, for our country, maybe for the world. They had found their career niche.

Italy it was.

First, Dad was to report to USIA headquarters in Washington, DC, for five days of debriefing, after which USIA would cover the costs of us visiting family in Minnesota and South Dakota.

Taking advantage of the flexibility in Washington's schedule, Dad secured us passage on a ship to New York City, from where we would launch the rest of our American stay.

* * *

In November of 1959, Mom and Dad made their protocol farewell calls on Ambassador and Mrs. Sparks and other senior diplomatic couples. They were fêted at a *despedida*, a good-bye party routinely thrown by embassy colleagues for departing friends—a *bienvenida* welcome party would follow for Dad's replacement. The comings and goings of embassy people is such that the party tradition ensures a smooth hand-off from the family on the way out and the introduction of the new people as they arrive.

Leaving Fina would be much, much more difficult. She had become part of our family, and the bonds of love between her and us little girls were as strong as blood ties. We had rooted ourselves as a family of five. I was six months old when we arrived in Caracas, and Susie was born there. Now, we were two little girls, spouting Fina-taught Spanish as our first language, singing, counting, imitating. Bicultural living and warm sunshine were our entire world. Fina was as much a part of our life as our parents were, and our

Spanish-language intimacy had forged a neurological pathway in me that would forever imbue the language with a primal sweetness. It resides in me to this day.

Fina had spoken hopefully of living with her *niñas en Italia,* my girls in Italy, but my parents knew that taking the Spanish-speaking woman on the journey to our next post was both impractical and unaffordable. Mom made arrangements for her to live with and work for close friends from Canada who lived nearby.

Much as she had imposed her calm on Fina's reaction to the departure of Pérez Jiménez on that January night in 1958, my mother asked Fina to control her emotions when it came time for her *niñas* to leave. Everything was to be happy and normal.

All Susie and I knew that November of 1959 was that we were going on "a wonderful *Santa Rosa* boat."

* * *

The black USIS station wagon pulled up past our mango tree and stopped at the gate. Ernie, the embassy driver, helped my father load our suitcases into the cargo area as my mother walked me to the car. Dad opened the rear door and Mom and I slid into the back seat. "*Avanti,*" Dad might have said, ready to spring from Spanish to Italian. Before long, I would understand what it felt like to be gone into a new life before I'd even left the old one.

I sat there, hands folded on my lap, doing what adults expected of me. Perhaps because I never had a baby shape, Mom speculated, she had always treated me like her little, dutiful companion. She told me I was toilet trained before I turned one—peeing and pooping on command, a therapist noted—and was walking immediately thereafter.

In a process that I would repeat seven times in the years to come, I relinquished my hold on the present. When it came time to go, you simply went. You did not protest. You did not look back. You moved on.

But being obedient was far from simple. I would struggle to hit the mark in everything asked of me for the rest of my life, saddling me with unrealistic expectations, a fear of failure, anxiety, and depression—all while acting happy and normal.

My sister Susie, on the other hand, was in no rush to hit developmental milestones. As a toddler on the cusp of turning three, she was strong-willed and refused to relinquish her rapidly deteriorating security blanket. As Fina carried Susie to the car, chatting about the wonderful *Santa Rosa* boat, my sister picked up on the tension and burst into tears. She gripped her blanket tighter and buried her head into Fina's broad shoulder.

"No! No!" she blurted. "I don't want to go!"

"Sure, you do," my mother said, reaching from inside the car. "That wonderful *Santa Rosa* boat!"

"No, no, nooo!" Susie sobbed.

She clung to Fina, who by now had lost control and was weeping openly. Dad pried Susie's limbs from her beloved Fina and placed my sister on my mother's lap. The doors closed, the engine started, and we were gone.

I have no memory of turning my head to watch Fina standing alone on our sidewalk, getting smaller and smaller until we turned the corner and home disappeared forever. The anguished crying that should have exploded from me simply did not. It stayed buried for more than a decade, and when the lonesomeness finally broke free, it was me alone on the sidewalk as my family drove away.

Fina stayed in the employ of American diplomats and expats in Caracas for the next thirteen years, and my mother sent her a Christmas card along with a photograph of Susie and me each December.

After Fina returned to Spain, her Amerson *familia* would see her one more time, although none of us could have imagined that in 1959.

My sister cried all the way across Caracas and halfway down the mountain to the coast before falling into an exhausted nap from which she barely woke as we walked up the ramp to the boat and into our stateroom. Just before dropping off for the night, Susie stated that she still did not want to go on the *Santa Rosa*.

The next day, with the boat docked off Nassau in the Bahamas, the four of us took a tender to shore for a bit of sightseeing. Looking out over the bay, Susie noticed the cruise ship bobbing gently at anchor. "What's that?"

"Oh, that?" Mom said, seizing the opportunity, "that's the *Santa Rosa* boat."

"Can we go on it now?"

"Great idea." We boarded the tender back to the *Santa Rosa*. America lay ahead.

* * *

The *Santa Rosa* dropped anchor in the Hudson River, and we caught a cab to La Guardia for a plane to Boston. Mary Caldwell Mudge, Mom's Macalester College roommate, and her husband, Art, met us at the gate and spirited us away to their New Hampshire farmhouse for the weekend.

My mother wrapped Susie and me in borrowed sweaters and relaxed. She had forgotten what it was like to be outdoors without looking over her shoulder. Mary had always made her laugh, and it was wonderful to chat without worrying about Spanish vocabulary or representing America.

We flew to Washington for Dad's required five-day consultation.

Things were changing in and around America's foreign service. Secretary of State John Foster Dulles, a staunch anti-communist, was out. His successor, Christian Herter, who was raised in France by expatriates, had a brief diplomatic career and a longer political career in Massachusetts before returning to the State Department. Herter's background and experience gave him a more moderate approach in his negotiations with the Soviets, a tone that suited Eisenhower.

Meanwhile, the Soviet leader, Premier Nikita Khrushchev, had made himself known to America. In the summer of 1959, television audiences were surprised to witness what the press termed a "Kitchen Debate" between the colorful Khrushchev and a remarkably relaxed Vice President Nixon. The impromptu discussion of the merits of American capitalism and Soviet Communism was a result of Nixon's attendance at the opening of the American National Exhibition of science and technology in Moscow.

That fall, Khrushchev became the first Soviet leader to travel to the United States. In summarizing their one-on-one meetings at Camp David, President Eisenhower and his Soviet counterpart both expressed a wish for a thaw in the Cold War.

* * *

Briefings complete, it was on to home leave, a foreign service officer's required return to his home on record to "undergo reorientation and re-exposure to the United States." That's what the law says. For me, it was a weird interlude with a family I barely recalled.

We drove a rental car to Winona, Minnesota, Mom's hometown, where her father ran the family hardware store. Dad must have marveled at the road improvements—the Interstate Highway System had been launched while we were in Caracas, and the smooth, wide highway was a welcome contrast to Venezuela's pothole-strewn, hold-onto-your-seat mountain roads.

We had visited Winona on summertime home leave two years before, and what little I remembered was nothing like this dark, cold place in mid-November. The bare tree limbs threatened like the branches of the mean apple trees in *The Wizard of Oz*. The sidewalks were gray and empty. The air pinched my nose as I stepped out of the car, nearly colliding with Grandma Robb.

"Hello, dear." She patted my head. "Just look at your curls!" She made a beeline for Susie, reaching out her soft, fluffy arms. "Ooh, I could just eat you up!"

Susie pulled away, crying. The lack of structure had played havoc with our napping schedule. Somehow, Mom got us fed and tucked into the twin beds in her old bedroom.

A good night's sleep helped, as did the General Mills cereals we hadn't seen—Kellogg's, not Betty Crocker, had the Latin American market. Grandma sat us in Grandpa's big corner chair to watch television. Captain Kangaroo reminded me of my German nursery school driver Onkel Otto, only with a much softer American voice. After my bath, Grandma pinched my hair with her fingers to make it wavy. Back when Mom was little, Grandma tied her wet hair up in socks to create Shirley Temple curls.

Grandma made a cake to celebrate my fifth birthday. Mid-afternoon, people I barely knew walked in the front door. Mom's brother, Uncle Jim, was a laughing hugger. Mom called him Jimmy. Aunt Beth kept a stern eye on our cousins—Ricka, about my age, and Becky, about Susie's.

While the other grownups sat talking in the living room, Grandma overcame our collective shyness by inviting the four of us little girls into the kitchen for a Play-Doh session. At some point in the afternoon, Becky nibbled a little too much of the flour-oil dough and threw up on her party dress. Aunt Beth and Mom took her upstairs for a change of clothes, which turned out to be my bathrobe. Dad's photos from the day captured that outfit for posterity.

The next day, we drove north to the Twin Cities to see two of Dad's younger sisters and their families. As we pulled up to a house, I practiced the names: Aunt-Snooky-Uncle-Bob, Aunt-Jeanie-Uncle-Carl. Carl's beard felt soft and warm against my face. They talked and laughed all afternoon while I watched Susie play with little cousin Julie.

In the morning, a whirlwind of cold air swept us west across the South Dakota border to the Amerson family farm. Grandma Amerson, a small, reserved woman who everyone else called Ma, and teenaged Uncle Terry, with a ready laugh and a winning smile, were planning an exit to California, where Grandma's siblings moved during the war. My Grandpa Amerson, who everyone else called Pa, had died unexpectedly just days after Susie's birth, so Dad's last visit to the farm had been rushed and unhappy. I knew nothing of that place and those people.

We drove back across the prairie to Winona where a traditional American Thanksgiving dinner with family awaited. There was little familiar about the food or the people.

Mom felt out of place in Winona. People in Minneapolis didn't know Caracas. Out on the South Dakota prairie, we might as well have been on another planet. Mom and Dad cut our home leave short, and soon we were on our way back to the foreign service.

I just wasn't sure where that was.

Part II

Milan

(1959-60)

*The distant glass ceiling of the Galleria Vittorio
Emanuele II hovered over us like a big spider web.*

1. Arriving

We flew into Milan-Malpensa airport just before Christmas. We were two time zones away from the Kremlin and a day's drive from Berlin, where the battle for control between America, its allies, and the USSR was underway. Dad and his college pal Fred had not been able to get into Germany during their post-college motorcycle tour of Europe, and Dad must have wondered if he would get there this time.

However, it would not happen with this assignment, a position that left him feeling hemmed in. My father was used to daily media access and a fair amount of independence after running a big media relations program out of the embassy in Caracas for four years. Now, as assistant branch public affairs officer in the two-person USIS branch office, Dad was the young understudy to the experienced, European-born PAO, Max Kraus. Milan was also a far more industrial and tightly organized city than Caracas, with sophisticated media and world-class art. USIS was lucky to get a few inches of print a couple of times a week in one of the dailies.

"Accommodating to the confines of my new assignment took some adjustment," he later wrote. I can see him raising his eyebrows and tilting his head as he wryly expressed being cut down to size.

Mom was going through her own transition. Four years into this joint venture and she was as miserable as a lonely kid at camp.

She thought she had mastered this foreign service thing. "After four years in Caracas I really thought I was a pro, ready to move easily from post to post," she later wrote. The friendliness of the Caracas embassy couples, developed while collaborating on ambassadorial receptions and other shared responsibilities, had created a close-knit community. Mom assumed that this was how things worked in each foreign service post.

She was wrong. "I quickly learned that posts were only as friendly as the people who were there on assignment," she later wrote. Milan was slim on staff and even slimmer on hospitality. There had been no "hello," no "here's who's who and what's where," no apartment or maid or school leads, no *bienvenida*. No one had sought out Mom to "make calls." The stuffy-sounding protocol was the quick way to introduce newcomers into the team of spouses, the "plus one" component of public diplomacy in those years.

It was downright lonely at the *pensione* residential hotel where we were stuck over the holidays. Worse yet, Mom felt overwhelmed by a deep depression, the first of what would become a private mourning period that followed every move. She did not reveal it to Dad, nor to us girls, holding the sadness inside while putting on a happy face.

She understood that her personal sacrifice was necessary to support her husband in his new work, and to help her children quickly acclimate to our new surroundings. But what a terrible loneliness it created in her.

It was only years later that she wrote of the devastating impact. "What a shock to find that our arrival in Milan was followed by those awful moving blues."

* * *

It was Christmas Eve. I leaned back in the metal café chair and watched my breath rise toward the distant glass ceiling of the Galleria Vittorio Emanuele II that hovered over us like a big spider web. I longed for the warmth of Venezuela—*flamboyán* trees the color of a Caracas sunset, the mosaic designs on the buildings near Dad's office in the embassy, the fruity perfume of the mango tree in our front yard. We hadn't seen much sun since we had arrived in Milan, and what light did filter into the gray city corridors lasted a fraction of the day I was used to. And there was no Fina.

"Finish your milk, girls."

My mother held a finger up and looked over Susie's shoulder toward the waiter's black jacket as he disappeared through the café doors. Her long, fancy red nails clicked against the tabletop as she picked up her coffee cup and sipped from where her crimson lipstick had left its kiss. Her skin looked as white as the cold air. The collar of her new dark coat tugged at the wisps of brown hair that had broken free of the French twist that had replaced her easy Caracas ponytail.

"Why didn't Fina come with us?" I asked.

"Oh, wouldn't that have been nice," she said, stealing a glance at my sister. Susie was working on her elephant ear pastry and calmly looking off toward the arcade, her straight bangs in perfect line with her eyebrows. "But Fina had to stay to help her new family in Venezuela. You understand?"

I nodded. I was the big sister, and that meant doing what grownups expected of me. I reached the parfait spoon down the tall glass to scoop up a few grains of sugar where they stood in the cooling milk. They crunched between my teeth like guava paste. I nibbled at the sticky golden flakes from my pastry that clung to my fingers.

The waiter arrived and Mom gave him some big bills. "*Grazie,*" thank you, she said, indicating there was no need for change. "*Prego,*" you're welcome, the waiter said and moved off to tend to another table.

"Here, Susie," Mom said, reaching across the little table. "Let's wrap up your elephant ear for tomorrow. Button up those coats. Time to get back to the *pensione* for Christmas Eve."

It was going to be a strange Christmas in the residence hotel. Mom was a traditionalist who treasured family customs. She had sustained some Minnesota holiday traditions in Caracas, like making Christmas cookies with us girls using her mother's cookie cutters.

Other traditions, like Christmas Eve *hallacas*—Venezuelan corn-meal meat pies—started in Caracas. Now we were in a new world, and this year was going to be pretty casual. In my mother's world, "casual" was a defeated fallback—"pretty casual" was a damning evaluation. However, there wasn't room in the small apartment kitchen to do much. Fish seemed to be what Italians ate on Christmas Eve, but that would only smell up the place. Things would be better when we moved into an apartment.

Mom pushed back her metal chair, the legs screeching on the floor. She reached under the table, retrieving the straps of her purse from around her feet. Only tourists hung their purses on the backs of their chairs, an easy grab for thieves. She slung the strap across her chest like a soldier's bandolier.

Taking us each by the hand, Mom guided my sister and me into the crowd. We flowed toward the Piazza del Duomo, the Christmas-festooned Galleria shop windows glittering with red and gold cellophane, silver-and-blue-foiled chocolates, and mounds of red-boxed *panettone*. Mom's heels clicked like a metronome on the glass tiles.

As we emerged from the Galleria, we passed a gypsy sitting on the pavement, her dirty skirts splayed out. A dull-eyed child about Susie's age sat listless on the woman's lap, and the mother's dark outstretched hand was accompanied by a pitiful voice saying something about the *bambino*, the child.

I tugged on Mom's arm. "Can't we give her money?"

"No," she said, but she slowed down and stepped us out of the crowd. The beggar's voice grew louder. "But how about food? Susie, shall we give your elephant ear to the baby?" My mother reached into her purse for the leftover pastry.

Susie frowned and shook her head. Her blond bangs shimmied. "It's mine."

"And you will be doing a very nice thing by giving it to this little girl who doesn't have anything else on Christmas."

Susie nodded.

"Here, Jane." My mother handed me the package.

I placed it in the gypsy's hand. "*Buon Natale*," Merry Christmas. The woman snatched it out of my hand with a sneer.

"Did I say that wrong?"

"You said it fine. And that was the right thing to do."

La Scala opera house was at the far end of the wide town square. The Duomo sat heavily at our end, its lit spires sculpted yellow and gray against the evening sky. Couples were gathered on the steps. I walked backward so I could keep my eye on them.

"Jane." Mom gave me a little tug.

A flock of pigeons rose like rippling gray smoke as we walked by. I stamped at one, watching it lift off its kernel of corn. We passed the red food kiosk as we left the piazza. I wondered if Santa would give me a lira so I could buy some corn there for the birds after Christmas.

* * *

Mom unlocked the *pensione* apartment door and flicked on the hall light. The apartment smelled of fresh tomato sauce. "Janie, how about turning on our tree?" my mother said. "I've got to get the pasta water on."

The fake Christmas tree was on the bedside table between our twin beds in the small bedroom Susie and I shared. I clicked on the tree lights. The teeny pretend candles lit up the two new decorations, a white felt angel for Susie and a lavender one for me. The two wooden Pinocchio dolls from the neighbors down the hall stood cheerfully under the tree. There was a lot of empty space next to them.

I heard the apartment door open.

"Do I smell dinner?" My father's tall frame was momentarily outlined by the elevator cage.

"Daddy!" Susie ran to meet him as he lowered his briefcase to the floor. He swung the door shut behind him. The hall light bounced off his slicked-back hair. Grandma Amerson told me in South Dakota that Dad's hair was as blond as Susie's and mine when he was our age.

I was right behind my sister. "Did you bring us anything from the office?" Our mail now was routed through an APO address—the Army Post Office delivered military and diplomatic mail through the nearby American bases. There would be no more having diplomats' letters intercepted by secret police.

Dad pointed to his attaché case. "Just reach into that there briefcase, and you'll see a letter or two." He stepped down the short hall to greet my mother. "Hi, honey."

They kissed, her dark head tilted up to his fair one. *"Buon Natale,"* she said.

"That's the spirit!" my father said, unbuttoning his coat. "What did I tell you, Nan? You're going to take to this place in no time."

My mother just smiled and took his coat. "Dinner's almost ready." Fresh pasta needed only a couple of minutes.

"Let me wash up."

Dad joined Susie and me at the tiny table as Mom carried in a platter of steaming spaghetti. "I don't know how you did this, Nan," Dad said. "Shall we say a few words?" We only did this on Christmas Eve. He reached for our hands. "Like how very lucky we are to be here celebrating our first Christmas in Italy." He looked at me.

"*Feliz Navidad,*" I said.

"*Buon Natale,*" my father corrected.

I knew I was using the old words, but they just felt so much more comfortable here at home. "*Buon Natale,*" I said.

My father nodded.

"*Natale,*" Susie said.

"And we're thinking about our families in Minnesota and South Dakota," Mom added.

It was a very quiet Christmas.

* * *

We moved into our apartment on New Year's Eve, Susie's third birthday.

After three weeks of pounding the pavement, with my parents taking turns at searching with one of us in hand, Dad and I had found a second-floor apartment that was just being completed. Even though we were still right in the middle of Milan, there was a big park across the street and a huge terrace outside of Mom and Dad's room.

Dad could walk to work. "We were just a half a block from the Duomo," my mother recalled years later. "The closer, the better the address, so we started out in high gear."

Dad managed to get a couple of mattresses out of the moving crates, but everything else was still packed away. Mom produced a magical bundle of *tramezzini,* small multilayered sandwiches special enough for a birthday dinner. She lit them with three candles, and we sang *Feliz Cumpleaños* as Susie blew them out.

"Isn't it nice to be done with the *pensione?*" Mom said as she pulled the candles out of the sandwiches. "New Year. New home."

Susie and I shared a bedroom, like always. We were used to each other's breaths, sleeping in the same room since Susie outgrew the bassinet.

Mom tucked us in. "Sleep tight, girls."

The modern smoky glass doors throughout the apartment looked very chic during the day but permitted lights any room—and the city streetlamps—to seep into every room after dark. As I drifted off, I knew that Susie and her "nighnee" security blanket would sleep happier in the brightness, too.

I was startled awake by car horns and a loud boom, and then another. A whole lot of something clattered to the street.

Susie sat up. "Mommy!"

Mom materialized at our side. "It's just New Year's, girls," she said, pulling the blankets up around us again. "Fireworks, just like in Caracas."

Something flashed at the window, followed by more clattering and a thud. A mattress whooshed by.

"And old pots and pans. Old furniture," Dad called from the living room. "Italian-style celebration."

Mom sighed. "Well, not quite like Caracas, but here we are. Let's get some sleep." She closed our door.

"Oh, good grief!" I heard her say a few minutes later from their bedroom.

I guessed she figured out just how bright these doors made our bedrooms at night. Right after breakfast on New Year's Day, she took out the Christmas paper she saved from our presents, and we taped it over all the doors.

That night, the Madonna and her baby were in six places on our bedroom door, and our room glowed blue. It was like living in the Duomo.

The world revolved into the 1960s, a decade that would witness our coming of age as an embassy family.

2. Bella Figura

The Milan USIS branch post was one of eight around the country that supported the work of the US Embassy in Rome. All offices were expected to maximize American exposure.

The pressure to produce was high in postwar Italy. Italians were traditionally friendly towards America, where so many of their countrymen had migrated. However, the decades of fascist leadership under Mussolini had left Italy vulnerable to the huge *Partito Comunista Italiano*. The Italian Communist Party had threatened to take over the country ever since the 1948 elections. In the Cold War atmosphere, the possibility of a communist government loomed darkly in the minds of Washington policymakers.

For my parents to do their part for democracy at cultural events, we needed to find a maid to look after us girls when Mom and Dad were out working for USIS. Finding help proved difficult. Many in the European servant class had, like Fina, found better-paying opportunities in South America. Post-war Italy was prospering, and domestic work was no longer the only option for lower-class women.

Eventually, Mom hired Maria Pia, a country girl, like Fina, but a social climber in the making, far more interested in improving herself than in playing with Susie and me. Her arms didn't form a hug just my size like Fina's. I have only one image of Maria Pia in my head—not in the pale blue uniform maids wore, but in a date-worthy dress, heels, and pearls—from her first day with us, when she taught Mom a lesson in how things were done in Milan.

* * *

Italy was governed by *la bella figura*, the practice of demonstrating the proper decorum when in public—even when you thought you were not in public.

Before she hired Maria Pia, Mom did our laundry. There was no utility sink as there was in our little back patio in Caracas, so Mom washed our clothes by hand in the tub and hung them to dry on a clothesline Dad strung up in one of the marble-floored bathrooms. To expedite the drying, Mom opened the bathroom windows, which faced an interior courtyard.

That lasted a day. The landlord came up to say that the neighbors across the way were offended by the sight of drying clothes. The *signora's ragazza,* the madame's maid, should know that clothes were to be dried on the roof. Mom just nodded. We had no *ragazza.* Lesson One in how things were done in Italy.

Lesson Two came via the large *terrazza* balcony outside Mom and Dad's bedroom, which accumulated soot from Milan's dirty, industrial air. One rainy day, Mom decided it was time to clean the terrace. She filled a pail, took off her shoes, put on her raincoat, and got to work. She looked up from her task a few minutes later to find the Contessa who lived across the way watching from her own balcony, open-mouthed, a cup of tea in her hand. Mom smiled, nodded, and finished the job. The next day, she watched as the Contessa's maid emerged onto the little balcony to dust the table and chair, after which the butler delivered a tray of tea and a newspaper, and then, the Contessa herself appeared, sat, sipped, and read. Lesson Two.

This was decidedly not Venezuela.

Maria Pia was Lesson Three in *bella figura*: it was essential to wear the right color coat, the right length skirt, the right poofy hairdo, whether you were a maid throwing out the garbage or a grand lady shopping in the Galleria Vittorio Emanuele II.

The first morning she lived with us, Mom asked Maria Pia to get some *ciriole* rolls from the *pasticceria* bakery down the block.

The maid said, "*Va bene,*" okay, and disappeared into her bedroom.

47

I thought she would just get her coat, but I counted all the way to one hundred in Spanish before Maria Pia came back down the hall—wearing high heels and a party dress. Mom's eyebrows went up and her lips pressed together into a small smile as Maria Pia went out for rolls.

Back in Caracas, Mom just swept her hair into a ponytail and slicked on bright red lipstick when she left the house. Now, she wore her hair in a French twist, and there was hairspray, eyeliner, and a box of bobby pins on the bathroom sink.

Proper conduct extended to children, of course. The first day Mom took Susie and me across the street in our play clothes for a romp in the city park, she saw that Italian children stayed off the grass, squatting instead on the pebble paths and drawing in the gravel with little sticks, careful to not get any dust on their good clothing. There was clearly no romping going on.

"Girls, please play like you see the Italian children doing." That's just how it was. To do otherwise would make a bad impression, a *brutta figura*.

"'Watch the rest of the children and do as they do' became our family mantra for the rest of our foreign service life," my mother would recall years later.

It was a skill that would serve me well throughout my childhood—with one dramatic exception—but leave me ill prepared to plot my own way.

* * *

With Maria Pia in place, Mom joined Dad in the after-hour activities that came with the job. Among the cultural ambassadors whom my parents hosted in Milan in early 1960 were the author Saul Bellow, winner of the National Book Award, and New York City Ballet's George Balanchine, whose company also appeared at La Scala during their 1953 European tour. What a kick it was for

Mom, just a few years retired from her own New York City dance career, to rub shoulders with Balanchine. Back then, she could never have afforded a ticket to the ballet. Now, Mom's attendance was mandatory.

Mom and Dad were also required to attend the opera at La Scala. The first time they went, Dad put on a tuxedo, and Mom put on a long black dress and white calf-skin gloves with little buttons all the way up to the elbow. Together, they looked like Fred and Ginger in *Shall We Dance*—Mom said it was one of her favorite movies when we saw it at the Centro Cultural in Caracas.

The next morning over breakfast, Mom told me about the evening. "The opera was *Aida*, about an Egyptian princess. We heard a wonderful new American singer, Leontyne Price. What a marvelous voice. She really wowed the Italians." Mom poured herself another cup of coffee. "We got to go backstage and meet her in the star's elegant dressing room. She was so gracious. Aren't we lucky to get these kinds of opportunities?"

* * *

Now that we were settled, Mom set about finding me a school—although I had begun kindergarten in Caracas, the transition to Milan had robbed me of three months of education. The English-speaking International School of Milan, housed in an old office building about two blocks from our apartment, had space for one more in their kindergarten room.

The next Monday morning, Susie stayed home with Maria Pia and Mom walked me to my new school. The kids in the classroom looked so much bigger than my school friends in Caracas. They were at round tables working with clay, like what Dad brought home for art projects.

The teacher walked over, smiling. "Hello, Jane," she said. "I'm Miss Lovey." She held out her hand. She did seem lovely.

My mother squeezed once and let go, and Miss Lovey walked me over to an empty chair at one of the little tables. I looked back at the door, but Mom was gone. "Everybody, can you say hello to our new friend Jane?" Miss Lovey said.

"*Ciao,*" the children said, then went back to work on the clay. The girl next to me gave me some of hers. "I'm Carol," she said. "I'm from England."

I lined up with Carol when Miss Lovey said it was time for the park. We walked across the busy street at the corner, Miss Lovey facing the traffic with a menacing look on her pretty face until we were all safely across. The rules were the same as Susie and I had observed at the park across from our apartment—children could walk, but not run, on the pebbled paths and were not permitted to step over the little fences onto the grass.

After the park, it was quiet time. Miss Lovey found me a mat next to Carol. Even though I had tried to play carefully, I was sweaty and the plastic of my mat stuck against my bare legs. After Miss Lovey turned off the lights, I faced the wall, curled my free fingers around the tip of my nose, and slipped my soft thumb into my mouth.

I hadn't needed to suck my thumb in Caracas. Colors were there. Warmth was there. Fina was there. Now, my thumb made me feel safe.

* * *

Spring finally made its way through Milan's industrial gray skies. Some afternoons, it was warm enough to wear our Caracas clothes when we played on the flat, concrete roof. It was up a flight of stairs from the service elevator, where Maria Pia now hung our laundry to dry. If you backed away from the walls, you could see roof after roof of clotheslines, television antennas, and little houses the size of puppet theaters which hid the stairs. We pretended ours was a castle. I was the queen and Susie was either the princess or the maid.

Mom became a regular at the USIS American lending library, one of the mainstays of Dad's work in Milan and throughout his career. "It was a blessing to have English language books no matter where we went," Mom said years later. "And the open stacks were amazing to people in other countries. The fact that you could browse the shelves and select your books directly—and not have to submit your request at a desk—was a huge novelty."

When the Milan library decided to decommission their children's section, my sister and I became the recipients of the Laura Ingalls Wilder *Little House* series, books I still have on my shelves. Susie and I played "Laura and Mary" for years, alternating the roles between the author and her blind sister.

Future home leave visits brought their adventures to life. Lake Pepin, the portion of the Mississippi River across which Pa drove the covered wagon—when the family moved from *The Little House in the Big Woods* in Wisconsin to *The Little House on the Prairie* in Minnesota—lies between Mom's hometown of Winona and the Twin Cities. Lake Pepin remains a mandatory stop when I visit Home Leave Territory.

School came to an end in June. At the closing ceremonies, Miss Lovey gave me a book for earning the Honor Award in my class. "It seems a bit early for starting out with a bang," Mom wrote home of my achievement. "Still, it shows that she is happy enough to be doing well. Susie now can hardly wait 'til October when she will start half-days."

That night, I lost my first tooth just as I was going to bed and Mom and Dad were getting ready for a USIS evening function. Mom put my tooth in a little box for the Tooth Fairy.

"And in the morning, you'll wake up and find your tooth gone and money from the Tooth Fairy!" She tucked it under my pillow.

As she was closing our bedroom door, I had a change of heart. I really did not want a strange lady, fairy or not, poking around under my pillow while I was asleep.

My mother thought fast. "How about if Dad and I take your tooth to the office for the Tooth Fairy to find there?" And, sure enough, I had money in my hand in the morning.

Susie saw a business opportunity. "I want to sell my nighnee to the Tooth Fairy babies," she announced over breakfast.

My mother could barely believe that my sister would give up her treasured security blanket. Together, they put the tattered thing into a box, and Dad took it to the office.

"By gum," my mother wrote home, "the fairy bought it, and Susie was thrilled to be paid. Lucky fairy babies."

3. LEAVING

My father's workdays were shorter than they had been in Caracas, and the job allowed for more off-hour independence. The four of us ate together most nights, and weekends were given over to exploring northern Italy in a used little pale-blue Fiat 1100, *la millecento.*

We visited Cremona, in the foothills of the Dolomites, where violins have been created for hundreds of years; Verona, its architecture said to have inspired Shakespeare's *Romeo and Juliet*; and Lago di Como and its stunning Alpine waters and shoreline palazzos. On the fourth of July, we drove to Lago Maggiore on the Swiss border and took a boat out to the tiny Isola dei Pescatori for lunch. A family picture memorializes my sister and me lifting our *acqua con gas*, fizzy water, with the Italian toast: "*Cin cin!*" Cheers!

In mid-July, we drove to the picturesque village of Soglio in the Swiss Alps to spend a long weekend with Mom's New York City roommate—and fellow dancer—Marty Howe and her husband. The hills were a lush green, with the grass cut for hay, and we took long walks up the slopes to see the cows and goats grazing.

Susie was enamored with the goats, helping them into the barn to be milked each evening. One evening, so that her favorite goat wouldn't be lonely without her, my sister placed a big goodnight kiss on its hind quarters. "The old ladies milking those goats had certainly never seen such a sight!" my mother wrote home.

* * *

Dad had two days of meetings at the Rome Embassy the following week, and Mom tagged along for some all-too-rare alone time. She luxuriated in the pleasure of walking at her own pace, browsing the chic shop windows on Via Condotti, and wandering through the burnt sienna alleyways in Trastevere. She downed a quick *cappuccino* at noon while standing at the bar like everyone else, chewing on a plain roll. She didn't want to risk a tastier meal that might have included garlic. She had an afternoon date with the Pope.

When Dad had brought home the two tickets to the Vatican—gifts from the editor of Milan's leading newspaper, *Il Tempo*—Mom was circumspect. Was it right for barely practicing Protestants to take such coveted spots away from devout Catholics? Dad was assured by the newspaper colleague that all were welcome at the papal audience. When Dad's embassy meetings conflicted with the event, his boss, Max Kraus, snapped up the ticket. He would travel down to Rome separately and meet Mom at the Vatican.

Mom returned to the hotel to change into her long-sleeved black dress and retrieve the veil she bought for the occasion. She practiced draping it over her head—it felt like putting on a pious costume for a dance performance.

She met Max in front of the Vatican, where they joined a group of about fifty people.

They were herded through a series of rooms, finally dead ending at the Pope Paul VI Audience Hall. Mom and Max, the lapsed Presbyterian and the Jew, lined up against the wall and waited.

She adjusted her veil.

Pope John XXIII entered without ceremony to muted clapping. He made his way around the room, pausing to speak with each person. Mom watched the protocol—head down, genuflect, kiss the ring. Non-Catholics were permitted to shake his hand, Dad said, but no one had done so before the Pope stopped in front of her. Mom lowered her head, sensing before seeing the hand being offered to her. She looked up as the Pope smiled, a gentle soul. Shaking his hand felt like the most natural thing in the world.

"Nancy Amerson, *ambasciata Americana*," American Embassy,

Mom said.

"*Molto bene,*" very good, Pope John XXIII said.

The Pope extended his hand to Max. As the diplomat shook it, he added a few words expressing the embassy's gratitude about the Vatican newspaper's recent pro-American op-ed.

As the group was ushered back out into the streets of Rome, Mom began composing her letter home. They would never believe it. She would send the veil to Fina. Imagine the thrill of owning a veil blessed by the Pope.

* * *

She told Dad about the experience as they rode the northbound train home to Milan.

He nodded appreciatively. "Another remarkable opportunity granted by Italy." He eased back into his seat as the ugly outskirts of Rome gave way to green fields. "So, here's something. I've been selected by headquarters to join the next graduate class at Johns Hopkins."

"Oh? In the States?"

"No, at their graduate school in Bologna."

"But we've just gotten used to Milan," Mom said. "I've only now put up the curtains."

"Yeah, I agree. Nine months has given us barely a taste. And the Rome Embassy wants me to stay put, too. They are looking for me to take over as director of the Milan branch next year."

"Good," Mom said.

"Though it is nice to be asked to dance," Dad said.

Mom patted Dad's hand. "Yes, it is. Just glad you didn't have to say yes."

By the end of the week, however, it became clear that Washington's request could not be turned down. Dad served "at the government's convenience," and that meant going where and when directed. We were moving once again, this time three hours south for Dad's year of postgraduate studies at the Johns Hopkins University School of Advanced International Studies (SAIS), the Bologna Center.

I don't remember being told we were leaving Milan, maybe because the city didn't yet feel like mine and maybe because it happened over my school's summer vacation. More than likely, Mom made it sound normal and happy, despite her fear of the moving "blues."

"We are moving. Again," she wrote home. "It's just that after really getting set here, the idea has taken a bit of getting used to. Such is the life in the foreign service."

Mom pushed away her foreboding as she took down the curtains. Maybe she could rise above the depression this time. One thing she would not do is reveal her feelings to Dad, much less to Susie and me. The four of us were off on our next adventure, and all she had to do was create a home.

Again.

Part III

Bologna

(1960-61)

The witch had a horrible long nose that quivered above an open mouth where a few yellow teeth poked out.

1. Arriving

As we drove down the Autostrada to Bologna in our made-in-Torino FIAT *millecento*, about 130 miles south along the middle of the boot, CIA pilot Gary Francis Powers was sentenced to ten years in a Russian prison.

Better Cold War news was happening in Rome, which hosted the 1960 summer Olympics. While the Soviet Union bested the competition with forty-three gold medals among the 103 it garnered, the runner-up was the United States, taking seventy-one medals, thirty-four of them gold. USIA produced a film for international audiences featuring America's Wilma Rudolph, the winner of three gold medals.

Compared to the cold industrial vibe of Milan, Bologna was quaint and historical. Although the city lost half of its industrial buildings to WWII bombings, the colonnaded medieval town inside the old walls survived. The city's heritage was reflected in Bologna's three nicknames: *la grassa,* The Fat One, for *bolognese* spaghetti meat sauce; *la dotta,* The Learned One, for the world's oldest university; and *la rossa,* The Red One, for its miles of terra cotta porticoes— and for being home to Italy's large communist party.

My father approached his new assignment from a decidedly different perspective—instead of strategizing against the communist USSR, he was to study it. The History of the Soviet Union—taught by an Italian, in Italian—was one of the graduate-level classes my father signed up for at the Bologna Center. He was one of three in that year's SAIS cohort chosen from the US Foreign Service, joining some thirty other mid-career European government practitioners and another thirty second-year American graduate students.

Dad dug into this delicious world of ideas, languages, and culture. In addition to boning up on the USSR, he enrolled in the Economics of Western Europe—where the postwar era had evinced huge changes—Italian History, and French, at last able to sate his appetite for the language that had been whetted by his 1951 European motorcycle adventure.

For Mom, the year in Bologna was a welcome break from doing what USIA wanted with colleagues who were hard to get to know. Although we still had our Rome Embassy affiliation and the perks that went with it—such as being able to shop at the Post Exchange (PX) at nearby military bases—there were no duties beyond enjoying being part of a graduate school community.

With the freedom came the costs. Without an established foreign service structure, my mother was once again on her own to figure out schools, shopping, and medical support. And, as she had dreaded, she hit the brick wall that she had come to call "the blues." There was no cure but time. Six months in, and the dark would give way to light again—she hoped. Perhaps the Bologna Center community would give her that sense of belonging that the embassy community in Caracas had given in abundance. In many ways, she missed Caracas more than she missed home.

Sara Mansfield Taber, my contemporary who was raised overseas as the daughter of a CIA officer, posits in her memoir *Born Under an Assumed Name* that there is an ardor that foreign service officers and their spouses often feel for the early posts. Maybe there was magic in those Caracas years. The couples my parents worked with became lifelong friends, and one of them, Allen Hansen, conducted my father's oral history interview for the Association of Diplomatic Studies and Training (ADST). His memoir—*Nine Lives, A Foreign Service Odyssey*—is among the ADST Memoirs and Occasional Papers Series listed in the opening pages of this book. In the year before his 2018 death, Allen became a correspondent of mine.

Magic.

* * *

My parents decided that home would be the ground-floor apartment of a hillside house, where the landlord, who was a doctor, lived with his family on the second floor. The house had served as the Nazi regional headquarters in Bologna during World War II. It was rumored that old armaments were still stored in a tunnel behind the house. Angela, the day maid, came with the house. Like Maria Pia in Milan, Angela was from the country, but, unlike Maria, she didn't live with us full-time. She took the train to and from our home four days a week.

My mother hoped there would be another international school for Susie and me in Bologna, but the only option was an Italian school in a villa on the outskirts of town. Susie would have none of it. After half a day, she stayed home in her uniform *grembiule* smock to play school with Angela's poor cat, while I put on my *grembiule* and rode the school's station wagon to first grade. I might be new, but I would look like I belonged.

It was a hard nut to crack. There was no one remotely like Miss Lovey in this rigid, rule-oriented school. Mondays through Saturdays, from the moment we arrived at eight until the five o'clock dismissal, we were mostly seated at connected desks like assembly line workers under the stern eyes of unsmiling women with high expectations. Cursive writing with dip ink pens, abacus-based arithmetic, and dictation—corrected in red pen—were our daily fare. No one spoke English, I was the only American, and I went by a new name—Giovanna, Jane in Italian. Still, I had succeeded at whatever had been asked of me so far, so I plunged in, determined that my conversational Italian from Milan would get me through.

However, first grade in Bologna was a dismal slog of being called on the carpet for making mistakes and learning the most Italian of ways to conceal failure—the *bella copia*, the notebook into which errors in language were made right with beautiful, India-ink penmanship as I recopied each morning's dictation. Mom covered the *cuaderno* notebook in Bambi wrapping paper, and Dad inscribed it in beautiful calligraphy: *Bella Copia.*

Unfortunately, this magic trick didn't exist for arithmetic. Thrown into an abacus-based math curriculum without having absorbed the basics about numbers, my solution was to give up and cry.

Not a great habit for a kid. As my husband could tell you, pouting is even less attractive in an otherwise accomplished adult.

* * *

As the lunch hour ended one fall day, I decided to try an escape. When the room monitor was looking the other way, I ducked my head under the table, licked my right hand's index and middle fingers, and quickly dabbed the saliva under each eye.

"*Signora,*" I said, raising my hand. I sniffed a bit as she walked over to me. "*Non mi sento bene,*" I don't feel well. I gazed sadly at the remains of my lunch, hoping my cheeks looked tear stained.

It was easy to look sick. The steam rising from the tin container smelled stale. The standard-issue Italian lunch pail looked like it might have been used in the war.

The woman glared at me with her eyebrows close together, then rendered her decision. "*Mangia.*" Eat. She sucked all the life from that wonderful word. I wasn't going to get out of the afternoon's arithmetic lesson.

My only friend, Gabriella, called to me from the foyer, risking being reprimanded for raising her voice. Her sweet smile and pixie haircut gave her the innocence of a young Audrey Hepburn, and she had no use for the name-calling and gossiping of the other girls in the class.

Gabriella was as nice as she appeared, so she was an outsider, like me.

We slowly climbed the marble staircase to the villa's second-floor classrooms. The abacuses were already on our desks when we entered the room. Signora Condoti was writing some numbers on the blackboard as we took our seats.

"*Allora.*" Now then. The teacher turned to face us.

I felt my brain go numb. She called on someone else.

I toyed with the pen in its inkwell.

"*Giovanna.*" I looked up. "*Giovanna,*" Signora Condoti repeated, pointing at the numbers on the board.

I had no idea. Real tears welled up in my eyes.

She looked at me for another moment. "*Va bene,*" okay, she said, and called on someone else. I tried to blink back the tears, but one slid down my right cheek. Gabriella caught my eye and smiled.

Mom was waiting at the foot of the driveway when the school station wagon dropped me off. "Hi, honey," she said, taking my satchel. "Good day?"

My stomach lurched. "Uh-huh," I said, hurrying ahead to where my sister was crouched in the mossy rose garden. A long line of orange and black hairy caterpillars stretched the full length of the walkway.

I reached for a stick. "Let's make them move." I poked at the center of the chain, and the links broke apart into fuzzy black balls. I squished one into blue ooze with the tip of my stick.

"Look," Susie said, standing up. "Snail tracks."

We followed the silvery threads laid down on the granite walk like swipes from a magic wand. It took us moments to cover the distance that had taken the snails all day. Four big brown shells, four sets of sticky antennae, four gooshy bodies. I reached for the biggest one, tugging against the gluey suction until, with a soft pop, the snail released its hold on the stone. I watched the antennae retract and the slimy body disappear into its shell. I lowered the snail back to the walkway and waited to see the gray slickness slowly emerge.

"Got salt?" I asked.

"No," Susie said and wandered off toward the house. I decided to melt the snail another day.

A glass of milk and slab of Nutella-coated bread were ready for me on the kitchen table. "Lots of homework?" Mom said.

"*Bella copia,*" I said, retrieving the *cuaderno* from my bag. "Signora Condoti gave us another *dettato* today. I need to copy it over."

I didn't say that my mistakes on the dictation had earned me a disapproving look and Signora Condoti's usual comments: *fai più attenzione,* pay more attention, *meno errori,* fewer mistakes.

"It seemed an unneeded burden for such a small tyke when kids her age in the USA were working on printing," my mother later wrote.

I switched out of my *grembiule* into a t-shirt and hand-me-down corduroys from our Winona cousins. I walked up the stairs no one used to the landing next to the locked door behind which our neighbors lived, where Dad had set up a small table and chair. I put my red-marked dictation notebook and the *bella copia* notebook side by side, the pure page ready to absorb my mistakes.

The small bottle of India ink was in its spot on the front right corner of the table. The clean pen nib lay on the clump of black-stained tissue. I inserted the nib into the long wooden holder and uncorked the ink, dipped the pen, and held it over the clean page.

Slowly, I traced the first cursive letters on the white cotton paper, feeling the nib's smooth path. I blew gently and watched the heavy lines seep into the paper and dry in perfect loops, settling solidly onto the middle blue line—the tip of each "t" touching the blue line on top, and the stem of each "p" reaching down to touch the line below. Finally, the whole page was filled, the corrected dictation fitting perfectly. I closed my eyes and stretched my arms.

My right hand tapped something. With a gasp, I saw the bottle of ink knocked on its side. I grabbed it and set it upright, but it was too late. A sea of black was seeping across the *bella copia* page, drowning my neat writing.

Mom tried to calm me, but I was miserable all through dinner. Regret mingled with fear. My stomach really was hurting now.

"May I be excused?" I asked.

"Maybe a little sleep is just the right thing," Mom said. "I'll come tuck you in."

Usually, her soothing hand on my forehead at bedtime was the best closure on the day. Tonight, though, I had something else in mind. I hurried into my pajamas.

"Okay!" I called.

My mother sat on the corner of the bed near my feet. "Now I lay me down to sleep," she began, the generic prayer from her childhood Presbyterian upbringing.

I chimed in. "I pray the Lord my soul to keep. When I wake up in the morning light, I'll do my best with all my might." My mother liked this version better than the one about "dying before I wake." But, tonight, the Protestant magic spell was not enough.

Mom kissed my forehead and went down the hall to help Susie get to bed. I waited for the tapping of her heels on the linoleum to fade, then started my school's Catholic routine, a better antidote to my misery.

I crossed myself. "*Santa Maria . .*"

"Are you saying something, Jane?" Mom called from down the hall.

"Nothing," I called back.

I waited another moment and started back in, but quieter. The words of the Rosary fell easily from my tongue. It was how we started school every day. My Italian face and my Italian voice would keep me from harm.

Ten hours of daily immersion in the dramatic singsong, start-and-stop of Italian slowly percolated through layers of English and Spanish and laid down a third language track. Soon, my communication repertoire borrowed as easily from Italian as it had from Spanish.

My chameleon toolkit had expanded.

2. La Befana

As I was struggling to master the requirements of Italian first grade, my mother labored to set expectations and boundaries for our maid, Angela.

Angela was canny. When my mother asked her to perform some new task, especially one that she would rather not do, she expressed amazement that such a thing could be done. *Ah, signora, mai visto,* oh my, madam, I have never seen such a thing. Mom held her ground. She had five years of maid-management and a year of Italian under her belt, and the private lessons she was taking with Berlitz were giving her new confidence.

Things came to a breaking point one day when my mother caught Angela pocketing the good silverware. There was no *"ah, signora"* to hide behind. As Angela handed over the goods, Mom took advantage of the upper hand—Angela was to go home and not come back for a week, and she would be on permanent probation thereafter. Mom told Susie and me that Angela was going to take a short vacation. She hid the rest of the silverware while the maid was out of the house.

Things ran much more smoothly when Angela returned.

* * *

The American presidential elections were held in November. Eisenhower had served two terms and was prohibited from running for a third time by the recently ratified Twenty-Second Amendment to the Constitution. Vice President Nixon was the Republican candidate. A young senator from Massachusetts, John Fitzgerald Kennedy, was the Democrats' choice.

Mom and Dad had sent their absentee ballots early, hoping that the unreliable Italian mail system would get their votes in on time.

Although they were registered Independents, in keeping with the neutral political stance expected of foreign service officers, my parents' liberal leanings were developed at Macalester College in Minnesota's traditional Democratic territory. Two Democrats held Minnesota's Senate seats—Hubert Humphrey, a one-time professor at Macalester, and Eugene McCarthy. In the presidential election of 1960, my parents voted for Democrat John Kennedy.

Kennedy won the presidential election by a narrow margin. Come January 1961, the Democrats would be back in office, with the youngest president in America's history and the first Catholic to inhabit the White House.

* * *

In mid-November, the American half of the Bologna Center student body decided to treat their classmates to a traditional Thanksgiving meal. Mom was in charge of the menu. As State Department staff, Dad and his foreign service colleagues Tom Fina and Dick Forschner had access to American goods via the PX. The Post Exchange stores were on the American military bases, bulwarks of democracy whose physical presence bolstered the Rome Embassy's diplomatic efforts.

Bologna lay between two bases. Joint Command South in Verona was about one hundred miles to the north. Camp Darby in Leghorn, as the military called Livorno, was about the same distance to the south. The plan was to get the turkey and trimmings in Verona, land of Romeo and Juliet.

At the last minute, Dad was up against a homework deadline, so Dick Forschner volunteered to do the driving in his brand-new Mercedes Benz. Mom rode shotgun, the Fodors guide open on her lap as was her habit anytime we traveled. Dick may not have expected a running commentary on the history of the area, but I imagine he got one as they drove past Ferrara's fourteenth-century historical center and on to Padua, home of Italy's oldest university, where Galileo had been on the faculty.

They arrived at the Joint Command South base in two hours and had all the fixings in the car in short order. All the fixings, that is, except celery, which was not to be found on the PX shelves. In Mom's book, there was no Thanksgiving without stuffing and no stuffing without celery. The vegetable was not an Italian staple. The PX at Camp Darby—in Livorno, four hours away—was the only solution.

Dick was a man on a mission, with a great ride and a lovely companion. He refueled the Mercedes and back they went past Bologna and on through the rolling hills of Tuscany to Livorno.

"With the determination of Sir Galahad," Dad later wrote, "ol' Dick headed the Mercedes over those narrow roads, seeking the grail of American celery." They emerged triumphant from the Leghorn PX, and an exhausted Dick and a quieter Mom drove back to Bologna.

The eight-hour, four-hundred-mile shopping trip resulted in a splendid Thanksgiving dinner that was a hit among the students and faculty who gathered at the Bologna Center on Friday, November 25, although the canned cranberry jelly probably got more attention than the celery stuffing. Our own family Thanksgiving the day before was nearly ruined by Angela's cat grabbing a turkey leg before being chased off the counter. Susie's habit of over-handling the animal in her pretend-school game seemed a little less wrong to Mom after that.

Dad loved a good machine—he had bought the Model A Ford that became his family's first car out on their South Dakota farm—so when he saw Dick's Mercedes, he needed one too. In December, my father took his own cross-country trip with Dick to check out a car at a dealer in Venice—the smart, navy-blue 190 model was smaller than his classmate's, but a Mercedes, nonetheless. With a diplomatic discount, the baby could be Dad's for a little over $2,000. He took the bait and drove it home, humming all the way.

Mom wasn't surprised, but her tight-fisted Scottish heritage equated extravagant spending with sinning. Maybe Susie and I picked up on Mom's disapproval, or maybe we simply liked the ping the pebbles made when we dropped them onto the Mercedes' roof from atop the garden wall.

That happened only once.

* * *

Christmas approached. A huge tree went up in the Piazza Maggiore, blessed by the statue of Pope Gregory XIII. The Santa Lucia Market arose along the walkway to Santa Maria dei Servi, its kiosks offering dried fruit, nougat *torrone,* and carved figurines. The cafés lining Bologna's medieval porticos sparkled with blue and silver boxes of Baci chocolates and cherry-red boxed panettone. On Sundays, families strolled arm in arm along the arcaded streets, walking on roads as old as the Roman Empire.

We found an Apennine fir and finally unpacked the Christmas boxes from Caracas, unspooling the lights from the Winona family's Robb Brothers Store and opening the tin foil packet of old tinsel. The decorations from the Milan Rinascente, including Susie's white angel and my purple one, filled in.

Although Italian mail delivery was sketchy at best, tantalizing brown paper packages from Winona and Minneapolis eventually arrived and were tucked under the tree. Cards, including one from Grandma Amerson in California that enclosed a check to "buy yourselves something nice," sat atop the television.

Angela was back in Mom's good graces. The week before Christmas, when I was home from school and Mom needed time to wrap gifts and decorate the house, she decided that Susie and I would go visit Angela's village with her by train for the day.

Mom tucked us into our Winona Knitting Mill sweaters. "Now, you girls have a good time at Angela's home. Remember, you're her guests. You can tell us all about your day at dinner."

As the train passed kilometer after kilometer of brown fields, I realized that Angela's commute made her day even longer than mine.

After a while, we slowed to a stop.

The pale sun barely warmed my face as Susie and I followed Angela down the steps of the train and right into the arms of a lady who had Angela's bushy eyebrows.

"*La mía sorella, Lucrezia,*" Angela said, introducing her sister.

Lucrezia pulled us into her black-sweatered chest. I squirmed back onto my own two feet.

"*Andiamo, bambine!*" Let's go, girls. Angela lifted our day bag and reached for me with her free hand. The train horn blared, and I felt myself tilting backward as the train pulled out.

Susie and Lucrezia followed us down the road away from the tracks. I scuffed my shoes as we walked, raising little clouds of dust. The beige single-story homes rose straight out of the road. The smell of frying onions streamed out of an open window. I caught a glimpse of a woman in black stirring something in a pan.

I tugged at Angela's arm. "*Ho fame.*" I'm hungry.

Angela smiled down at me as we hurried along. "You'll see what a feast we'll have at my house," she said in Italian.

A few blocks from the train station, we stopped in front of a small house. "*Benvenuti,*" welcome, Angela said as she opened the door. She didn't use a key.

The sister ushered Susie in behind me and closed the door. The dim interior slowly came into focus as my eyes recovered from the bright sunlight. We were in a large room, part kitchen, part living room, dominated by a wooden table and mismatched high-backed chairs. On the far side of the room, a radio sat between two easy chairs. A couple of doors on the right wall were probably the bedrooms.

A rooster crowed. Angela threw open the back door, letting in a bright grassy-green rectangle of light. "Are you girls ready for a real country lunch?"

She disappeared outside. Lucrezia gestured toward the table. We sat as she set out plates, a round loaf of bread, and some of that salami with white pieces like teeth in it. You have to swallow those fast, so you don't choke. Lucrezia began hacking at the bread.

Angela returned. She held her hands behind her back. "Guess what I have here?" she said. She brought her hands forward revealing four eggs. "Fresh from the *gallina*," the hen. She set three of the eggs on the table and reached for a spoon. "And this is how we eat them here." She cradled the fourth egg in her palm and gently tapped its top until a bit of shell popped off. Angela lifted the egg to her mouth, tilted her head back, and swallowed.

A whole raw egg in the mouth?

Angela reached for another egg, tapped off the top, and offered it to my sister.

The corners of Susie's mouth turned down.

"Oh, come on," I said, reaching for the egg myself.

The warm shell nested in my cupped hand. The golden insides looked up at me. I remembered Mom's words—we were guests, and guests do what the host asks. I raised the shell to my lips. A warm gooey syrup filled my mouth and slid down my throat. I licked the gummy crust off my lips, tasting salt.

"*Brava*," well done, Lucrezia said, squeezing my shoulders.

After lunch, Angela picked up our bag, and we walked a couple of blocks deeper into the town, where there were apartment buildings. Susie and Lucrezia followed us up some stairs to a second-floor apartment.

We were greeted by a smiling lady not wearing black. "*Oh, ecco le bambine!*" Here are the girls, she said.

We had just gotten seated on the living room couch when there was a knock at the door. "*Chi è?*" Angela called. Who is it? There was no answer.

She walked toward the door, looking at Susie and me over her shoulder. She put her hand on the doorknob. "*Chi è?*"

Still no answer. Angela slowly opened the door.

There stood a witch with stringy black hair. Her horrible long nose quivered above an open mouth, where a few yellow teeth poked out. She lifted her broom of gray sticks like a weapon.

Susie let out a yell. I grabbed her hand, and we ran into a bedroom, slamming the door behind us.

"*No, no, bambine,*" Angela called from the living room. "This is the Befana, who brings you Christmas."

I heard feet approaching the bedroom door, slapping on the linoleum. Angela opened the door a crack. "Only the Befana."

Well, get that witch out of here. I shook my head and hugged my sister tighter.

The adults were laughing. "*Bambine,*" Lucrezia called out. "The Befana has brought you presents."

"And not coal like she brings to the bad children," Angela said over her shoulder. "*Non è vero, sorellina?*" Right, little sister?

"Oh, I wouldn't know anything about that," Lucrezia said.

Angela stepped into the bedroom. "*Sta bene,*" she said. It's alright. "*È andanta via.*" She's gone.

I let my hand slip into Susie's and kept my eyes down as we followed Angela back into the living room. When I dared to look up, the witch was gone, and in her place was a different grownup, wearing pants and a sweater, with her hair tied back. A pretty Christmas box of candy sat on the coffee table.

"*Grazie,*" I said to no one in particular as I picked up the candy and walked it over to our bag.

It felt like forever before we were back on the train and headed to the safe harbor of our parents.

I held my breath until Christmas morning, but instead of coal, there was a half-nibbled carrot and an empty glass of milk. "Rudolph loved the carrot, Janie and Susie!" It was signed, "Santa."

We had evaded the Befana. We were still *stranieri*, foreigners.

We celebrated Susie's fourth birthday with a week in the mountains of Garmisch, Germany, at a US Army winter sports recreation area. In that strange nest of American English, hamburgers, and apple pie, I felt my Italian self growing pale.

I wasn't sure whether to be happy or sad about that. But my thumb reassured me.

3. Leaving

My father's year at the Bologna Center expanded into France in the spring of 1961 when the class traveled to Paris to visit the recently relocated headquarters of the North Atlantic Treaty Organization, NATO.

Just a dozen years old, NATO had grown out of the post-war economic and security needs of the nations of Western Europe. Washington viewed an economically strong and rearmed Europe as a key Cold War bulwark against communist expansion. The Soviet control of East Germany and the Soviet-sponsored coup in Czechoslovakia had given rise to real concerns that Western Europe would be similarly co-opted. The NATO agreement addressed the region's collective security issue—members were sworn to consider an attack upon one as an attack upon all. NATO put the United States on the side of Western Europe, while the Soviets held the East under the Warsaw Treaty.

Italy's significant Communist Party gave its membership in NATO strategic importance. The United States became concerned that a winning leftist coalition would pull Italy into the Soviet Union's sphere of influence with the elections of 1948. It was rumored that the new Central Intelligence Agency had intervened to support the pro-American Christian Democrats against the pro-Moscow Socialist Democrats. A monumental anti-communist letter-writing campaign was promoted from the pulpits of Italian American Catholic churches. The relatives back in the old country got the message—the American-backed coalition took the election.

Imagine the conversations in Dad's course on Soviet History as the Bolognese professor laid out these issues. Not for the first time would my father have argued that the CIA and USIA were not the same thing. How freeing it must have been to be a student and not a spokesperson for a year.

The Bologna Center class also traveled to West Germany's Ruhr Valley, where industry dismantled by the Allies and rebuilt under Allied control—through the Marshall Plan's massive influx of aid—was now being called the Miracle on the Rhine. Volkswagen, whose American sales were climbing because of a Madison Avenue marketing campaign, hosted the class's visit.

However, travel to Germany was complicated by the impasse over West Germany—the former British, French, and US zones of occupation—and East Germany, the former Soviet zone of occupation. Berlin posed an additional problem—it was surrounded by East Germany and divided into four sectors occupied by the United States, Great Britain, France, and the Soviet Union.

Three years before, Soviet Premier Nikita Khrushchev issued an ultimatum that the Western powers withdraw from Berlin. Although he withdrew his threat, Khrushchev had pulled the United States and its allies into negotiations. He continued courting America with a 1959 "goodwill" tour during which he met with President Eisenhower on the topic, and a Paris summit was called. Then, the CIA's Gary Powers was captured by the Soviets, and the summit was called off. Uncertainty was the status quo.

Nonetheless, travel between the Berlin sectors remained unrestricted in 1961, and an estimated three thousand East German refugees flowed daily into West Berlin. Dad and his classmates had a sobering morning visit with the refugees in the American military barracks where they were being housed. The class had the afternoon free, and Dad and his state department colleague Tom Fina crossed under the Brandenburg Gate into communist-controlled territory, something the Berlin Wall would prohibit just months later.

"We were allowed to cross the Brandenburg Gate line into East Berlin, and we walked for hours along the barren streets of that forlorn city," my father later wrote. "The train carried us back across the forbidden and forbidding territory of East Germany."

Within months, the Soviets would suddenly close the border crossing points and construct the Berlin Wall, isolating the three western sectors of the city from both East Germany and the Soviet-controlled East Berlin.

Before that happened, Dad would get a chance to be part of history.

* * *

My father was in Germany when I began running a fever accompanied by a sore throat. Aspirin and a day in bed seemed to do no good. Mom's home remedies failed to help—chilled washcloths on my forehead practically steamed, and the cool handkerchief wrapped around my neck with one of Dad's socks and fastened with a diaper pin made no impact. By the second night, my fever was on the rise, and my neck had swollen to twice its size. I could barely turn my head.

Mom had seen this before. An adored cousin, her scandalous Aunt Winona's out-of-wedlock toddler Janie, was struck by diphtheria while staying with Mom's family in the 1930s. Baby Jane had died. Mom carried the sorrowful love in her heart until she gave the dear child's name to her first-born baby. Now, the illness was threatening to take me, too.

Trying not to panic, Mom knocked on the upstairs neighbors' door. The signora had become, if not a friend, a good acquaintance—she had given my mother the name of her dressmaker, a gift no Italian woman bestowed easily. Her husband, our landlord, was a doctor. He answered the door.

"*Buonasera e scusatemi,*" good evening and pardon my intrusion, Mom said. "My daughter is very sick. My husband is in Germany. You might perhaps advise me?"

"*Certo che si.*" But of course. The doctor picked up his black bag and followed my mother back down the stairs.

The doctor confirmed the diagnosis—it was diphtheria. He gave me a *bomba*, medicine delivered via a suppository, and cautioned Mom to keep me cool and hydrated.

It was a long night. My fever broke just before dawn, and my mother and I both dropped off into a deep sleep. By the time Dad got home, sick himself with the flu, I was on the mend; but Mom now had two of us to care for.

Angela earned her pay keeping Susie entertained, and Mom must have felt awfully far from home.

* * *

The Rome Embassy was keeping an eye on Dad during our year in Bologna, and he went down for various meetings to stay in the loop. Towards the end of his year at the Bologna Center, he interviewed for what he considered one of the best assignments in USIA—press attaché, Rome Embassy. The position floated just under the public affairs officer (who directed the country's USIS programming) and touched on all embassy activities that concerned the public.

He got the job. I don't remember being told we would be moving to Rome, maybe because I had known all along that Dad was in school only for the year, just like me, and maybe because I had bigger things to worry about as the Italian school year neared final exams.

It didn't matter how you did in class if you didn't pass the national oral and written examinations. Failure meant being held back, or, worse yet, getting kicked out of academic studies and shuffled off to trade school. I was treated no better, and no worse, than any other first-grader. We were given the date and location of the exams, and everything else came to a halt.

My mother and I climbed the dark granite staircase of the Bologna school administration building, our footsteps echoing off the cavernous enclosure. I ran my free hand along the cool stone wall—the rough surface heightened my senses, and I needed to be sharp. I had dressed in my red plaid pleated skirt and a white blouse ironed with extra starch, and my socks were folded at the same point on each ankle. I reminded myself to check my patent leather shoes for dust.

I had been practicing the assigned poem all week. "*Lumaca, lumaca, dove vai?*" Snail, snail, where are you going? We had learned to recite it slowly and in a sing-song Italian, with big arm gestures for emphasis. I had rehearsed it in our rose garden using my best wriggly Italian face with my lips showing off their muscles and my forehead pulling at my eyebrows. The snails paid me no attention.

Mom reached the landing a step ahead of me and paused while I made up the distance between our locked hands.

"Do you know what always helped me do my best?" she said. "Well, I'd hook my little finger with Grandma's, like this," she said, taking my pinkie in hers. "And she'd say, 'I do, I do, I do.' So, I do, I do, I do." She squeezed my finger. I squeezed back.

We turned to the right off the landing into a large hall bordered by hard wooden benches. The room was filled with children and mothers, some standing, some sitting, everyone talking and fussing.

My mother and I worked our way through the milling crowd toward an empty spot on a bench on the far side of the room. "*Scusi, scusi.*" Sorry, sorry. The word acted like a horn in Italian traffic, and it worked about as well—one body would shift out of the way, and another would slip into the space before we could make much progress. Somehow, there was still a little bit of room on the bench when we reached it.

"Maria Elena Scotti!" A woman in a dark suit was at the door at the far end of the room.

She looked down at the paper in her hand.

The room hushed so fast it was like someone put a lid on us. The lady next to my mother popped up and lifted her little girl off the bench. *"Eccoci qui."* Here we are.

She pushed the girl ahead of her into the hushed crowd. As her mother urged her forward, the girl looked back at me. I smiled. She bit her lip and turned toward the door. People stepped out of the way as if the two of them were contagious. They reached the stern woman. Papers were exchanged, and then the girl disappeared behind the door, alone. Her mother faced us, shifting her weight from foot to foot.

It seemed like the whole room let out a breath. Then, the activity started up again, the mothers a little more fidgety, the children starting to get loud. I brushed the dust off my shoes and tucked my curls behind my ears.

My mother patted my hand. "Okay?"

I nodded. I knew the poem. This was only a test of how good I was at being Italian. It was pretend.

The door at the end of the room opened again. "Giovanna Amerson! Amerson, Giovanna!"

I scooted off the bench, the soles of my shoes sliding a bit as they hit the tiled floor. I turned to face my mother. She smiled and extended a crooked little finger. I didn't need it.

"Don't worry, Mommy," I said, patting her on the cheek. "This really doesn't matter. I'm an American."

As I walked across the room and through the door, I had no idea that within weeks I would feel far from sure about that identity.

* * *

Dad got a bonus volunteer assignment tacked onto his academic year—working the press operations at the Kennedy-Khrushchev summit in Vienna.

Nikita Khrushchev's 1959 Camp David meeting with President Eisenhower—and Vice President Nixon's subsequent visit to Moscow—had established a working relationship for ongoing negotiations. A new American president was in the White House—John F. Kennedy, the Catholic Democrat from Massachusetts. And a new Cold War battleground was in play—Cuba.

Fidel Castro had severed ties with the United States after nationalizing industries, including American-owned businesses, and he began forging economic links with the Soviet Union. In April 1961, US-sponsored Cuban exiles failed to oust Castro in a three-day fiasco called the Bay of Pigs.

Kennedy resolved to meet with Khrushchev to establish an open line of communications and refresh negotiations between the United States and the Soviets over the control of Berlin.

Kennedy and Khrushchev would meet in Vienna on June 4, 1961. The open borders in the separate Berlin sectors that permitted Dad's informal tour of Soviet-held East Berlin were at risk, as were America's power and influence.

There were widespread fears within the diplomatic community that Kennedy might misjudge Khrushchev. The premier's affable manner—the person who had laughingly debated Nixon and eaten corn dogs in Iowa—cloaked his determination to expand Communism.

The four of us piled into the new Mercedes and headed north through Trieste and Yugoslavia and into Austria. Dad made himself helpful in the press center, where *The New York Times'* James Reston and other seasoned reporters worked off copy provided by the White House.

Mom took Susie and me on the enormous Ferris wheel and to

Viennese coffee houses for *Apfelstrudel* and *Linzer Torte*. As the summit concluded, the two leaders emerged on a stone balcony above a tree-lined avenue from where Mom, Susie, and I watched. Kennedy was wearing a red tie. He seemed to wave to me, and I waved back. Mom told Susie and me that we voted for him. I didn't remember that, but she seemed very sure and happy about it.

The summit was a failure. Kennedy's inexperience did not prepare him for Khrushchev's body blows. Within two months, construction began on the Berlin Wall. The Soviet leader had bested the American.

The president resolved to take a hard line in future international conflicts. There was a storm brewing in Indochina—the communists were at work in Laos and Vietnam. Kennedy vowed to stick to his guns there.

We returned to Bologna only long enough to oversee the movers. "Again leaving a group of friends that we had come to enjoy and count on," my mother wrote about uprooting ourselves for the third time in eighteen months.

A process that had become normal to me would never feel normal to her.

Part IV

Rome

(1961-63)

The sky burst wide over a sea of canvas booths that had overtaken Piazza Navona at Christmas.

1. ARRIVING

Edward R. Murrow, the celebrated journalist, was the new USIA director. Morrow's radio broadcasts from war-torn Europe set the bar high for eyewitness reporting, and his television series, *See It Now*, helped bring down anti-communist crusader Senator Joseph R. McCarthy.

He did not shy away from controversy. During his Senate Foreign Relations Committee confirmation hearings, one senator asked Murrow if he intended to tell the bad about the United States along with the good. Murrow responded, "If the bad is significant, it is going to be reported anyway, and we must report it honestly; otherwise, it will be distorted."

President Kennedy would echo these words a year later, telling USIA's broadcasting partner, the Voice of America, "You are obliged to tell our story in a truthful way, to tell it, as Oliver Cromwell said about his portrait, 'Paint us with all our blemishes and warts.'"

There were serious blemishes. The US image abroad was dominated by Southern segregation and racial discrimination. Violent attacks on Black protesters and interracial Freedom Riders were dramatic news copy, and the pictures and television images told an alarming story.

The resulting damage to foreign relations, Murrow said, could not be blamed on the communists. America was doing this to itself, and even the great Black musicians like Nat King Cole and Dizzy Gillespie—designated by USIA as American cultural ambassadors—could not drown out the truth.

It seemed a shame that Americans would never see USIA's film about Wilma Rudolph, the Black track and field athlete who had won three gold medals at the Rome Olympics. Surely promoting her success was a story that Americans needed to see, but USIA's enacting legislation prohibited the domestic dissemination of its films, propaganda created for non-US audiences.

* * *

Being on the sidelines at the Vienna summit had whetted Dad's appetite for his new job.

The press attaché kept his finger on the pulse of the Italian press for the ambassador and his direct reports at the mission. Dad was the embassy contact point for the hundreds of American reporters based in Rome, coordinating their interviews with embassy officers. Drafting ambassadorial speeches and handling special work as it came up—including dealing with visiting American dignitaries—were also part of the job.

While we were in Milan and Bologna, Ambassador James David Zellerbach—a businessman—had been chief of mission in Rome. Our arrival coincided with that of President Kennedy's new appointment as ambassador to Italy—a career diplomat with a stellar reputation, G. Frederick Reinhardt. His illustrious career already included serving as ambassador to South Vietnam, the United Arab Republics, and North Yemen. Dad was joining an elite team in the Eternal City.

Slipping back into the familiar connections of embassy life felt like a homecoming to my mother as she made her calls on Mrs. Reinhardt and the other senior wives, introducing herself into the system. The office helped my parents find our new home, a sixth-floor apartment in a comfortable gated high-rise community, Vigna Clara, an American enclave. For the first time in our lives, Susie and I heard English being spoken in our surroundings, including the community swimming pool and the wooded park behind the apartments where children played freely without the surveillance of mothers or uniform-clad maids.

The embassy had also secured spots for Susie and me at the Overseas School of Rome, an American-credentialed institution. I was beginning second grade, and Susie, having overcome her reluctance to go to school, was ready for kindergarten.

However, what my mother must have found happily familiar was not at all comfortable to me. After my year of Italian submersion, this American environment felt foreign.

* * *

The week before school began, I joined the Girl Scouts' Brownie ranks at a meeting of other American second and third graders who lived in our apartment complex. We spent most of our time sitting cross-legged on the neighbors' living room carpet, singing tunes I had never heard.

"Kookaburra sits in the old gum tree . . ."

As I mouthed the words, I looked around the circle. It sure seemed like every girl knew the lyrics. Jennifer, across from me, bounced her beanie-clad head from side to side as she sang, her hair sweeping her badge-laden vest. My mother had ordered my vest and beanie. Sooner or later, I would look like a Brownie, but I wasn't sure I would ever feel like one.

Jennifer's mother struggled to her feet. "Well, girls, that's it for this week. Shall we close with our Brownie pledge?"

I tugged my anklets out of my shoes as I stood. I watched Camille, my new friend. She raised her right hand and tucked her thumb over her ring finger and little finger. I worked mine into the same shape, raising a two-finger salute.

Jennifer's mother began, "On my honor, I will try . . ." I kept my eyes on her, moving my lips in what I hoped was a good bluff. I longed for the familiar words of the Rosary. At last, she dropped her arm. "Off to work on your badges!"

I lowered my head and walked quickly toward the apartment's front door. I had almost made it when I felt a tug on my sleeve.

"Jane!"

Someone had figured out that I was an impostor. I turned, and my fear melted into relief. I had forgotten that Camille was having lunch at my apartment. It was the first time I had ever invited a friend to come over.

We walked alone across the sloping asphalt that separated Jennifer's building from mine. "Look," Camille said, pointing toward the piazza that lay beyond the gates. "You see where that taxi just went? That's where the bus will pick us up on Monday."

Camille was also going into second grade, but she was not new to the Overseas School.

"What number bus?" I asked. We had taken the bus into the embassy several times, and other buses to the outdoor market.

"Not a city bus," she said, raising her eyebrows. "Our school bus."

"Oh."

My mother had Campbell's tomato soup from the embassy commissary ready for us, along with grilled provolone cheese sandwiches. She called Susie out from her bedroom, where she had been coloring, and then Mom sat with the three of us while we ate lunch.

Camille chatted away about school. I listened and learned.

* * *

On Monday morning, I put on my Bologna exam outfit—the pleated skirt and pressed blouse might just give me the confidence to play my new role, an American girl. I checked myself in the hall mirror. Those darned buck teeth. It was just that my thumb was so satisfying, even when Dad put a Band-Aid on it to get me to stop sucking it.

Mom and Susie walked me to the bus stop—my mother had agreed to drive Susie to school the next day, so this first day was mine alone. Camille was waiting with her older brother and sister, along with a bunch of other kids and their maids and mothers.

A tourist-sized sky-blue bus pulled to a whooshing stop. The kids all clustered around it and boarded, sweeping me up with them into the crowded aisle. Camille saved me a seat. I was too far from the window to see Mom and Susie as we pulled out. A flood of English filled the bus.

Way out on the Via Cassia, the bus turned left into a huge parking lot.

"Come on, Jane!" Camille said, taking my hand as I got off.

She pulled me into the crowd. Our hands came apart almost immediately, but the group moved me across the tarmac, up a broad set of stairs, and onto a landing.

Camille found me. "We're down here." She led me to our classroom. Mrs. Holt, it said on the door. Not *Signora* Holt. Mrs. Holt.

The room was huge and bright. The desks were in rows with lots of room in between, not lined up tight against each other like my old school. The blackboard was on the wall instead of on a swinging frame, and the walls themselves were decorated with pictures on squares of colored paper, their vivid colors illuminated by the oddly white ceiling lights.

"Look for your name," Camille said as she walked toward a desk at the back of the room.

And there it was, on the second seat from the front—Jane Amerson, hand-drawn in strong black letters on a piece of pink paper and taped to the corner of the desk where the inkwell should be. How strange, and how nice, to see in public the name I used at home. I patted my pencil case—I might not be needing those pen nibs after all.

I was right. Instead of cursive writing with dip pens, we spent the morning doing simple block lettering in pencil, copying what Mrs. Holt wrote out on the blackboard. No guessing, no dictation, at least not yet. The teacher handed out clean pink notebooks with wide lines on some pages and no lines at all on some pages, so we could use the whole page for drawing, not just a little square like in Bologna. I had barely used my colored pencils at all last year.

By mid-afternoon, I'd almost forgotten we were in Italy.

Mrs. Holt's end-of-day announcement reminded me that we really were in Rome. "Please have your parents sign this permission slip," she said as she handed papers out to the front row. "It's for our field trip to the Etruscan ruins."

Wow. I could hardly wait to tell my parents and Susie that there was a whole other civilization to see. The four of us spent one Sunday afternoon walking around the old Roman Forum and the Coliseum, where Susie and I counted cats while Mom read to us from the blue guidebook. Maybe I would be an archaeologist when I grew up.

I headed for the bus back home to work on my English spelling. The word "people" was strange: it sounded like *pipel* but was written *peh-oh-pleh*. And "because" was *beh-ca-u-ze*.

I still spell them out in my head.

2. PIAZZA NAVONA

D ad's year of study in Bologna had impressed the brass back in Washington. Recruited at a level six and rising to level four in Caracas, USIA lifted him to level three with the new job at the Rome Embassy.

"We are now a three!" Mom wrote home. "As the ranks only go up to one, we are feeling pretty lucky. The added pay is substantial and will mean just that much more that we can put away for our house in Washington."

At some point, like all embassy people, we would rotate through the home office stateside. One day.

* * *

With its iconic location on the renowned Via Veneto and its palatial and historic building, the US Embassy in Rome was in a league of its own. The building from which the beacon of American democracy beamed had been home to both Italian royalty and the Mussolini regime.

The place had seen some history. Via Vittorio Veneto 121 was a grand house of the Renaissance Revival known as the Palazzo Margherita, referring to its original tenant, Queen Margherita of Savoy. The Queen Mother lived in the palace for the first quarter of the century, during the rule of her son, Vittorio Emmanuele III. When she died, the palace became Mussolini's headquarters. America bought the building after Mussolini's execution in 1946. Palazzo Margherita and the separate ambassadorial residence, Villa Taverna—another grand historical home—are among the thousands of buildings owned or leased for use in United States diplomacy listed on the Department of State's Register of Culturally Significant Property.

Dad's office was located on the embassy grounds in yet another *palazzo*. As press attaché, Dad, along with his staff of three Italians, scanned the morning newspapers and distributed an English-language mimeographed summary of the significant items to all embassy offices before the mid-morning coffee break on the Via Veneto. The remainder of a routine day could involve connecting with the Italian press on topics of the day, arranging for American press interviews, or drafting ambassadorial remarks.

While Dad networked with the Italian press to promote his country, his colleagues in intelligence made sure that Rome's English language newspaper, the *Daily American*, stayed pro-democracy and anti-communist. With the discontinuation of the American military's European publication, *Stars and Stripes*, after World War II, three GIs started the *Daily American*. It was the only local English-speaking daily—the *International Herald Tribune* was published in Paris and took days to reach Rome.

* * *

Two Saturdays before Christmas, Camille told me that there was no Santa Claus. We were at my house finishing our sandwiches after the Brownie meeting. I asked my friend what she hoped Santa would bring her for Christmas. I expected to hear a book or a bike. Instead, I got a lecture.

"There is no such thing as Santa Claus."

I had never even considered this possibility. "Yes, there is."

"No," Camille said. "There isn't."

It dawned on me that this was yet another thing that I had never known I didn't know, like the Brownie pledge and how Red Rover worked. But those were just *things* I didn't know—

Santa was a whole *world* that I thought was there. A baby world for little kids, not for second graders. I felt stupid. I felt embarrassed.

I hated Camille.

Dad drove Mom, Susie, and me to church the next morning. The Ponte Sant'Angelo Methodist Church across the Tiber from the ancient Mausoleum of Hadrian felt like the Presbyterian church my mother had grown up in, an extension of the small-town feeling that she wanted my sister and me to absorb. My father normally stayed home on Sundays to read, or he played tennis with an embassy colleague, but today was the Christmas play.

I had my shepherd costume on my lap—somehow, a handkerchief-and-rope hat was holy. Susie's angel outfit—her fluffy bathrobe and some tinsel Mom saved from last year—was already at church. Dad's movie camera lay on the seat between my parents. Mom was saying something about not filming in church. Dad knew that. The camera was for later. After church, we were going to Piazza Navona.

We had been to the iconic Roman meeting place for lunch a few times on our Sunday outings. The crispy breadsticks and steaming plates of pasta at the Tre Scalini restaurant were my favorites. You could see the Bernini fountain from the table by the window, its marble people soaring into the air. Mom said that Piazza Navona was a real carnival at Christmas.

The church show went fine, and then we were off to see magic.

It was a cold ten-minute walk, even in the noonday sun. A ribbon of bright blue sky ran between one side of the street and the other, interrupted only by laundry hung like flags. Everyone in Rome was home on Sundays, their cars on the sidewalk, so we went single file alongside the rough walls of the old *palazzi*. The smells of garlic and olive oil drifted from the barred windows. A man hugging a paper bag of *focaccia* to his chest scuttled across the sidewalk in front of us. He pushed open a wooden door, revealing a sunny stone courtyard and a stairway leading up into gloom.

Dad wandered into the street with his movie camera on. "Okay, Nancy, now you and the girls walk ahead. No, don't look back at me. Just go ahead. Act natural."

We heard this a lot.

The sticky sweet smell of fried dough curled around the next corner, where the sky burst wide over a sea of canvas booths that had overtaken Piazza Navona. People were everywhere. Bunches of balloons floated in the center of the crowd.

"Wow, it's really full," I said. "You can't even see the Bernini."

Dad asked me to repeat that for the camera.

Mom steered us into the crowd, with a kind of drawn-out "Bohhb" that meant please cut out the filming and take one of the girls. Susie reached for his hand.

We wandered from booth to booth, the four of us reflected in huge gold balls, pink balls, red balls. A bunch of silvery glass grapes shimmered in the sun; the light trapped inside like Tinkerbell. Tin birds with tails of spun glass hung mid-flight. Twirling stretches of green tinsel spiraled up and up and up. The sun danced from booth to booth, marking the path like an airport runway at night.

As Mom paused to touch special pieces, the vendors would start in. "*Signora, un buon prezzo.*" Madam, I can give you a good price, and an amount in lire. "*Eh!*" Her response delivered just the right amount of skepticism. What would the lady wish to offer? "I could pay . . ." she responded, loud enough for Dad to hear how good her Italian was now. Done. The knotted string bag she pulled out of her purse began to take shape as she nestled in her newspaper-wrapped purchases.

On the other side of the piazza, in the deep cool shadows of canvas tents, was a whole new Christmas universe—the makings of the traditional Italian *presepio*, the manger scene. Hills of spongy green moss; sandy paths and rocky ledges; gnarly clumps of wood stuck in clay bases; tin foil waterfalls springing from cork mountain walls; wooden bridges crossing rivers of glass. Atop a hill, there was an entire village with a winding pebble street flanked by houses festooned with hanging laundry. Down in the valley, shepherds stood with their lambs slung across their shoulders. A farmhouse sat nearby, with pottery mules, oxen, and chickens littering its yard.

The Three Wise Men in brilliant gold and ruby robes climbed a hill toward the little thatched hut surrounded by silver angels. The Madonna perched on her invisible chair and Joseph stood in the hay, gripping his staff. They gazed at the empty cradle. No one puts Jesus out until he is born on Christmas.

Susie helped me choose the best pieces for our own manger scene. Soon, Mom's bag was bursting with moss, bark, and figurines, and I had figured out the best way to build.

"It has to go up high," I said. The square of cardboard that Dad had brought home for art projects earlier in the week would fit right on top of the antique trunk from Winona, ready for newspaper hills under a draped sheet.

"No," Susie said. "Under the tree."

"Look, it needs to be where we can move the Wise Men," I said. Susie needed a lot of explanations, it seemed to me.

My analysis was cut short by a squealing sound at the far end of the piazza.

"Bagpipes!" Mom said. "Just like your Robb ancestors in Scotland." She took us each by the hand, and we strode off in the direction of the noise, the string bag bumping between us. Dad followed, movie camera running.

A long whine reeled us in. A wavering tune balanced on top of the hum. The crowd made room for us blonde *ragazze*. The green *loden* wool of strangers' coats scratched gently at my cheeks as we squeezed through.

Two men stood in the clearing. They wore woolen hats and leather vests, and their legs were wrapped in sheepskin bound by ropes. Their boots drooped around their ankles.

The shepherds each held a pouch from which they were squeezing music with their elbows, bulging cheeks pushing air through a long instrument like a recorder, fingers protruding from fingerless gloves to press upon the holes.

The gentle tune was repeating now, the notes flowing simply into each other, the melody floating up with winter's breath. The bagpipes whined to a stop, and the last note hung in the still cold air.

One of the men pulled off his hat and carried it around the gathered crowd. "*Grazie, grazie, buon natale, grazie, buon natale.*" Thank you, Merry Christmas.

Dad dropped a few lire into the hat. The melody of the shepherds' song rang in my ears as we walked slowly back to the Mercedes.

On our way home, we stopped at the stand of Christmas trees in the piazza behind Vigna Clara. As Dad parked the car, Susie and I ran ahead of Mom into the fresh forest. We poked and tugged. Each tree seemed perfect, and then each tree seemed terrible, and then a tree was just right, but we lost track of it. By the time Dad walked over from the car, we were worn out. He stepped in, picked a tree, and we drove off with it bobbing out of the trunk.

The tangy, golden smell of pot roast enveloped us as Mom unlocked the front door. It was quiet. Our Rome maid, Giovanna, was out as scheduled every Sunday, probably walking in the Borghese Gardens with her *carabinieri* policeman boyfriend. His dress-up uniform was a splendid cape and a hat with a red plume.

"Jane, run let your father in," Mom said as she headed for the living room with the string bag bundles.

I opened the back door just as the service elevator dinged open. "Hello?" Dad said from behind the bushy tree.

I kept the elevator door open with one foot. Susie hopped out into the corridor, mostly in the way.

"Watch out." I held Susie's shoulder as Dad and the tree shoved by us into the apartment, leaving us littered with needles. I squished a couple between my fingers and sniffed, sending a blast of Christmas up my nose. I rolled the tacky sap on my palms into little balls like old snot.

"Okay," Mom called from the kitchen. "Time for dinner."

Dad stepped out of the laundry room. "Tree's drinking. Let me wash up and put on some special music."

Susie and I were in our seats at the dining room table as the first notes played. "It's the shepherd song!" I said.

"*Tu Scendi Dalle Stelle,*" Dad corrected, sitting at his place at the head of the table. "This is the new Alpini album." The a cappella singers were the elite infantry recruits from the Alpine villages of northern Italy. "The lyrics are on the back of the jacket."

Mom walked in with a platter of steaming pot roast and mashed potatoes. "And you guys can learn the song, but after dinner," she said. "Food's getting cold."

As the music flowed over me, I realized that it didn't matter if there was no Santa Claus. There was enough Christmas in the shepherd's music, the fragrant tree, and the string bag full of magic.

* * *

Mom started a new Christmas Eve tradition: tacos. It was a deconstruction of the Venezuelan cornmeal meat pies that Fina procured for us our first Christmas in Caracas. The blend of ground beef, beans, tomatoes, onions, and shredded cheese—enfolded in canned El Paso tortillas that the Naples PX stocked for the Mexican American GIs—made a festive table and the leftovers rolled into Christmas Day omelets.

For Susie's fifth birthday, we went to Sicily—a place, Mom wrote home, "that has been conquered so many times by so many different cultures that it is filled with every style of architecture and ruins." My class was studying the ancient Greeks, so to stand in the remains of their temples was exhilarating. Susie and I both loved the donkey carts decorated in bright colors, with the donkeys wearing red harnesses, bells, and feather hats. Mount Etna smoked on New Year's Eve while the Sicilians threw 1961 out their windows.

Fifty-four hundred miles to the west, Fidel Castro declared himself a Marxist-Leninist and asked the Soviet Union to protect his socialist nation. Within nine months, Khrushchev would assemble missiles just ninety miles from America, jarring the world to the brink of nuclear war.

And in February, captured CIA pilot Gary Francis Powers was exchanged for a Russian spy on a bridge in Berlin.

3. HOME LEAVE TERRITORY

By the summer of 1962, we were overdue for a month's home leave. We had been in Italy almost three years, and we were nearing the statutory requirement by which a foreign service officer must return to the United States for a month's reorientation. As the *Winona Sunday News* reported during our visit: "Home leave, Amerson said, is not only enjoyable but is required for all USIA personnel overseas for renewed exposure to the attitudes and atmosphere of the country."

Of our prior home leave in 1957, my mother later recalled, "You must stay in America for thirty days, not counting the five consulting days in Washington or weekends or holidays. We slept in eighteen beds with a six-month-old and a two-and-a-half-year-old." She laughed. "I remember little of that first home leave." I remember none of it.

This time, Susie and I were older, ready to participate in and remember roundtrip travel to Dad's address-of-record in South Dakota, by way of Winona, and back to Rome, by way of California. It was the longest journey of our foreign service life—some thirteen thousand miles in thirty days by boat, plane, and car.

The trip wove a vivid tapestry of impressions that became part of my DNA, a fixed daydream of America.

* * *

The SS Independence towers over the low dockside buildings in the Naples harbor and the little outdoor table where we eat our pizzas with knives and forks. Two long blasts of the boat's whistle, and we board.

The man at reception is from England, and his quick thank-yous come out as "Q!" The four of us say it to each other (and quietly to him) for the rest of the trip. We zigzag down the long interior corridors heavy

with warm air and swing in the ocean-made waves of the small pool
that lift us up the tall glass walls.

Mom and Dad wake us before dawn as the ship arrives in New York
City. The deck is crowded but so quiet that you can hear the water slipping by. The Statue of Liberty breaks through the mist as people mumble prayers and clap. Mom squeezes my hand. "Welcome to America."

A yellow cab takes us into the shadowed, empty canyons of Manhattan
as the sun rises. In front of the hotel, a smoking grate in the sidewalk is
a secret passage to the subway. There are no ruins in New York. Dad
brings us breakfast in paper bags—soft rolls, salty butter, and powdered sugar donuts that leave white mustaches on our upper lips.

The sidewalks are so wide that we don't have to step into and out of the
street, and we stride four-abreast without being bumped into by someone every second. The flat gray skyscrapers are not much of a contrast
with the pale sky. The ochre and burnt sienna colors of Roman buildings
make our sky look so much bluer. When we cross the street on white
lines, no one runs, and the cars staying stopped at the red light without
beeping or gunning their motors.

Mom treats us to dinner at the Automat, where rotating displays like
tiny shop windows present little plates of American foods—macaroni
and cheese, a baloney sandwich, banana cream pie—for just twenty-five
American cents. When she was a dancer in New York City, Mom made
soup out of hot water and ketchup for dinner. I'll bet it was great—she
makes the best minestrone.

* * *

We take an airplane to Minnesota, where we get into a station wagon—it is as big as two Fiats put together with an enormous back seat
for Susie and me and even more room behind us. It has black and yellow
California license plates. No one knows we are from Italy.

We follow the Mississippi River south to where it becomes so wild and
wide that it's called Lake Pepin. In the winter, it freezes over as hard

as a highway. Laura Ingalls Wilder crossed Lake Pepin in Pa's covered wagon from the little house in the big woods to the little house on the prairie.

The sweet and tangy sip of my first A&W root beer, lips tucked over the icy glass mug, makes tiny explosions in my mouth. My teeth sink into the gooey layers of hamburger, cheese, lettuce, tomato, and gooshy American bread. Salty strips of potato and chewy cheese curds make my mouth pucker.

The road rises high above the brown Mississippi, the swaths of beige sandbars glinting in the afternoon sun. Sugar Loaf, the mountaintop rock, stands against the evening sky like a sentinel over Winona.

Grandma's soft arms and belly envelop Susie and me. She smells like an Italian bakery. I lift her hand skin and let it go. It melts back into place in slow motion. Grandpa kisses the top of our heads as he brings out the tricycles he brought home from his store for us to ride. Mom hugs Grandpa and lets us ride down the empty sidewalk alone, the wheels going thump-thump as we hit the cracked cement. Susie rounds the corner. Mom just stands there with Grandpa.

Lake Winona's water is gray-green and muddy even in the bright sunlight, and the sand closes over my toes as soon as I step in. In Capri, you could see right down to the bottom, so at least I knew what was there. I watch Susie wade out to the slide with our Robb cousins. After baloney sandwiches and watermelon, we go to the playground in our suits and play barefoot without grownups. Grandma takes us to Dairy Queen, where the ice cream is as soft as the cotton candy in the Borghese Gardens.

Robb Brothers, Grandpa's store, has everything: red wheelbarrows, blue bicycles, green rakes, and black barbecue grills all lined up shiny on the sidewalk. Inside, it smells like fresh cardboard, new plastic, and warm metal. The blue-white air lies like a layer of shellac on the crimson garden tool handles, the silver metal pot covers, the blue cardboard backs of slim sewing scissors. Grandpa folds himself almost in half to come down to our height, a gentle smile lifting the droopy part of his cheeks, and gives Susie and me each a crisp dollar bill. I buy a doll to remind me of Mom's Shirley Temple doll that lives in the ottoman on Grandma's front porch.

* * *

We follow the Mississippi north again towards the Twin Cities, the high road matching the river like soprano harmony following an alto melody. Dad's sisters, Aunt Snooky and Aunt Jeanie, and their husbands-the-uncles, laugh and hug and eat and sing.

I watch Mom re-do her French twist, bobby pins in her mouth, licking her finger to slick back a few stray pieces of hair and smooth down Susie's bangs. She refreshes her pink lipstick. Dad's laugh mingles with the happy chaos of being with kid sisters. We barely make a dent in bowls of potato salad and bean salad, platters of fried chicken, piles of steaming sweet corn, and baskets of those wonderful American rolls with salty butter.

Aunt Snooky gets out her guitar, and the party shifts to the living room. Susie wanders over to the couch as Dad flips through the songbook for another cowboy tune. I settle into Mom, feeling the gentle rise and fall of her ribcage.

* * *

We caravan west to South Dakota on a ribbon of gray sunlight splitting the endless emerald cornfields. The tires bump a rhythm like a heartbeat. The deep-blue sky arches overhead, and you can see the horizon in every direction. Ragged columns of clouds in various stages of puffery parade by. Shimmering silver silos and red-painted barns, twinned like Romulus and Remus, appear here and there, the pop-up cluster of trees hiding the farmhouse that completes the set. Dad says the trees protect the houses from being covered by the winter snows, but that a summer tornado can uproot a tree and drop it right on the house. I check the sky.

At our boy cousins' farm, we eat again—fresh-picked corn, Jell-O-mold salads, layered fruit bars. Butter runs down my arm and grass tickles my bare legs. Susie and I put on the boys' jackets that smell like hay and smoke. We shovel green food pellets out of a little wagon for the sheep, and balance on the wooden fence slats watching enormous grunting pigs slurp slop. Aunt Marie shows me how to reach under the sitting hens for their warm eggs, but I'm pretty sure I'll get pecked so, no, thank you.

There is a bar of soap in the bathroom that grinds the dirt right off. The stairs leading to the boys' bedrooms are like the steps to the loft where Laura and Mary lay on their straw-filled mattress. Aunt Marie makes bread and pie while Uncle Eugene sits at the kitchen table smoking his pipe and making conversation as the Farm Bulletin plays on the radio.

It is heaven.

* * *

The road to California runs flat through swaths of prairie with barely a windbreak or silo to challenge the vista. This is cowboys-and-Indians country. Even in summer, the grass whispers of loneliness. I bunch my sweater into a pillow, lulled by the soft familiar tones of Mom and Dad speaking quietly.

The whirring movie camera records our journey. We meet a real American Indian at Mount Rushmore, watch cowboys ride down Main Street in a pioneer-days parade in Deadwood, see big brown bears wander across the road in Yellowstone. I taste the Great Salt Lake, and hot pain flashes behind my ears. I have the mumps.

The modern Los Angeles house of friends from Rome is ours for a night. It has green shag rugs, chaotic paintings, and a Kodachrome brilliant backyard with a bright-green manicured lawn and a waterfall. Something in the rugs nips at our ankles—fleas. I leap into bed from the tiled floor, hoping that fleas can't jump this high. I jiggle all night, my ears and face aflame.

Old people come, Grandma Amerson and her sisters, who made that long drive from South Dakota in the olden days. Uncle Terry, Dad's baby brother, is a teenager. He puts an orange peel over his top teeth and smiles like a crazy monkey. The old people bring out potato salad, green

Jell-O, and pans of cookie bars.

It's been a long trip. Mom says that we are tired of America, and Americans are tired of us. It's time to go home.

4. President Kennedy

Susie and I were inspired by American commercials in our tape-recording sessions that fall. "Chick-chick-chickorina soup," we sang. "It's nutritious and delicious. Mmmm boy! It's good!"

Dad's public relations expertise had normalized the idea of recording reel-to-reel tapes at home. Running the machine ourselves, my sister and I sang, played our Italian *ocarinas* clay flutes, read our own poetry, explained our lives, and acted out plays—*Goldilocks and the Three Bears* featured me as the heroine, Susie, Mom, and Dad as the bears, and the closing moral of the story, "I'll never leave home again without asking!" I can still recreate that line in my little Janie voice.

The confidence with which we used the tape recorder would blossom as we grew and technology developed—still cameras, cassette recorders, video cameras—such that later in life we were the ones who could program a VCR or figure out the connections of a computer. I still thank Dad when I solve a mechanical problem.

When Susie and I tired of playing with each other, we used the blank side of Dad's USIS press releases for other creations. I wrote poems and stories—"Jane loves words!" Mom wrote home—while Susie drew and painted. "The girls both appear to have some talent in this direction," wrote Dad, whose love of doodling made its way into our annual Christmas card. "Although I think Susie has the edge, as far as innate ability goes."

Dad's portrait of Lorenzo de' Medici, after the Macchietti painting in the Uffizi, hung in our entryway. He loved words, too—Mom knew she could count on a poem for her birthday.

* * *

Susie was now in first grade, and I was in third. It was good to not be the new kid this year, but instead to be welcoming new arrivals. The student body at the Overseas School of Rome was an ebb and flow of diplomat, corporate, expatriate, and Italian children who understood the nomadic norms that governed our lives.

Not everybody was nice, however. I was now wearing glasses, and I forgot them at home on the first day of third grade. The teacher put me in the front row so I could see the blackboard, and Johnny, the class bully, teased me for being blind. The teacher saw my tears, assumed that it was eye strain, and moved me to the back of the class to do whatever I wanted for the rest of the day. It felt like a little victory over that mean boy.

Johnny bragged about how he was going to be in a movie about the Egyptian queen, Cleopatra. On and on he went, but his story failed to materialize. Then, we found out the truth—Johnny had lost his role as Cleo's son. His movie career was over before it had even begun.

Mom and Dad knew the bigger story. *Cleopatra*, being filmed at the Cinecittà movie studio on the outskirts of Rome, was in trouble due to the affair between the leading stars, Elizabeth Taylor and Richard Burton. As the love story played out in the headlines, the filming budget ballooned, and the shooting schedule exploded. Mean Johnny grew too old to play Liz's son. I was very happy.

The movie made an unexpected appearance on Dad's embassy schedule. At the invitation of 20th Century Fox, a contingent of congressmen flew in to generate publicity and support for the film. It was my father's responsibility to escort them to a room someone had set up for the event.

The congressmen stood around until, finally, a door opened and in walked Elizabeth Taylor, or rather, Cleopatra. She was obviously between takes and complying with the studio's request. The men shuffled and stared, ogled even, while Liz looked uncomfortable.

No one said anything until one of the congressmen sidled towards the movie star and announced tremulously, "I came, I saw, I conquered!"

Dad later wrote, "The episode still seems to me one of the more bizarre sidebars to an assignment in the Eternal City."

* * *

Of all the dignitaries who visited Italy, it was White House visitors who created the greatest volume of work for my father and his staff. Advance people arrived a few weeks early to work out the detailed schedule, from logistics to media coverage. It was up to Dad to see that the visit stayed on track, from the officials' arrival at Fiumicino Airport to press conferences and audiences with Italian dignitaries, including the bedazzled denizens of the Vatican.

Jackie Kennedy swept through Rome for two days in March of 1962 on her way to India, where her sister, Lee Radziwill, lived. Dad's preparation for Jackie's visit included setting up her private audience with Pope John XXIII. He accompanied Mrs. Kennedy and her official escort to the Vatican but stayed out of range of the newsreel cameras.

Jackie and her children Caroline and John-John came through Rome again in early August for a few days at her sister's Trastevere apartment before continuing to the Amalfi Coast. I hoped that Caroline would come to Vigna Clara to play with Susie and me. We settled for seeing them on television and in the newspapers. The *paparazzi* were all over them.

* * *

Lyndon Johnson, who visited thirty-three countries as Kennedy's vice president, showed up in Italy three times during Dad's stint as press attaché. Most of his trips abroad were representational functions. Perhaps Kennedy sent Johnson away to keep him busy. Perhaps Johnson sought the kind of recognition abroad that he was not getting in America.

LBJ's September 1962 trip to Italy was part of a strategic goodwill tour of Southern Europe and the Middle East suggested by the State Department. Greece, Turkey, and Italy were among the United States' original and staunchest Cold War allies, and the American military bases in these countries were critical to Soviet containment. Likewise, our alliances with Iran, Lebanon, and Cyprus helped to stabilize the Middle East.

The vice president's meetings with top government officials in these countries, as well as with influential private citizens, supported essential alliances on the southern fringe of the communist world. The vice president reassured these allies of continued US commitment to assist them in resisting Soviet bloc pressures.

LBJ and his thirty traveling companions completed this tour in Rome. The one topic of substance in his formal talks with the Italian government was to increase its purchase of American military equipment. Dad organized visits to a shipyard and an aerospace research center, as well as a luncheon with the American Men's Club of Rome.

The vice president treated the trip as a campaign event, as was his style no matter where he traveled. His limo stopped traffic frequently so that Johnson could wade into the crowded sidewalks and physically press the flesh of the puzzled *romani*, who probably had no idea who this big *americano* might be.

"LBJ's legendary ego translated into American arrogance," my father later wrote. "The press was to capture only his favored left side—can you imagine trying to control that?"

Johnson's style went over much better in Naples, where he spoke to NATO forces. *TIME* magazine reported that the crowds shouted: "*Viva Johnson! Viva America!*"

The vice president responded in kind: "*Viva Napoli!*" The Italian press was effusive. LBJ flew back to Washington in his glory.

The alliance with Italy took center stage just weeks later during the Cuban Missile Crisis. For two weeks, the world held its breath while Kennedy and Khrushchev stared each other down across the Straits of Florida, with Soviet nuclear missiles deployed in Cuba matched by American nuclear missiles in Italy and Turkey. Kennedy won the contest when the Soviet leader agreed to withdraw Russian weapons from Cuba.

Khrushchev's failure precipitated his fall from power two years later.

* * *

President Kennedy himself made the embassy work the hardest.

Rome was the final stop in the president's triumphant 1963 European trip, which *TIME* called "a rock star tour." In Germany, President Kennedy was an immediate hit with his *"Ich bin ein Berliner,"* I am a Berliner, speech to hundreds of thousands of West Berliners jamming the streets.

Irish President Éamon de Valera and throngs of cheering crowds welcomed Kennedy when he arrived in the land of his ancestors. In England, he was met by Prime Minister Harold Macmillan.

The president's final stops were Rome and Naples. My father worked closely with Press Secretary Pierre Salinger and his White House staff on the schedule for Kennedy's arrival and subsequent moves around the city and in Naples. Ambassador Reinhardt and his family vacated Villa Taverna for the presidential party.

Kennedy emerged alone from Air Force One, glamorous and handsome, waving to the small knot of observers. His open-air limousine was escorted by elegant *carabinieri* on horseback. He made his protocol visit to the Quirinale Palace, the seat of the national government. The president's call on Pope Paul VI came just days after the pontiff's installation upon the death of John XXIII. The media noted this historic meeting between the first Catholic American president and the head of the Catholic Church.

However, Dad learned that the White House handlers were disappointed in the Romans' lack of enthusiasm as the president drove through the streets in an embassy limousine. Jackie was adored, but Dad said that *romani* had seen too many parades of triumphant leaders during the last two thousand years to be bowled over, even by this American president.

Before departing for Naples, President Kennedy set time aside to meet informally with embassy families at Villa Taverna. The four of us lined up with about thirty other people on the pebbled walkway between the ambassadorial residence and its garden. Mr. Kennedy came out the front door wearing a gray suit and a pretty purple tie. I watched him make his way down the receiving line, stopping to speak with every person. The first time we had seen him was on the balcony in Vienna three years before. Now, I noted that he was shorter than Dad and had Mom's hair color. My mother tugged me back into place as he approached us.

The president shook Dad's hand. "Thanks for making all this work," he said, with a sweep of an arm. "Nice gathering."

"Glad to help, sir," Dad said. "This is my wife, Nancy, and our daughters, Jane and Susan."

"Hello," President Kennedy said as he shook Mom's hand. He bent down to our level and shook our extended hands. "Hello, girls."

I looked the president in the eye. "Hello." Kids in the foreign service know how to shake hands.

When we got home, I pulled out an old press release—our art projects paper—and wrote this poem: "He is a man, an important man, in a gray suit and purple tie. Today at Villa Taverna, he stopped by to say hi. Villa Taverna, as you must know, is pretty in rain or snow."

* * *

The crowds in Naples were larger, louder, and more demonstrative. Perhaps the strong ties between Italian immigrants and this southern city made the difference. Perhaps Vice President Johnson had warmed up the crowds with his visit the year before.

"I shall leave this country with regret," Kennedy said at NATO military headquarters before departing Naples, adding that the NATO "pledge is as strong and unshakeable today as it was when it was made."

The Washington spinners must have smiled as they boarded Air Force One for the trip home, leaving my father and the rest of the embassy staff to wrap things up. Dad kept to himself the rumor that the Villa Taverna delegation included a White House staffer expressly to keep Kennedy company in the bedroom. "My puritanical propensities inclined me not to accept this as one-hundred percent true. Alas, evidence that has surfaced regarding JFK's predilections removes any lingering doubts."

"Sooner or later," Italians said, "everybody comes to Rome."

And, sooner or later, all of us at the Rome Embassy would leave.

5. Leaving

Our maid was the first to announce she was leaving. "Giovanna has plans to go to Tunis to work for the Italian ambassador," Mom wrote home. "I'm afraid that she is not quite the adaptable type, and that North Africa may be more than her provincial soul can take. I'm sure we will miss her, but no one is indispensable."

Fourth grade got underway with the British Miss Holt, no relation to the American Mrs. Holt. My friends were back—my skipping club pal Susan, our music teacher's son Josh, and Danny, whose father was a painter and whose mother was Mom's friend. Mean Johnny was also back. Camille's father had been posted to Washington, so she was gone, and I was fine with that—I had not forgiven the whole Santa thing.

My parents assumed that we would be in Rome for another two-year tour, then eligible for home leave and transfer to a new assignment. But their expectations had not fully taken into consideration the nature of this foreign service career: we had signed on to be moved "at the convenience of the government." Just as Susie and I were settled into our school year, Dad got orders from Washington.

USIA needed Dad in Bogotá as public affairs officer, heading up the countrywide USIS operation in Colombia. It was an unexpected promotion. His replacement as Rome press attaché, Jock Shirley, was already in Rome, having just finished a USIS assignment in Trieste and Venice. Years later, Jock would again fill Dad's shoes at the Rome Embassy, this time as PAO.

To Mom, the surprise move felt like having her feet cut out from under her. After the chaos of seeing our life upended three years in a row, she had finally put down roots in Rome. For the first time since Caracas, Mom felt at home. She knew her way around the alleyways off the fashionable Via del Corso, the high-end shops of Via Veneto, and the stalls of the flea-market vendors at Porta Portese.

"We had a dinner for some Latin Americans including the head of the post-revolution junta in Venezuela. Someone asked if I hoped to return to Latin America, and I blithely replied: 'Oh, yes, I'd love to someday,'" Mom later wrote. "I reacted to Bob's announcement the next morning that we were going to Bogotá as PAO with less than shouts of praise. A move? And as the boss's wife? I could barely realize it was a fact."

Orders specified that Dad was to make a direct transfer, doing without a personal vacation during the transition to the new post. He was expected at USIA headquarters in Washington on November 18 for five days of consultation and was then to report to the embassy in Bogotá. Although it had been a year since we had seen family, there would be no time for visits with the Amersons and the Robbs. Pulling Susie and me out of school midyear felt doubly cruel to our mother.

The foreign service, Mom later said, did not treat families quite right. It would be years before the State Department acted on that oversight by creating the Family Liaison Office to help foreign service officers and their families with resources like an Employee Assistance Program and a Deployment Stress Management Program "to increase your resilience or manage any concerns." The world has become so much more complicated for current foreign service families.

Our parents told my sister and me that we were leaving Rome by way of promising us a pet. I wonder now if Dad had promised to get a guard dog to keep us safer in our new home. Bogotá was decidedly more dangerous than Rome.

"How would you girls like a dog?" Dad said.

Susie was immediately enthusiastic. "Wow! Yes! What kind?"

I was not at all sure. Dogs terrified me. One of our Vigna Clara friends let her dachshund run off his leash in the play area behind our apartment building, and the sight of that yippy thing careening around the sandy lot sent me running. A dog was just so unpredictable.

Mom noticed my hesitation. "We'll get a little puppy that you can take care of," she said.

"But what about my birthday ride?" I was fascinated by the ubiquitous, colorful sidecar attachments to Rome's hundreds of motorcycles and scooters, and my mother had promised me that I would get to ride in one as a present for my birthday in mid-November.

"Maybe before we go," she said.

Time for my sidecar ride ran out as Dad prepared the press attaché assignment for Jock Shirley and Mom got us packed. My last day of school was November 14, my ninth birthday.

Mom brought my party to school, with individual pizzas for the entire class. It was good-bye to Susan, Josh, Danny, and Johnny. I had spent more time with these classmates than anyone else in my life, except Mom, Dad, and Susie. I chewed my pizza while choking down tears, the dough becoming pasty mush.

I guessed I wouldn't become an archaeologist after all. We were moving to our next life.

* * *

Two days later, we were at the Francis Scott Key residential hotel in Washington, a short walk from USIA headquarters. Mom told us that the hotel was named for the man who wrote the words to America's national song. My favorite part of the hotel was the store where they sold grape-flavored hard candies so tangy that they made my mouth water and my lips pucker in a weirdly good way.

On Monday, Dad began a week of meetings on his upcoming responsibilities in Colombia. The Kennedy administration's new Alliance for Progress—*Alianza Para El Progreso*—was generating a breeze of hope and optimism throughout Latin America, and Colombia was a major showcase for the *Alianza's* economic-social program of cooperation, assistance, and self-reliance. After the relatively superficial press attaché work in sophisticated Rome, the challenge of having real involvement with a country's development filled Dad with excitement.

He had lunch with his PAO predecessor, Keith Adamson, who had been recalled from Bogotá to Washington after just two years to take a position at the Voice of America. The VOA, which operated under USIA's control, created a tremendous volume of Spanish-language recordings using Colombian actors. The country's Spanish was recognized as the least accented in Latin America, just as Midwestern English was the generic voice of the evening news in the United States.

Adamson informed my father that his wife was arriving to help orient Mom to the job of PAO's wife. Dad mentioned it to her over dinner.

Sure enough, a day later, the hotel's front desk called our room to announce that a Mrs. Adamson was on her way up. Mom yanked the curlers out of her just-washed hair and covered her head with what she hoped was a very chic scarf. The wife entered with great fanfare, like a movie star. It soon became clear that she was not especially interested in helping Mom understand what life in Bogotá would be like but rather in evaluating her successor's credentials.

* * *

Our transfer week drew to a close on Friday, November 22. Dad completed all his staff-level meetings that morning and was scheduled to see USIA Director Murrow after lunch. It would be Dad's first personal encounter with the journalism icon. Over the noon hour, Dad picked up our air travel tickets, managing to get us all upgraded to first class in the process, an unexpected treat. He wondered if he could parlay the travel into a kind of gift for Mom. It was their eleventh wedding anniversary the next day.

While Dad was finishing up at USIA, Mom, Susie, and I took a tour of the White House. It was not as old and fancy as Roman palazzos, but it was very clean and pretty. Somewhere upstairs, in President Kennedy's bedroom closet, was that gray suit and purple tie he had worn to meet us at the ambassador's house in Rome. I wondered if we would see him, but Mom said that Mr. and Mrs. Kennedy were on a trip to Texas. Caroline, of course, was in school like all the other kids who were not on their way to a new home.

The plan for the afternoon was to pick up new school shoes for both of us girls. Italian shoes were expensive, and the selection of American options was limited at the Naples PX.

Washington's big department store, Hecht's, was only a few blocks from the hotel.

We got to the store a little after noon. Mom ushered Susie and me into one compartment of the revolving door, and it spit us out in the makeup aisle. The store directory said the shoe department was on the lower level. Mom herded us to the escalator, and down we went. Rows of shoes pulled us off the escalator like a magnet. I had never seen so many varieties. In Italy, there was pretty much one style in one color for a whole season, which changed completely by the next. We waded in alongside Mom.

"They shot the president!"

My head jerked up. A saleslady standing at the end of our aisle had her hand up to her mouth. The next few minutes passed in slow motion as if we were all underwater. Grownups reached out for each other, their mouths twisted, but I could only hear my heartbeat.

Mom gripped my hand harder than I could ever remember, and she pulled us back up the escalator and through the revolving glass doors. My face felt hot against the cool fall air.

"What about the shoes?" I asked.

"Yeah," Susie said.

"Right now, we need to find Dad," Mom said.

All around us, people were stopped, talking like friends. Mom steered us around the clusters. She was very good at this, Italian sidewalks being way more crowded. We were used to it, too, but there was a whole other energy today.

"What happened, Mommy?" I asked.

"Walk," Mom said.

The news of Kennedy's shooting had hit USIA even faster, canceling Dad's meeting with Director Murrow, and my father was in our room when we got back to the hotel. The television was on. They said the president was dead. The television stayed on until dinnertime without any of the fun American commercials.

That night, we retraced our steps back to 1600 Pennsylvania Avenue, where a quiet crowd stood gazing at the White House. It shone in the night air as bright as the Roman wedding cake, the Vittorio Emanuele II monument. Just that morning, it was where my Man-in-the-Purple-Tie lived. It wasn't anymore. Caroline and John-John's daddy was dead. No one's daddy should die.

I heard grownups around us crying, the kind of noise you might hear in a movie but not in real life. I kept one hand in my coat pocket, my fingers playing with leftover lint. Mom had a grip on my other hand, the tips of her nails firm against my palm. Susie danced at the end of Mom's other arm, bouncing to keep warm. Dad's hands were on our shoulders.

So, this dark sadness was death. I pulled my hand out of my pocket and hooked a couple of warm fingers around Dad's cold ones. Poor

Daddy, feeling this punch in the stomach all alone on the airplane from Caracas to South Dakota when Grandpa Amerson died. I wished I remembered him, and then I was glad I didn't because I would be feeling sad all over again. I looked up at my father. His cheeks glistened in the glow of the streetlight. Mom's, too. I had never seen my parents cry. Poor Caroline and John-John. I tightened my grip on Dad's hand, and he squeezed me back.

* * *

The next morning, we drove out to the Maryland suburbs to spend the day at Camille's house. I was excited to watch Saturday morning cartoons. Instead, we all sat in what they called their family room while the adults monopolized the television. The programming was as boring as Italian news. I was impatient, but the adults' faces warned me from saying anything. The novelty of hearing American English on the TV screen made up a little for the disappointment.

Mom and Dad's anniversary was forgotten.

On Monday, while the presidential funeral procession was getting underway down Pennsylvania Avenue, we flew into our new lives in Colombia. The tragic death of our country's young leader seemed to add a new dimension to my father's assignment. The Peace Corps, the Voice of America, and the Alliance for Progress were emblems of the martyred president's ideals, and all three programs had a strong presence in Colombia.

Dad felt the zeal of Mormons and other true believers sent around the world to "win hearts and minds." The embassy's presence was, after all, called the US Mission.

Part V

Bogotá

(1963-66)

The wall meant to keep the Amerson and Cárdenas homes apart became instead the place we gathered to play.

1. Arriving

Twenty-six bombs went off in Bogotá the night we arrived, including one at the home of a newspaper editor a scant two blocks from our new house. Although the era of narco trafficking had not yet dawned in Colombia, it was a country at war.

At his briefing in Washington, my father was reminded that, like much of Latin America, Colombia had many political, economic, and social problems. The country was in the seventeenth year of a brutal and barbaric civil war—*La Violencia*—born of an intense political feud that would result in the deaths of more than two hundred thousand people. One regime was overthrown by a military coup, and the military dictator was then himself driven from office. A fragile political alliance, the National Front, had been in place for just a handful of years, managing to implement an agrarian reform law and to initiate national economic planning for development. The centerpiece was the economic support of the United States through Kennedy's Alliance for Progress.

Colombians felt a close kinship to Jack and Jackie, who visited the country in December of 1961 in a South American trip that had also included a dinner with Venezuelan President Betancourt in Caracas. "President Kennedy and Jackie had visited Colombia," wrote my father. "After his death they were almost deified, which gave us representatives of the US government, of the Kennedys' country, an aura of glory tinged with sadness."

Washington knew that some Colombians saw their country's economic dependence on the United States as a problem. Or, at best, as not enough of a solution, for Colombia's economic growth had come almost to a standstill while inflation was running rampant.

More serious trouble was brewing. Marxist guerillas, including students trained in Castro's Cuba were lurking in the background.

The embassy was aware that the Soviets were connecting with the Colombian communist movement.

Singing the praises of democracy in the face of decades of inequality would be tough going.

* * *

My mother's concern was her children. The explosions on our first night had been much too close. More disturbing still was the very real threat of child kidnappings. The feuding factions needed money, and rich Colombians paid handsome ransoms for the return of their children. Teusaquillo, the well-to-do neighborhood in which we now lived, was a target community. There were no front yards on our street. Kids played instead in private gardens behind the houses, protected by tall walls. Julia, the housekeeper, and Rosanna, the cook, kept an eye on us and on the house.

In her letters home, Mom revealed how traumatic this transition was. "Last night, as I tucked Janie into bed, she said, 'I do hope there are no more bombs tonight,' and there was a loud boom. Eighteen more through the night but none near us," she wrote, ending on a positive note despite her fear: "The rosy side of it is that if the bombing does go on for a certain length of time, we become a hardship post with a nice increase in pay!"

All that Susie and I knew was that we were never to leave an adult's sight. New rule. No questions.

My mother dispelled her anxiety through action. There was no time to give into "the blues." Her family needed to get settled, and the first order of business was to get Susie and me into school.

There were two English-speaking options school options in Bogotá—the prestigious Colegio Nueva Granada, CNG, an American-style college preparatory school like the Overseas School of Rome, and the English School, which followed a British curriculum. CNG would have been the ideal fit, but, as Mom had anticipated when Dad announced the mid-year move, the school did not have room for both a new fourth grader and a new second grader. The English School had space, although it was difficult to assess how welcoming the administration would be. The headmistress, Mrs. Masson, sounded curt on the telephone, or perhaps it was just the accent.

In short order, Susie and I were outfitted with the English School uniform—brown blazers and matching pleated skirts. I was thrilled. We might be new, but we would look like we belonged in this school. At least we would have language on our side during the day.

Our Spanish, however, was buried under four years—about half our lives—of Italian.

* * *

My father arranged for the embassy car to take Mom, Susie, and me to school on our first day. As we pulled up to a large, gated villa in a residential street, a tall woman exited the gate and strode across the sidewalk to meet us. Her wool jacket strained at its buttons, and there were horizontal folds across her belly where the heavy skirt rode up.

Dad's chauffeur, Bonifacio, opened the car door for Mom. "Hello, Mrs. Masson," Mom said. Susie and I climbed out behind her. "Girls, this is your headmistress."

Mrs. Masson bent into the creases of her skirt and extended her hand. "Hello, Jane. Hello, Susan."

I couldn't help but smile. She sounded like the British man in reception on the *SS Independence.*

"Did I say something amusing, dear?" Mrs. Masson said, taking my hand in two of hers.

She pressed my fingers a little too tightly. Her cheeks drooped down her face.

Mom gently held onto my shoulders as I pulled my hand free.

"On your way, Mummy!" Mrs. Masson said, stepping between us.

She marched Susie and me through the gate and locked it behind her. I heard the car pull away. Mrs. Masson walked us briskly across the empty asphalt-covered yard. I caught Susie's eye and attempted to smile. She looked like she was trying not to cry.

"It's okay," I mouthed.

I wished I felt that for real. Mrs. Masson walked us past the villa to a metal hut that butted up against the back corner of the property. It looked like where workers eat lunch when they are building an apartment house. She propelled me up two wooden steps and pulled open the door.

"Hello, Mrs. Ospina. This is your new student, Jane Amerson. Good day."

The door swung shut behind me. I barely registered my sister's departure as my eyes adjusted to the dim interior. A dark-haired woman stepped away from the blackboard, the front of her black sweater smudged with chalk. She looked annoyed.

"Oh, yes," she said, looking over my shoulder. "Silence!"

I turned toward the students, about fifteen of them, seated at old wooden desks. Mrs. Ospina pointed toward an empty desk in the dead center of the group.

"Please sit. I will speak with you at recess," she said.

All thirty eyes watched me as I made my way down a tight aisle, trying not to let my bookbag bounce against anyone's shoulders. My chair squealed on the wooden floor as I pulled it back, and again as I sat down. I felt the cold seat against my legs where my cotton skirt had pulled up. I prayed that my underwear wasn't showing and held my bookbag tighter. Recess was done by the time Mrs. Ospina finished giving me the work I needed to complete to catch up with the class. There were some books that I couldn't wait to start, but there was also a whole bunch of arithmetic. I nodded my head as she hurriedly reviewed the assignments.

At noon, I followed the kids to the villa's attached garage, which served as a lunchroom. I had my lunchbox from Overseas. Mom had also given us each some Colombian *pesos* to spend for a little extra, but there was nothing being served here. I spotted Susie sitting with some of the second graders—she waved but got right back to her new friends. I found a seat toward the back and pulled out my chicken sandwich and *mamoncillo* fruit. I occupied myself with pulling the tough peel off of each fruit and gnawing the coating of pulp off the mouth-sized pits.

Mrs. Ospina's impatience flared up throughout the rest of the day. At one point, she threw the board eraser at a boy's head. Her aim was amazing.

Mom was in the embassy car at the front gate at dismissal.

The next morning, she walked us to the English School bus stop a couple of blocks from the house. The bus, a diesel-spewing, clattering contraption of corrugated metal, was a far cry from the sleek, comfortable ride we had at Overseas.

"See you at four!" Mom called as we climbed aboard. Mrs. Masson had advised my mother that the bus would not drop children off if the designated person was not there to meet us.

Kidnappings were a very real threat.

Mrs. Masson stalked the yard as we arrived, during recess, and as we left for the day, her red hands clasped behind her back. Her husband, who was as little as she was big, trailed behind her like a dinghy pulled by a tugboat. He liked us. On days that the school had snagged little containers of ice cream as a lunch treat, Mr. Masson gave us a heads-up at morning recess. "I scream, you scream, we all scream for ice cream!" He smiled like a happy elf. Mrs. Masson just glared at him, and at us.

I started looking forward to classroom reading time. We took turns reading out loud from a funny book called Canterbury Tales about some very cartoony characters traveling across England and began a play by Shakespeare that was also really silly. Susie's class was reading it, too. We nearly fell off our dining room chairs at dinner one night laughing so hard at how that one character had run away from the other. Mom and Dad just shook their heads.

"And Mrs. Ospina told us that after New Year's," I said, "we'll be learning how we lost the colonies."

"Honey, we *are* the colonies," Mom said.

Thus began my two-and-a-half-year immersion in all things British. Shakespeare and Chaucer, kings and queens, adventure stories about children, kippers, and puffins by Enid Blyton, blue uniformed Girl Guides, a girls' magazine that included recipes for scones, and spelling "color" as "colour."

Susie and I slowly adopted very slight English accents.

* * *

Christmas came on fast. Our things were not scheduled to arrive until the new year, so Mom had to make do without her rolling pin, mixer, and cookie cutters that created sugar cookies in the shapes of trees and stars. Instead, she baked several batches of Grandma Amerson's lemon bars with powdered sugar topping and Grandma Robb's nutty Viennese crescents.

The Sunday before Christmas, as always, the four of us went tree hunting, settling for a thin cypress at the Carulla supermarket where people from the hills outside Bogotá had set up shop. At another pop-up down the sidewalk, we bought a manger—built from the cardboard frame of a Fab detergent box and decorated with Colombian pebbles and dried grasses—and new figurines of Mary, Joseph, and baby Jesus.

The Christmas tree sucked up water in one of Julia's buckets while we had Sunday dinner. The beef tenderloin called *lomito* came from the German butcher down the street, a post-war emigré like Tante and Otto who ran my Venezuelan school. Susie and I were excused from doing the dishes, our once-a-week chore when the maids were out, so that we could help Dad carry the refreshed tree into the living room.

Mom appeared with the packages from the supermarket and then surprised us with something remarkable—new tinsel, untouched in its cardboard sleeve. Mom always picked the tinsel off the tree after Christmas and folded it in tin foil for the next year. Last year's tinsel was somewhere on the Atlantic, along with the lights, the glass grapes from Piazza Navona, and the cloth angels from Milan.

Mom had also managed to find El Paso tortillas in Washington, so our taco Christmas Eve dinner and Christmas Day breakfast traditions made Bogotá feel more familiar. On New Year's Eve, we celebrated Susie's seventh birthday with Italian Asti Spumante. We toasted each other in Italian, now our private family language: "*Cin, cin!*"

I felt the comfortable confines of our four-person unit wrap around me. As the world rolled into 1964, we were home again.

2. AMIGOS

By the end of the first week of January, the ship carrying everything that made a house our home was nearing the Panama Canal, through which it would access the Pacific Ocean and Colombia's west coast port of Buenaventura. While the ship waited to pass through the Canal, however, diplomatic relations between Panama and the United States blew up.

It had been sixty-one years since President Teddy Roosevelt's treaty gave America control over the Canal Zone, but Panamanians were far from reconciled to the fact. On January 7, a couple of so-called "Zonian" American teenagers took down the Panamanian flag from in front of the American school. Full-scale rioting broke out two days later. The embassy in Panama City was evacuated, the consulate in Colón was stoned, and the USIS library was burned down. Panama broke diplomatic relations with the United States, pending a commencement of negotiations on a new treaty for control of the Canal Zone.

The event resonated in Colombia, whose jurisdiction of nearly eighty years in Panama had been eliminated by the 1903 treaty creating the Canal Zone. As the new head of the United States' public affairs program in Colombia, Dad was grateful for the goodwill toward America that Kennedy's presidency, and his death, had granted.

Finally, our ship continued through the Canal. Its cargo included the Mercedes, but the car's delivery was in question. My parents hadn't realized that they were supposed to have made a request for entry, so it was possible that the car might sit in port for a couple of months, or even be taken back to Panama.

Colombia hadn't allowed the importation of cars since 1954, part of its economic balance of trade equation. What cars there were on the road were mostly very old, and used cars sold for a tremendous price—Mom wrote home that a 1952 Ford had sold for $2,000, about two-thirds of what brand-new models cost in the States. At the embassy, Dad heard that diplomats who were allowed to bring in cars made a killing selling them on the local market when they left—he made a mental note.

Not having the car wasn't a problem for Dad. His embassy driver, Bonifacio, was at our door by 7:30 each morning to take Dad to work in a long black limo. Mom appreciated having Bonifacio at her disposal later in the morning.

"I had Bonifacio take me to the Gold Museum, housed in a bank vault in the center of town," she wrote her parents. "It is an absolutely breathtaking collection of golden ornaments, relics of the past Indian culture. I hope this week to see more of the other interesting museums and the like. It is too easy to just live day-to-day keeping the house unless one makes a real effort to look around."

Still, my mother made selective use of the chauffeur's time. There was something distasteful to her about parading privilege.

* * *

The English School got underway after the holidays. The lesson I dreaded all Christmas break was on the morning schedule—the times tables. My fourth-grade class in Rome was beginning to learn the nine times tables in November when we left, and I hoped that maybe I had outrun some portion of arithmetic altogether. I had not.

I watched Mrs. Ospina scrawl the dreaded numbers and their symbols on the blackboard. She turned to face the class, holding her chalky, bony fingers out like she was casting a spell—the evil arithmetic spell.

"Please calculate the answers," she said, squinting her eyes slightly as she scanned the room for trouble.

My brain froze. My mouth got dry. I tried to look casual as I glanced across the room at my Welsh friend Katherine. She was working away at her paper. I tapped the shoulder of the boy in front of me. Pedro was Cuban, where I supposed boys were nice to girls. I knew I could get us both in a huge amount of trouble for talking, but it was this or failure today. Pedro turned halfway in his chair to look at me, curious at the distraction.

"I don't get it," I whispered.

Mrs. Ospina was arranging papers on her desk, her eyes down. Pedro was still just looking at me. Then he turned to face the teacher.

"She don't get it," he announced.

Mrs. Ospina called Mom that night to offer to tutor me in arithmetic. Mom thought this was a lovely idea, and so one day a week I went home with Mrs. Ospina for an hour of just arithmetic. I couldn't believe my parents were paying for this torture. At least Mrs. Ospina included me in the creamy sweet *arequipe* caramel she set out for her sons, what was called *las onces*, the elevenses, just like the Famous Five children in the Enid Blyton books.

I wasn't sure I would ever remember the nine times tables.

I included Pedro when I gave out Valentine's Day cards a few weeks later. Mom called it having class. Pedro called it stupid and ground the card under his foot in the dirt outside our classroom shed.

* * *

Our things finally made their way to Teusaquillo at the end of January, including, much to my parents' surprise, the Mercedes. With the car in place, the four of us resumed weekend outings, Dad driving confidently and aggressively, and Mom riding shotgun, a new Colombian guidebook opened on her lap and one hand ready to brace herself against the glove box.

Bogotá sat at more than eight thousand feet above sea level—making it hard to catch your breath, as I had discovered climbing our marble staircase to my bedroom—on an Andean altiplano plateau. A half-hour drive on the sabana plain past huge flower farms took us to the Salt Cathedral, a church carved out of an old salt mine. When we drove off the altiplano and down to the five-thousand-foot level, we were rewarded by the bananas and poinsettias of *tierra caliente*, hot country, the tropical climate which warmed the bones of chilled *bogotanos*.

One Sunday, Susie and I thought we were going to the salt mines when Dad turned down a dirt road and pulled over. Beyond the barbed wire stretched a stubbly field, at the end of which sat a small, white-stucco house and an outbuilding. A farmer in an old, straw cowboy hat was walking toward us, his arms hidden by his black wool *ruana*, the traditional Colombian shawl.

Dad got out of the car. Susie reached for the door handle.

"Hold on," Mom said. Susie squirmed.

The farmer separated a small bundle from his ruana and lifted it across the barbed wire to Dad, who set it down at his feet before handing the man something from his pocket. The bundle wiggled.

"A dog!"

Susie was out the car door before Mom could react. She crouched at Dad's feet and opened the blanket. A little brown and white muzzle poked out, and a pink tongue licked Susie's fingers.

"Mommy, Janie, come see!"

I held Mom's hand as we walked across the road. This little puppy was way too cute to be scary. I sat next to Susie on the dirt as the dog clambered out of his blanket and onto my sister's lap, where he curled up, scrunching his rear end to make a nest.

"He's a boxer," Mom said, stroking the puppy's head. "A brindle, see his stripes? What would you like to call him?"

I knew immediately. "Caesar. Caesar Augustus." Roman history was still fresh in my memory.

"But he's a baby," Susie said. "A *niño* baby."

And so, we added Caesar Augustus Niño Baby to our family. Dad made it clear that Caesar was not a toy or a person, but a dog. He would be allowed into the house during the day but kenneled at night in a wooden doghouse on the covered patio by the maids' room. Dad would see to his training when he had time.

No one else ever walked Caesar but Dad.

* * *

Susie and I now had a whole backyard where we could play by ourselves. It was protected by the house, the kitchen garden, and an eight-foot wall that separated our property from that of the neighbors. "The girls and the dog have lots of playing space and are rarely in the house," Mom wrote home. "They are worn out by the end of the day, but everyone here folds early. It must be the altitude."

We were following Caesar around the yard one weekend, being careful to avoid his piles of poop, when a clod of dirt came flying over the brick wall, narrowly missing Susie's head.

"Hey!" I yelled. I jumped back as another clump of dirt soared into the air. "*Mannaggia!*" Italian was my best defense. Spanish was beginning to sound familiar, but I still counted on Italian to express myself when it really mattered. It was such a good language to be angry in.

I grabbed Susie and turned toward the house. A shock of cold hit me right between the shoulder blades. I pivoted. A wiggly stream of water from a hose held high over the neighbors' side of the wall wavered in the air like a wary snake.

"*Cretino!*"

Another soggy clump of dirt flew through the air and dropped at my feet. I reached down, took a few steps toward the wall, and heaved the clump back over the top as hard as I could. The stream of hose water died down. We were fighting back.

I took a deep breath, feeling not very filled, and peeled off my sweater, never minding the cold damp of the gray afternoon. I led Susie to the edge of our yard, where the fragrant leaves of a eucalyptus tree hung in long twists like icicles.

I knelt and spread my sweater next to the dirt. "Help me." We quickly covered the red wool with old leaves, dead grass, and dirt and tied the arms together. I lifted the weapon by its buttonholes, ready to launch.

Instead, more dirt came flying back at us. Both of us yelled this time, and suddenly Julia and Rosanna were next to us, screaming at the wall in Spanish and herding Susie and me back into the house. In moments, we were seated at the kitchen table, wrapped in Julia's and Rosanna's bright wool *ruanas*.

Julia fussed at us, shaking her head at the ruined sweater. She had worked and lived at this house for Dad's predecessors, and she spoke a little English. "Cárdenas children bad! ¡*Maleducados*!"

So, our enemies were named Cárdenas. I swung my leg into Susie's foot. "We will win this." It was good to feel confident about something.

Julia carried the ruined sweater out to the laundry tub while Rosanna stayed at her stove, shaving dark chocolate into scalded milk. She whipped the milk into a brown foam with a wooden paddle she rubbed between her palms.

She poured out two big cups. "*Tomen, niñas.*" Here you are, girls.

The milk and tangy chocolate spread their warmth until I felt hot both inside and out.

* * *

The following Saturday, I was pushing Susie on the tire swing Dad rigged up in the backyard, like the one near the lake in Winona. I kept an eye out for projectiles.

Instead, a boy's head popped up over the wall. He looked at me in surprise and disappeared. Then, the head of another boy appeared and disappeared.

Susie climbed out of the tire swing, and we walked over to the wall as the two boys straddled the flat top. I side-stepped a pile of poop.

The bigger boy, who looked to be about my age, raised empty hands, grinning sheepishly.

"You are not Adamson boys, yes? We fight boys, no girls."

I put my hands on my hips. Confusing us for the boys who used to live here was not okay.

"*Malos*," bad, I said. My Spanish was not much better than their English, but I wasn't going to let them get off the hook that easily.

"Yes. Sorry," the boy said. His smile grew a little bigger. "*Soy* Luis." I'm Luis.

"Andrés," the other one said, nodding.

It was only polite to follow suit. I used the names that Julia and Rosanna called us.

"Juanita," I said. "*Y* Susi."

"*Hola*," Susie said.

"*Hola*," Luis and Andrés said in unison.

I took a step back and felt my foot land with a squoosh right in the poop. There wasn't anything to do but wait the boys out.

"*Adiós*," Luis finally said. Andrés waved, and they disappeared.

"Yuck!" Susie said, pointing at my shoe.

"I know, I know," I said, avoiding the smooshed stuff as I limped toward the edge of the grass to grind it off with dirt. My shoe smelled the whole rest of the weekend while it aired out in the laundry area.

* * *

That Sunday, Dad dragged a cement block to the base of a peach tree whose branches hung over the wall. He tied a rope to one of the branches and helped Susie and me work our way up the rope, hand over hand, walking our feet up the wall until we could sit astride the flat top.

The wall meant to keep the Amerson and the Cárdenas homes apart became, instead, the place where we gathered each day to play. The strategy avoided the Colombian formalities—asking permission to go next door, shaking the hand of the parent when you got there, shaking it again when you left—and was instead informal, fun, and spontaneous. Whoever was around would clamber up the wall under the peach tree and wait to be joined by whoever else was free. In addition to Luis and Andrés, there were Luis' twin Isabel and the youngest Cárdenas, Teresita. They had an older sister, Magdalena, called Mai, but at fourteen, she was way too old to play.

Mom wrote home, "They are happy just to sit up in that tree and talk." Luis and Isa were having guava paste for their *merienda*, their snack—would we like some? Mom had just baked chocolate chip cookies—would they like some? They had a *finca*, a farm—maybe we would like to ride horses?

Other plans evolved. Let's do a play together, Luis suggested. We could invite the neighborhood, I said. So, we did.

The silly lines still play in my head, coaxing a smile. Luis plays the illiterate *campesino* farmer, who wants to send a letter, along with a bottle of wine and a loaf of bread, to his sweetheart, Beba. Andrés is the scribe. "Dear Beba," begins Luis. The scribe confuses the girl's name for the command "drink!" and lifts the bottle of wine to his lips. Luis, lost in his letter reverie, doesn't notice, but the audience begins to giggle. "*Coma,*" the *campesino* dictates, which is also the command "eat!" (Don't ask why someone who is illiterate knows where a comma goes.) The scribe takes a bite of the bread. The audience collapses into laughter. The wordplay and the antics roll on as the scribe writes, eats, and drinks until the letter is done, the bottle is empty, and the bread is gone.

The corniness of vaudeville has nothing on the story of *Coma y Beba*.

Without any effort, the Cárdenas children retaught Susie and me the Spanish we had first learned from Fina. Something clicked into place in my heart.

3. GRANDPA

Ambassador Fulton Freeman, a career foreign service officer, directed the Bogotá Embassy, along with his deputy chief of mission, Henry Dearborn. The Dearborns had hosted our *bienvenida*, welcome reception, and quickly became family friends. Mom and Dad's calendar filled with embassy activities designed to strengthen the relationships among staff.

As the senior USIA spouse, Mom hosted a luncheon for the other embassy wives, acknowledging the calling cards that the women had left at the house in December. What the folks at home might toss off as stuffy protocol was, to Mom, simply good manners tempered with kindness. It made a group of strangers into a working community that could help each other out, as family or neighbors would have done back home. Making it obligatory made even the shyest and most introverted get out, meet people, and become part of the whole.

With the arrival of the new year, the Colombian mourning period for President Kennedy lifted, and my parents' evening schedule filled with social engagements that connected the embassy community to their Colombian hosts. They attended one cocktail party for a group of college students leaving to study in the States, and they hosted another for a group of returning Fulbright students, all beneficiaries of the international cultural exchange program established in 1946 by Senator J. William Fulbright. Susie and I put on our party dresses so we could pass out what Mom called "finger food"—Rosana's *empanadas*, meat pies, and Venezuelan *tequeños*, cheese sticks—before we went to bed.

Our parents felt themselves engaging with Colombians in a way they had not with Italians. "The people had a special quality it seemed to us," my father wrote. "Maybe this was optimism."

As the boss's wife, my mother took an active part in Bogotá's Centro Binacional Colombo-Americano, USIS's outreach arm providing English classes, US university counseling, and the US-style library. The Centro's programming success—some two thousand Colombian students were enrolled—soon overwhelmed its class space, and it lacked an auditorium suitable for performances by US cultural ambassadors, visiting musicians, and notable authors.

A new location was identified. Bonifacio drove Mom to see the building and meet the Centro's new American director and his wife, eager young people ready to move the work forward quickly in the new space. They were delightful, and my mother organized an evening of dinner and music to introduce them to the Bogotá cultural community.

Ever aware of opportunities to represent the States, Mom directed Rosanna's preparation of a true Midwestern cold buffet—turkey, ham, potato salad, and molded cranberry salad. Everyone raved that it was the prettiest and tastiest buffet they had ever had in Bogotá. Maybe they were being polite—cold cuts were far from the Colombian norm for a dinner party.

News that the Centro's young director had been killed by a terrorist bomb shortly after we left Bogotá broke my parents' hearts.

* * *

By March, Mom and Dad were well-acquainted with both the embassy staff and their Colombian host community, and Mom was ready to show her parents around when they arrived on a rare overseas trip. Although they had visited us in Bologna three years before, that was in our old life, and I now had them firmly cemented into 478 Wilson Street, Winona, in the America of our 1962 home leave.

Dad warmed up the Mercedes in the dark to be at El Dorado Airport for our grandparents' 4:00 a.m. arrival, and Susie and I were so excited that we were up and ready as well. The English School was on vacation for *Semana Santa*, Holy Week.

"Well, you girls will need to sit on your grandparents' laps," Mom said. That sounded great to me. On the drive home, I played with Grandma's soft hand skin, reassured by the way it still lifted off her bones and stayed there for a moment like whipped cream when it's ready.

Dad stepped out of the car to open our front gate with that familiar squeal that I associated with homecoming. As he pulled into the driveway, Grandma Robb marveled at the size of the house.

"Why, Nan, you could fit three 478 Wilson Streets into this place!"

Julia opened the front door, dipping her head to our guests. "*Bienvenidos*," welcome. She wore her usual pale blue uniform.

"Mother, this is Julia," Mom said. "And here's Rosanna." Our cook stood behind Julia, a tentative smile on her face, her hands flat on her apron.

"Your cook?" Grandma said.

"Yes, Mother, as I've explained in my letters," Mom said. "They've lived in this house for a lot longer than we have."

"And Francisca irons," I said.

"Oh, my, a laundress?" Grandma said.

"Once a week," Mom said.

Grandpa nodded at Rosanna and Julia as he and Dad carried in the luggage. Mom and Susie followed them upstairs.

I was anxious to show Grandma the rest of what I now realized was our huge house. "Okay, so this," I said, opening the half-bath door, "is our *emergencia*, very handy for last-minute stops before the bus."

"Jane, leave Grandma alone to get some rest," Mom called from the second floor.

"She's giving me the grand tour," Grandma called back. "Okay, honey, next?"

I showed Grandma the study where we practiced piano, the living room where Caesar slept during the day, the dining room where we ate every meal, and the back hall leading to the kitchen, laundry, and maids' rooms.

"Maids' quarters," Grandma said. "Pretty fancy."

I started up the backstairs, but Grandma took the steps slowly. "My, it is harder to move at this altitude." I had forgotten all about the eight thousand feet.

Mom met us at the top of the stairs. "Oh, goodness, Jane. Mother, don't strain yourself."

As I followed Mom and Grandma to the guest room at the front of the house, Grandma said, "I didn't realize that you embassy people live entirely different lives from the rest of us."

I felt exactly the same way about Winona.

* * *

The next morning, Dad began Grandpa and Grandma's sightseeing by driving the six of us to the foot of Mount Monserrate, the Andean foothill that rose out of central Bogotá. We took the cable car to the top, watching the city fade into the haze and the little white church at the top of the hill take shape as we approached the summit.

Mom and Grandma walked arm in arm toward the church to have a look at the golden altar, while Susie trailed Dad as he scanned the view with his movie camera, narrating to himself. Grandpa looked out at the view of Bogotá and the altiplano savanna, then wandered around for a few minutes taking photographs and speaking with several Colombian families. They weren't long conversations—he didn't speak Spanish, and they didn't speak English.

"Dad Robb, so tied to his work responsibilities in Winona, showed his adventurous/poetic side," wrote my father later. "Talking with people as possible, soaking it all in."

Grandpa wandered over to a bench and pulled his notepad and pencil out from his jacket breast pocket. I recognized the unseeing gaze—he was building a poem.

I hoped he would share it with me, like Mom shared my poems with him in her Monday letters. I liked the challenge of rhythm and rhyme, finding the words with the right beats. I liked figuring out how I felt.

I made it a point to stand by Grandpa on the downhill cable car ride. "Did you make a poem?" I asked.

Grandpa pulled his gaze away from the receding peak and looked down at me. "Not quite yet," he said. "It needs to sit in my head and in my pocket for a little while."

"Then it'll be ready?"

"Maybe," he said. "Maybe not. You never know, right?"

"Right," I said. "It's not like baking a cake, like my birthday cake."

Grandpa allowed himself the smallest smile. "You remember that, Janie? When you two and your two cousins sat with me in my big chair?"

I wasn't exactly sure if I remembered, but Mom had the pictures of my fifth birthday in Winona in one of our photo albums. "Sure do," I said.

The gondola approached the landing pad and jerked to a stop.

Grandpa reached for my hand. "Let's see how my little poem is doing in a couple of days."

Poet-hand in poet-hand, we followed Dad, Mom, Susie, and Grandma back to the Mercedes.

* * *

The week flew by. The Cárdenas kids got permission to come over so they could meet our grandparents, and Grandpa took our picture at the front gate with Caesar. We went swimming and horseback riding at the Bogotá Country Club—they had the best *empanadas* and little hot dog snacks. Grandpa and Grandma went to the open-air market with Mom, where they bought traditional black-and-white straw cowboy hats for Uncle Jim and Aunt Beth. Dad took Grandpa to a bullfight—us girls didn't need to see that.

On Maundy Thursday, my grandparents left for a two-day trip to Popayán, a colonial town renowned for its daily Holy Week processionals—pious adults carrying ancient religious images through Popayán's historic streets every morning, and their devoted children doing their own procession every afternoon. My grandparents were back by Saturday, and all of us went to church on Easter—Union Church was the English-language, Protestant congregation of Bogotá, where my school friends were in my Sunday school class. I was sorry that we didn't have a parade.

The morning our grandparents were flying back to Winona, Grandpa called me into the guest room.

"It's been so nice to be with you, Janie," he said, "and to get to know the country that you live in." He reached into his jacket and pulled out the little notebook, along with a piece of folded paper. "I wanted you to have the very first copy of my little poem about this wonderful place." He unfolded the paper and placed it in my hand. "Let's read it together, shall we?"

"I cannot leave this place

This town
Or any land
But must look back
And then I see
One beckoning
And gently waving hand."

I didn't understand it, but I thought I might when I was a little older.

* * *

James T. Robb, Sr., came from a family of letter-writers and poets. When he died only three years after visiting us in Bogotá, his friend and pastor the Reverend Harold Rekstad wrote: "Jim had the soul of a poet. He sensed and saw the world about him and felt deeply what is missed by the casual observer."

Grandpa didn't talk much, and his smile was even more rare. He reserved his emotion for his writing. I'm so glad I glimpsed it all with him in Bogotá.

4. CHEATER

La Violencia had been raging in Colombia for years. A long-term battle between opposing political parties—the Liberals and the Conservatives—and the huge imbalance between the "haves" and the "have-nots" created a climate in which war-like events were commonplace: bombings, assassinations, kidnappings that funded the warring factions.

Our house was never left empty. Julia and Rosanna kept vigil whenever our parents were out. Susie and I were supervised by an adult any time we were on the street, and it was drilled into us to stay in view.

Many years later, my mother recalled these years in Bogotá: "I knew where the children were all the time. Once, we were out in front of the house and Susie skated around the corner and didn't come right back. My heart stopped. The perceived danger was an overwhelming accumulation of feelings."

* * *

The point was driven home when my American classmate Lisa invited me over to play in El Chicó, the expat American neighborhood at the other end of town.

It was the first time I had heard that expression, "expat." People like Lisa's family were plain old civilian Americans living abroad outside the protective force field of the embassy. I felt kind of sorry for them.

At Lisa's house, we played Barbies for a while, changing them into different outfits and having them take turns going on walks around Lisa's bedroom with Ken. Then, Lisa announced to her mother that we were going down to the corner for a snack. As if a kid could go down the block alone.

I couldn't believe it when her mother said, "Okay, dear. There are pesos on the hall dresser."

We walked out the door and started down the sidewalk. It felt like there was a spotlight on us and a megaphone blasting, "American children alone!" We turned the corner, and now we were completely out of range. Lisa continued chatting away, but I couldn't hear her above the loud voice in my head advertising us. "¡*Americanas!*"

Halfway down the block, Lisa walked into an ice-cream store like the ones in America. I had no idea there were such things in Bogotá.

She stepped up to the counter. "*Dos* Black Cows."

"What's that?" I asked.

"Haven't you ever had a Coke float?" she said.

I didn't tell Mom about the two Black Cows or walking alone when she picked me up. I had broken a family rule for an ice cream treat that did not taste nearly good enough to have warranted the risk. Sitting in the backseat of the Mercedes, I felt my real world firm up around me—the world in which a grownup walked you to the bus stop; the world in which you did not go around the corner alone; the world in which I was safe.

The next time Lisa asked me over, I said I couldn't go.

* * *

The school year rolled on toward June. I continued to struggle with arithmetic. My sister, however, was showing a talent for math as well as reading. Susie came home one day mad at a classmate who accused her of pretending to read a Bobbsey Twins book on the bus. "She told him she was also reading Nancy Drew and so there!" Mom wrote home.

We were both doing beautifully in Spanish, thanks to our long conversations with the Cárdenas kids on our wall hang-out. Susie was after Dad to teach her French, too.

A final hurdle loomed. The end-of-year examinations were essay questions written in England, mailed across the Atlantic to the English School, and mailed back to England to be graded. I imagined a line of stern women, stuffed into tweed suits like Mrs. Masson, hunched over our papers like Andean vultures on a dead cow.

Exam week arrived. The back of the Monday afternoon bus became a spontaneous discussion group as kids who had taken the test that day filled the rest of us in on the questions. The ground materialized beneath my feet. What a great support system. I settled into preparing for my Thursday exam.

On Tuesday evening, I excused myself from the dinner table before dessert. "I need to call Lisa," I told Mom as I stood up. "Can't remember exactly what this one exam question is."

Mom looked up from the Laura Ingalls Wilder book she was reading to my sister and me, as she often did over our dinner when Dad worked late. "You're going to do what?"

"Call Lisa about Thursday's questions." I turned toward the foyer. Sometimes Mom was a bit thick. I heard the book close with a thwack.

"You come back here, Jane, and sit down."

I stopped, startled, and looked back at my mother. She never spoke this loudly. No voices were raised in the Amerson household. Ever.

"Susie, you may be excused," Mom said.

My sister scooted past me and into the TV room. I sat back down at the table.

"Are you telling me that you are cheating?" Mom said, her voice quiet again.

"Cheating?" The foreign concept hung in the air. "No." I hurried to explain. "This is what they do. I mean, we were just talking." Weren't we?

"But you're finding out what the questions are ahead of time, and then you're studying those things, and then you're taking the test. Right?"

Well, when it was put that way. I nodded. My face was on fire.

Mom looked me in the eye. "So, you're cheating," she said. She sat back, tapping her fingers on the arms of her chair for a very long time. I waited.

"I'm very disappointed in you." There it was.

I wondered how my face could feel so hot with all the blood drained out of it. My stomach tightened into a hard pit. I could barely stand to hear anymore, but there was more. "I'm going to have to tell Headmistress Masson at the school show on Friday. Now, go to your room."

I ran upstairs and threw myself onto my bed. A hundred headmistresses whirled around me, glaring down at this horrid little American cheater.

Mom didn't bring up my illegal behavior at breakfast, and Dad was in his usual cheery hurry to get out to the embassy car. I barely talked to anyone all day.

Thursday was the exam. I did all right, but it was over for me. They would not let a cheater go on to fifth grade.

Friday evening was the English School year-end program at the Unity Church. Susie was all chatty about some Scottish song her second-grade class was performing. I tried to remember the words of the Ogden Nash poem I was to recite. I couldn't get beyond the first line: "Isabel met an enormous bear." A Headmistress Masson bear.

My turn came up. I walked onto the stage and into the spotlight. Could they see the word cheater written on my face? I took a breath and began.

"Isabel met an enormous bear." My right arm traced an arc as tall and wide as the whole headmistress. Another breath, and the poem came to life. "Isabel, Isabel, didn't care." I lifted my left arm, trapping bear Masson. Performance magic propelled me through the poem. "She washed her hands, and she straightened her hair up." I lifted my chin and declaimed the final line. "Then Isabel quietly ate the bear up."

If only. My arms dropped, and I shrank back into reality.

I peered into the wings—no headmistress. Susie passed me as her class assembled. I took her seat between my parents. Mom patted my hand. Dad mouthed, "*Brava!*"

The performances ended. Headmistress Masson stalked onto the stage, her face pink and blotchy under the lights, her mouth puckered into a fake smile. The arm of justice was about to come down.

"Thank you," she said and walked off. The parents clapped. The lights came on. We went home.

Mom had not told.

Some sixty years later, it occurs to me that I was only following my mother's prime directive of our foreign service life: "Do what the other children do." How it might have changed my state of mind to have been able to raise my voice, to declare that being moved into a new school with a foreign curriculum on a new continent halfway through the year was completely unfair and that I was doing my best to stay afloat.

I wish I could have said to my mother, as I had back in Bologna: "It doesn't matter. I'm an American."

Instead, I pledged to never again make a mistake.

* * *

As school summer vacation got underway, Mom made a surprise announcement over breakfast after Dad had left for the office with Bonifacio.

"Girls, what would you think about going up to Winona for a little visit?"

"Now? Is it home leave again?" I asked.

"Well, like an extra trip," Mom said. "Just us girls."

"Not Daddy?" Susie said.

"No, not this time," Mom said. "He has work and trips of his own to take care of. And Caesar."

"Daddy doesn't like Caesar," I said.

My father frequently muttered something about the "damn dog," especially when Caesar farted while lying in front of the fire. Or, worse yet, when he started peeing at the top of the stairs and Mom scooped him up and carried him downstairs like a baby, his little yellow fountain trickling puddles on the marble steps.

"Well, now, that's just not true," Mom said. "Dad wants to give Caesar some attention so that we can all get along even better."

Which is how Mom, Susie, and I flew up to Winona for a week while Dad trained Caesar to lie down and stay. My father even took a movie of our boxer shaking with the effort of restraining his fury as a little street dog meandered by.

What no one said—before we left, while we were in Winona, or when we got home—was that Grandpa had cancer. He would be gone by the spring of 1967, when I was a lonely seventh grader struggling to survive an American junior high, Susie was thriving in a happy crew of fifth graders, and Dad was in Uruguay on State Department business. Mom would fly out to Minnesota alone to bury her father.

"He was what you saw: a simple, forthright, kind gentleman of utmost integrity, inspiring qualities of character," said the Reverend Harold Rekstad at First Congregational church in Winona.

5. UNCLE TERRY

A sea change was underway. New leaders were in charge in Moscow, in Washington, and at the Bogotá Embassy.

After nine years as leader of the Soviet Union, Nikita Khrushchev was out. His protégé, Leonid Ilyich Brezhnev, was the new Soviet Premier. Secretary of State Dean Rusk prepared to deal with a very different personality from Khrushchev's feisty belligerence. Perhaps Brezhnev would introduce a new approach to the Cold War.

Rusk would continue reporting to President Lyndon Johnson, who, along with his running mate, Minnesota's Senator Hubert Humphrey, had been elected to the term that began in January 1965. My parents' Macalester College friend Walter (Fritz) Mondale replaced Humphrey in the US Senate, joining Democrat Eugene McCarthy. Mom updated her Christmas card address list with Fritz and his wife Joan's new Washington address.

There were changes in USIA, as well. Edward R. Murrow, a chain smoker who was almost never seen without his trademark Camel cigarette, resigned. Lung cancer would take his life by April.

Carl Thomas Rowan was the new USIA director. He was a Southern Black journalist with a degree and journalism credentials from Minnesota, and he came to his post at USIA with diplomatic experience—under President Kennedy, Rowan had served as assistant secretary of state, delegate to the United Nations, and ambassador to Finland.

A big change had also taken place in the Bogotá Embassy. President Johnson replaced Ambassador Freeman with Covey T. Oliver, a fellow Texan. Ambassador Oliver was neither a career diplomat nor a rich businessman, but a professor of international law. He was fluent in Spanish and had some first-hand understanding of Latin American social issues from his childhood near the Mexican border.

Ambassador Oliver and his wife, Barbara, a Smith College graduate with a passion for social justice, were hearty outdoor types who tended to de-emphasize protocol in a most likable way. Mom wrote home, "They are tops, in our book. New to the game but so interested in what is going on." Mrs. Oliver put her interest in child welfare to use on the local board of the March of Dimes, something that would soon matter to me.

* * *

Mrs. Ospina moved up with us to fifth grade, and the class migrated from the Quonset hut to a room in the villa where Mrs. Masson had her office. Susie's third-grade class moved into our shed.

A bigger change was in the offing. Mrs. Masson spoke with the parents about the plans to move the English School to the outskirts of Bogotá. That meant danger to Mom. The poorest of the poor lived outside the city, and terrorists. The finca where our dog Caesar was born blew up when student bombers accidentally detonated themselves.

I had a more immediate problem—buck teeth. Stupid thumb. Although I knew better, there were times I still went for it. Sucking my thumb was like patting my own head or eating warm bread with American butter, but I hated that my teeth stuck out. Wearing glasses was bad enough. It was time to stop the baby habit and get myself in shape—at least, that's what my father said. Mom made an appointment with an orthodontist recommended by embassy friends. When she picked me up at school a few days later, I was surprised to see Dad in the driver's seat. He never did family stuff with us during the week.

"Hey, kid," he said with a smile.

We drove downtown to Chapinero, and Dad pulled the Mercedes

into an indoor garage. The last time we had parked on the street, someone had stolen the car's star emblem.

From the fifth floor waiting room you could hear the traffic and smell the diesel rising from the busy street. I wondered if you could hear your own school bus—Susie and the rest of the kids would be coming this way in a little while.

I got four permanent teeth pulled that afternoon, Dad holding one hand tight, and Mom holding the other. It turned out that my thumb wasn't to blame for my protruding front teeth—my mouth was simply too small. I held my eyes open as wide as I could, and my mouth even wider. My glasses got speckled with tooth goop. My throat ached.

The orthodontist said that it would take two years to move my remaining teeth into place. On the next visit, he said, he would wrap metal bands around my teeth, upper and lower, and thread through the entire set with a wire.

"So, this we will tighten each month," he said. "¡*Y pronto, una sonrisa bella!*" Maybe a pretty smile at some point, but not before a lot of very shiny smiles.

I touched my puffy lips and sighed as we got in the elevator. "Suffer to be beautiful, right?"

Perhaps it was the Novocain that stimulated my first sleepwalking episode that night, the first of many that year. The pattern was the same—about an hour after I turned out the light, a recurring nightmare with a relentless pounding soundtrack would pull me from my bed, weeping and wandering the upstairs hallway until my mother or father would awaken me.

I remember standing in my parents' second-floor bedroom trying to open the window that let onto the backyard, and it's only now that I realize my mother's fear as she held me—had I been ready to jump? She consulted our Colombian doctor, who recommended warm milk laced with rum. That seemed to knock me out.

The terrifying nightmare soundtrack with its unyielding drumbeat held sway in my dreams for years. It re-emerged one final time as I slipped out of consciousness before wisdom teeth surgery in college, and then released me. Brought on by Novocain and killed off by the stronger stuff, this troubling response to pressure had run its course.

* * *

We weren't the only Amersons in Colombia that fall. Dad's brother, Richard Terry, whom we had last seen at the end of home leave in Los Angeles, showed up in Dad's office one September afternoon. For a minute, Dad assumed this tall, well-dressed hombre with a full beard was looking to have my father do something for him. Then he realized that it was his kid brother. Sadly, the handsome beard vanished the next day with the same notice my uncle had given us of his arrival.

Terry injected youthful energy and good humor into our foursome. He sang along with his new Smothers Brothers album. He walked us to the bus stop, Susie skipping at his side, and he was waiting for us when the bus brought us home. Mom said he reminded her of Dad when they first married. "Terry is a joy to have in the house," she wrote her parents. "Each meal he sighs and says: 'I haven't eaten so well in years! This is living!' Reminds me of how Bob inhaled every meal when we were newly married, after almost ten years of being on his own."

Terry socialized with my parents' friends, his charismatic ways making for easy conversation. He joined Mom and other embassy wives for golf at the country club, laughing with them as they all, to use Mom's phrase, "fully utilized the fairway." Terry also picked up an English teaching job at the binational center, where he expanded his social circle to include people of his own age. Soon, he had a Colombian girlfriend, Alma. Susie and I thought she looked like a movie star.

* * *

At the end of October, Susie hosted a Halloween party for her school friends. Terry and Dad created a mysterious fortune-reading room in Dad's art studio, complete with scary music, hanging paper bats, and cloth ghosts. Dad shrouded himself in great-great-grandmother Robb's paisley shawl and hunkered down in the far corner of the room with a crystal ball and a deck of cards.

I had my own Halloween party to get ready for. It was a boy-girl party at my friend Vicky's house in El Chicó. It was a miracle that Mom allowed me to go. Her moral compass made lax parenting a sin.

When I brought it up over dinner, she exploded. "Fifth graders? A boy-girl party for fifth graders? What is wrong with these parents?"

I actually felt exactly the same. But everyone was going, including a boy I had a crush on, Peter.

"I know, Mom, but . . ." I couldn't say the part about Peter without giving too much away. "But maybe I could go just for a little while. Dad?"

My father did one of his "harrumphs," tipped his head to one side, and lifted his chin. There was an announcement coming,

"Well, sure, Janie. How about it, Nan? I can take the kid over for an hour or so. Mike from the office has some new records he wanted to show me, so I could swing by their place for a drink and a little music and have us both back not too late."

"This is just not age-appropriate," Mom said. "What's the rush? These kids are barely in the double digits."

Mom felt this way pretty strongly. One of my American friends got a new watch for her birthday, one of those slim, bracelet styles like grownups wore. When I asked for something like it, the answer was no. "You have the rest of your life to wear adult things. You don't need a dainty watch that could crack against the wall when you're climbing up to play with the Cárdenas kids."

She was right. I had jumped into the country club pool completely forgetting that I was wearing the Timex that Grandpa and Grandma brought me from Robb Brothers Store, and I spent an agonizing evening praying that the beads of moisture inside the glass would evaporate. No, I really wasn't ready to be a grownup or even a teenager, but this party meant a lot.

In the end, it was the fact Susie was having a costume party that tipped the scales in my favor, and Mom relented. "Well, let's make sure you have the very best costume, then."

She dyed an old sheet purple, the color of royalty, made a few seams, and voilá—a floor-length toga fit for Caesar's wife. Julia picked some lavender from the garden and tucked it around one of my Italian hairbands.

"*Muy linda,*" she said. Very pretty. I hugged her tight. "*¡Qué perfume!*" I hoped that Peter might get close enough to agree that I smelled good. But not so close he would get tangled in my braces.

We were all dancing together to Petula Clark's "Downtown" when someone put on a slow song. Peter walked over. "Would you like to dance?"

He sure was nice. And small, like me, just my height. Why did I hear my mother's voice in my head?

"Oh, gee, um." I sounded like an idiot. I could just imagine Mrs. Ospina whacking me over the head with the board eraser. "Maybe later, when it's faster music?"

"This is a great song, Jane." Peter smiled.

"You know, I just don't think my mother would approve." Had I actually just said that out loud?

"Approve of me?"

"No, no, it's not about you," I rushed. "It's just slow dancing."

Peter looked at me. "It's one song. I'm sure one song is all right." He smiled again. "I'm absolutely sure."

And so, Peter smelled my lavender despite me. I confessed the whole thing to Mom over breakfast the next morning. I was so glad that I didn't have to be a grownup for a long, long time.

* * *

For my tenth birthday in November, Mom took me and my friends to see the Beatles' *A Hard Day's Night*. Mom said that the band wouldn't last. I cut out their faces from *Tiger Beat* magazine and hung them on strings from one corner of my bedroom to the other like a big X. Everyone loved Paul, but I loved George—I thought he was probably lonelier. I was planning a band at recess. I was pretty sure we could become famous. My friend Katherine from Wales was the only one interested, so far. Susie was glad to be left out of this club.

Back in Bologna, the landlords had left us a piano. Mom brushed off her sight-reading skills, Dad taught himself to use both hands at once, and Susie plunked away while I was at school. A piano of our own had arrived in Bogotá in a huge wooden crate that made a wonderful playhouse in the space behind Rosanna's garden. Susie and I started lessons, but I found reading music discouragingly challenging, like arithmetic. Years later, when I read about the relationship between music and math, I understood my frustrated young self; it was only as a young adult and an emerging choreographer that I re-discovered the spatial relationships between numbers that my old Italian school's abacus lessons had tried to impart.

I preferred the simplicity of harmonizing and blowing on ocarinas, clay flutes, and recorders while Dad played guitar. We had new Colombian songs in our repertoire—Susie singing the soprano melody and me on alto—that we would sometimes perform for the guests at our parents' parties.

Susie and I were also taking ballet on Thursdays after school in a house close enough for Mom to walk us to. In Rome, I danced in the apartment wearing Mom's old cotton leotard that zipped up the back from when she was a dancer in New York City, but now both Susie and I had new pink tights, black leotards, and ballet slippers, which we also wore when we jigged around the house to the bagpipes record Grandma had left for us.

* * *

On the Sunday before Christmas, Terry came with us to get a tree outside one of the nearby grocery stores. The rocky Andes bore few pines trees like those from the Apennines. The tree we picked out was more like a couple of yews tied together.

Dad and Terry pulled the Christmas boxes out of the attic. It had been nearly two years since we had seen our Rome decorations, so opening each box was like Christmas itself. Unwrapping the blown-glass birds, grapes, and bells from Piazza Navona was like reaching back in time. The fragile pieces were nestled in pages from the Rome newspaper, *Corriere della Sera*, dated January 5, 1963. How odd to think of a day in which we had never even heard of Bogotá, when we had been as at home in Italy as we were now in Colombia.

After decorating the tree, Susie and I got to work on the presepio. The new manger we'd gotten for our first Colombian Christmas inspired us to create a huge scene on one of the card tables Julia reserved for large dinners. We balled up pages of the *El Tiempo* newspaper that Dad brought home from the office, dropped a sheet over the paper and moss over the sheet, and we had the hills of Bethlehem. Aluminum foil became a stream over which we put a small bridge. Plaster shepherds and their sheep lay under twigs in clay representing trees. Baby Jesus took his place behind the hut, waiting for Christmas morning.

On Christmas Eve, we got ready for the Amerson traditional taco dinner.

With Julia and Rosanna off for the holiday, Mom set the dinner table herself and bustled around the kitchen, browning the hamburger and heating the canned tortillas in sizzling oil. The smells wound up the back stairway and past Uncle Terry's room, but Mom shooed him out of the kitchen when he followed his nose down the back stairs.

The doorbell rang while Susie and I were putting on our party shoes. We hurried down the marble staircase to see Julia letting in Terry's girlfriend, Alma. She was the most beautiful person who had ever been in our house—dark eyes, lots of mascara, long brown hair. We agreed on our way down the kitchen hall that since I was the oldest, I would sit next to Alma at dinner.

I scurried back to the dining room with my arms loaded with what Dad called "the fixin's" only to find that Terry had seated his girlfriend on the corner at Mom's end and had stationed himself where I should be. I put the bowls of shredded *queso blanco*, cheese, and chopped lettuce from the garden within Alma's reach. She smelled even better than I had on Halloween.

Mom rushed in with the steaming tacos and browned ground lomo, beef. "Everybody here? Food's going to get cool." She sat, a proprietary eye on the table.

Dad said, "Shall we count the many ways we are lucky and grateful?"

We held hands and each said very few words—my mouth was practically drooling—before digging in, hot sauce dripping down our forearms as we competed to eat the most tacos.

* * *

Uncle Terry left after Christmas as spontaneously as he arrived. Alma cried. Susie and I did, too.

I have no recollection of the drama that played out around me that December, and my parents' writings don't shed any light. It was my

Aunt Snooky who told me a few years ago—after my parents were gone—that Terry and Alma were to be married, and that my aunt and Uncle Bob had flown down from Minnesota for the wedding. However, Dad pulled rank and forbade the marriage, sensing perhaps that Alma and her family believed they would be benefitting from the US Embassy connection, while young Terry would probably tire of the game and leave everyone on bad terms. Whatever the rationale, Dad made it clear that this was his turf and that there would be no wedding. Terry flew back to the States with my aunt and uncle.

Four years later, when he parked a re-purposed hearse at the tidy suburban curb of our Maryland house, Uncle Terry was a long-haired hippy with a tie-dyed girlfriend in tow. Of the whole Bogotá affair, my uncle recently wrote me that he and Dad had patched up their differences.

I am glad to know that the brothers forgave each other.

6. Yard Sale

The Johnson administration continued to make Colombia the showplace for Kennedy's Alliance for Progress, his economic development program legacy. Dad's USIS program publicized and encouraged these efforts, partnering with his embassy colleagues from the Agency for International Development, another of President Kennedy's creations. "The halcyon years for Latin America," wrote my father, "were the years of the early Kennedy Administration and the Alliance for Progress when everything was expanding and hopeful and optimistic."

One of the most visible Alliance projects in Bogotá was a large, low-cost housing community built on the grounds of an old airport on the outskirts of the city. Ciudad Kennedy was dedicated in the name of our fallen president shortly after we arrived in Bogotá. Dad represented the embassy at the event, and Mom, Susie, and I went with him.

After the ceremony, the four of us walked with the mayor of Ciudad Kennedy to his home, a tidy, three-room cinder block building with a concrete floor. We shook hands with his wife, and I patted their little boy on the head. On the longest wall of the living room, photographs of President Kennedy and the Pope, and a painting of Jesus presided over a collection of votive candles.

On the way home, Dad told us that the United States had built that house and many more, replacing those constructed with cardboard walls and corrugated tin roofs that didn't last very long in rainy Bogotá.

* * *

As wife of the PAO, Mom had a leadership role to play in Colombia. For the first time in our embassy life, she found like-minded women interested in community service. "I found some marvelous volunteer experiences with a group of women I'd have liked in any country," she later wrote, "extraordinary women who were doing amazing work on a shoestring."

Bogotá had an active community of *señoras de bien*—well-off women—who considered it their *deber*, their duty, to do something for the poor. American women from the embassy and the expat community contributed their shared experiences in volunteering.

My mother was one of two American women asked to join the newly formed board of the YWCA—the international organization had been highlighted as a model in Pope John XXIII's ecumenical work. The work took Mom back to her roots—she and her mother had been part of many community projects through the Winona YWCA—and she sought board-development materials from home. "We'd like to show how cooperation can accomplish so much for clubs, families, and the country," she wrote to her mother.

Mom was also on a binational board supporting Ciudad Kennedy's daycare program, the Jardín Infantil, the Kindergarten. "I loved being with women who felt strongly about these issues," she later said.

One Saturday morning in late spring, Susie and I accompanied Mom to a program the children of the daycare center had prepared for their benefactors. The air was cool, but the sun was shining, and my new green *ruana* was cozy on my shoulders as we stood in the yard waiting for the performance.

A very small, serious boy emerged onto the yard, beating a steady rhythm with the claves, wooden sticks. He marched in time to the rhythm, but mostly side to side, so it took quite a while for him to advance. Gradually, a series of other somber children emerged behind the boy, marching, and beating at the air with tambourines and claves. The line crossed the yard as slowly and steadily as Bologna's linked caterpillars.

The children were tiny. Julia told Susie and me that many children in *el campo*, the countryside, ate nothing but coffee and *panela*, brown sugar, for breakfast, which sounded yummy, but which was terrible for their teeth and their muscles and bones. Mom's group raised enough money to provide a full nutritious meal to these children every day.

Eventually, the ladies in charge ended the parade with applause, and the kids scattered toward their teachers and the few mothers who had managed to take a morning off from their jobs. Susie and I coaxed the children away from those attachments with bags of cookies, toys, and clothing that we had assembled with the Cárdenas kids using donations from the Colombian cookie company Ponque Ramo and the American Women's Club. The children's eyes were enormous as they accepted their gifts.

The effort of Mom and her colleagues was recognized by none other than Ambassador Oliver in his weekly staff meeting at the embassy. He noted a letter to the editor in *El Tiempo*, the Bogotá daily, that had been published around Christmas. "The gist of the letter," Mom wrote home, "was that our work with the Jardín was real diplomacy, and it mentioned Mrs. Oliver, Maria Rosa Dearborn, and Nancy Amerson. The ambassador said he sent a copy to Washington so that we would have 'official recognition.' It is surely a nice extra to have what we try to do recognized as being of some worth to the joint effort."

Wives had long been rated as part of their foreign service husbands' annual evaluations, but having her work be publicly recognized was a high point of Mom's "trailing spouse" life. Still, she knew it made little difference in the larger picture. She wrote home: "I sometimes wonder why foreign service families knock themselves out when the taxpayers have little or no appreciation of the fact that they are getting their money's worth from most of their government servants overseas."

* * *

There were lots of Colombian children wandering alone in the streets of Bogotá. *Bogotanos* called them *cochinos*, dirty pigs. One Saturday afternoon, I was doing my homework in my room when I heard clanging in the street and looked out. A small group of *cochinos* was across the street rummaging through garbage cans. The tallest kid handed a piece of something to a very small boy, who put it in his mouth and sat down against the building, slumping like an old man.

Garbage for dinner? No. I ran downstairs, calling for Mom. I found her reading in the living room.

My mother listened, pressed her lips together, then stood up. "Okay," she said. "Let's ask Rosanna to put some food together for these children." She never called them *cochinos*. Rosanna frowned and shook her head but placed some leftover *lomito* and yucca on one of our older plates and sliced four big chunks off a day-old bread loaf.

"*Y arequipe*," I said, pouring ribbons of the caramel syrup across the bread.

Mom followed me and the plate out our front door and down the driveway. As our gate clanged shut behind us, the children turned, ready to run.

"*Niños*," children, I said, extending the plate. "*Comida*." Food.

The three smaller children looked at the older boy, who gave a small nod. They ran toward me. As they approached, I saw for the first time up close why people called them *cochinos*: their faces were lined with dirt, their hands and legs were filthy, and their clothes were ragged and caked with grime. Their shoes were nothing but cardboard wrapped onto their feet with some old string.

I extended the plate toward the older boy. Our eyes met. He was about my age but the most tired person I had ever seen, with deep circles under his eyes, his lips cracked and dry, his cheeks hollow.

He lowered his eyes and took the plate; for a moment, our fingers were only inches away from each other.

The boy turned away and squatted on the sidewalk, with the other three huddled around him. He doled out the bit of food, starting with the littlest child, who couldn't have been more than four. His nose was runny, as were his eyes, and his belly was bloated by hunger, protruding above pants that were way too big for him and were held together by a safety pin. There were cuts on his right cheek, as if he had fallen.

I looked at Mom, who was leaning against our low front wall, hands clasped at her waist. "Mom, he's hurt."

She pushed off the wall and stepped over to look at the boy. "Yes, honey. Let's do what we can." She stepped toward our gate. The children's heads turned, their eyes wary. "*Esperen*," she said, holding her hand up. Wait.

I stayed with the group while Mom went into the house. They finished the food and clambered back up to their feet. "*Esperen*," I repeated.

Mom returned with a basin of soapy water, an old washcloth, and Band-Aids, and set them down on the sidewalk.

"*Señora*," the oldest boy said, lowering his eyes as he handed her the empty plate.

Mom took the dish as if it were a gift from a visiting dignitary.

I knelt next to the basin of water and motioned to the littlest boy. He approached as if in a trance, his eyes empty. He seemed to barely register the feel of the washcloth on his face as I wiped at the dirt, the washcloth coming back brown. I patted at the scratches on his face and laid a Band-Aid across his hot, dry cheek.

"Okay," I said, standing.

The leader looked at me directly one more time. "*Gracias,*" he said.

I nodded. They wandered off down the sidewalk. We never saw them again.

* * *

That night at dinner, Mom and I told Dad and Susie what had happened that afternoon. "I knew we needed to help," I said, recounting how I wiped some of the dirt off the little boy's face. "But I'm not even sure what difference it made."

"Anything at all was a good thing to do," Mom said, passing the mashed potatoes to Dad. "Making a difference is why we are here, after all," Dad said, taking the bowl. The mashed potatoes, stopped, midair in my father's hand. "No person is unimportant in a democracy."

He nodded at his own pontification, and Susie retrieved the mashed potatoes. Dad looked across the table toward me, but not quite at me. I followed his gaze and passed him the peas.

"Isn't that what the embassy wives are working on, Nan?" Dad said, adding a slab of butter to his peas. They put lots of butter and cream and milk on everything in South Dakota.

"With the Colombian ladies, yes. We're modeling volunteerism. It's somewhat of a new concept here," Mom said.

She took a sip of wine. In Italy, pretty much everyone drank wine, even the kids. Mom and Dad had kept up the custom here in Colombia, having wine with their dinner.

My mother put her glass down and looked at me as if she had made up her mind about something. "The March of Dimes," she said.

"Who?" I asked.

"The March of Dimes, that's who is helping kids all over the world get a better start in life, including here in Bogotá. Mrs. Oliver, the ambassador's wife, is on the board. Maybe we can't help every street child, but we can help the organization make a difference." My mother rested her elbows on the table and leaned into her argument. "Like Henry. His polio could have been prevented with better education and better health care." Francisca's son came with her on ironing days, sitting on a chair with his iron braces unlocked.

"Polio?" Susie said, looking at Dad. "Didn't he get the sugar cubes like you brought home?"

"You got those because you are a very fortunate American child," Dad said. "We are all very fortunate. And, yes, I think that supporting the March of Dimes would be a fine thing to do, Janie."

I could hardly wait to tell the Cárdenas. We were going to raise money for children.

* * *

We kids worked out a fundraising plan under the moniker of AMCA, for Amerson/ Cárdenas. Our backyard show had been an AMCA production, as was our one-issue neighborhood newspaper with the single paid ad from the candy store across the street. We thought people might give us money if we went door to door. Mom waited on the sidewalk while Luis, Isabel, Susie, and I took turns climbing up and down the stoops, smiling at the baffled maids as they looked around us, trying to figure out our scheme. We left empty-handed.

Luis came up with the idea. "Sell old things," he said.

"*¡Sí!*" I said. This was exactly the sort of thing that they did in the Honey Bunch and Norman books. "A yard sale."

"*Un llard esale,*" Luis repeated, looking pleased.

The following Saturday, the front wall of our house was covered with items for sale. Dad donated an old electric razor and some art materials. Mom sorted through the pots and pans for a few we could do without, and she gave us several scarves and some old jewelry she said was "paste" even though it was not sticky. Susie and I contributed toys we had outgrown—like the one-eyed camel on rollers that the little boy with polio, Henry, now enjoyed—and American hand-me-down dresses, like Pollyanna wore, to be handed down again. Even Julia joined in, giving us some little figurines that she collected.

Luis and his siblings added books, some sweaters, and other things, including fake flowers I had seen in their dining room. It was a good thing that Mr. Cárdenas was away on business that weekend because he would never have approved of his children selling their household items like some street vendors.

Mom kept an eye on everyone and everything.

We raised an entire jar of pesos, mostly in coins. During *Hechizada*—the *Bewitched* television show—that night, I dumped the change on the coffee table in the den and counted it out—fifty-five pesos. After school on Monday, Mom drove the six of us kids to the March of Dimes office, where we proudly delivered the jar to a surprised receptionist.

"I get such a kick out of seeing them so enthused," Mom wrote home.

It was my first taste of community service. People can make a difference.

* * *

In late April 1965, President Johnson ordered troops to the Dominican Republic, where a revolution was threatening to create what America feared would be "another Cuba." Angered by the US intervention, a group of Colombian student activists quietly filtered into the Bogotá Embassy, one by one, then suddenly commandeered the ambassador's office. Ambassador Oliver was a former university professor, and his willingness to listen to the students' concerns defused the situation. After a few hours of nervous tension, the students left peacefully.

The police found fifteen sticks of dynamite in a closet just outside Dad's office ten minutes before they were set to explode.

And when Mom drove home from grocery shopping one afternoon, there was a can lying right in the middle of our driveway between the gate and the house. She left the car at the curb and walked around the can and into the house. While she was calling Dad, Julia walked out and picked the can up—it was just baby powder. But no one in our house used baby powder.

Susie and I knew nothing of these matters.

7. LEAVING

In the fall of 1965, the English School moved to a rural potato farm about 45 minutes out of the city. Our sixth-grade classroom was in what had been the villa's first floor living room.

After two years of crabby Mrs. Ospina, it was a relief to have calm, British Miss Baker as our teacher. She read to us from *King Solomon's Mines* after lunch and gave us lots of writing time in class. She was so smart that when I needed an artist's name to rhyme with "he," she immediately said, "Klee." It was my first encounter with that name. When I saw a Klee in a Paris museum in 2018, I thought of Miss Baker.

My Cárdenas-built Spanish was now strong enough to move me into the advanced class with the Colombian kids. I knew my accent was good when a Cárdenas cousin asked me where I was from. "*Soy americana*," I'm American. His immediate response was that he, too, was American—South American. To this day, I remember being chastised and humbled. "*Norte americana*," I mumbled, even though North America included Canada.

Susie's fourth-grade classroom was in a brand-new building a few hundred yards away from the villa. The building looked like the motel in Wyoming where we stayed during home leave—a line of prefab cubes connected by a long, covered porch. Susie's classroom faced a field where everyone had gym, stumbling over stray potatoes as our legs became coated in gray dust. We collected tadpoles from an irrigation ditch and played tag near a tree that housed a large nest of cat-sized white rats. The English girl who was taking hormones to stop growing aimed for me and my Welsh friend Katherine in games of Red Rover on the abandoned tennis court.

We didn't tell Mom about the rats.

My Canadian crush, Peter, asked me to go steady. Of course, I couldn't go on dates with him or anyone else yet, I told Mom, but it was very nice to be asked. I tried to keep my mouth closed when I smiled because I knew my braces glinted.

"Susie couldn't care less about boys," Mom wrote home, "but she thinks her gang of girls is about tops. It is fun to watch them go through these stages and not have the worries many parents do about school and study habits." My sister was at the top of her class without much effort—and had held the class Bible when we graduated from church camp—while I regularly dissolved into tears of frustration for failing to hit impossible goals.

"Jane is now and then a worry wart of sorts over not being perfect," Mom wrote home. "I tell her that it is not what we expect, and I think it relaxes her a bit. She sometimes tries to justify her lack of doing by bursting into tears. I hope that she does not make a habit of this, as other kids could really make life miserable for the poor thing."

I pulled straight A's for so long that when I was finally handed a B minus by a college professor when I was in my twenties, I sobbed as if I'd lost a family member. My husband watched, open-mouthed. "Well, that was some time in coming," Ray said. I sniffed, smiled, and got on with my life.

* * *

Carl Rowan's tenure as USIA director lasted barely a year. He was replaced by Texan communications lawyer Leonard Marks, who had guided Lady Bird Johnson's radio and television assets into immensely profitable—and politically useful—holdings.

It was another of LBJ's Texan friends that gave Dad his ultimate Colombian adventure.

Ambassador Oliver was an outdoorsman with a love of guns. Dad—still the South Dakota farm boy at heart—often joined the ambassador on weekend bird-hunting trips organized by Colombian officials. Dad admired the shirt worn one Sunday by the beefy brother of the minister of agriculture—who would later become president—and the next week, the shirt showed up in a package on Dad's desk.

Colombia's southern jungles were a fascination to the rugged ambassador and his equally outdoorsy wife. An outpost on the Amazon, Leticia, became the destination for a hunting trip. A US Navy airplane operated by the embassy's Military Advisory Assistance Group was secured, and Dad was among the staff who were invited along.

The plane left El Dorado Airport, soaring above the small white church atop Monserrate then on for hours over dense, trackless jungle. The pilot nailed a miraculous landing in a tiny field next to the miles-wide Amazon. A small crowd of local people, delirious at the chance to greet the American ambassador and his *señora esposa*, his wife, materialized out of the jungle carrying a feast on banana leaves; and the group was soon settled into spartan accommodations in one of the wooden buildings hugging the shoreline.

The ambassador's hunting guide in Leticia—Mike Tsalikis—was Busch Gardens Zoo's wildlife source, and he kept a menagerie of birds, monkeys, alligators, and snakes. He offered to loop his twenty-foot boa constrictor around anyone's body. Ambassador Oliver stepped forward and appeared to enjoy having his biceps hugged by the powerful reptile.

The trip's main event took place that night. Mike flew the group over to an Amazon tributary in an even more remote section of the jungle, where native experts in two dugout canoes carried the visitors down the dark waters.

One man, the gunner, stood at the prow with a shotgun ready and a bright light affixed to his head, scanning back and forth along the waterline. The other man, the rower, stood at the rear, silently propelling the canoe forward. The challenge, for the gunner, was to spot two bright reflections—the eyes—separated widely enough to indicate a sizable alligator, valuable for its meat and hide. The rower then had to get the dugout close to the animal before the alligator sensed danger and slipped below the surface.

Dad took a turn as gunner. He spotted two eyes, set far apart, and kept them in the beam of his spotlight as the dugout glided ever nearer. Dad held his rifle's sight steady on the space between the two reflections, and the timing was right as he got off his shot. Two of Mike's staff were in the water immediately to grapple with the wounded beast, their hands around his dangerous snout. They heaved the six-foot animal onto the dugout and held him down as he expired from the gunshot.

My father had mixed feelings about killing the alligator, so the only trophy he carried back home was a flash photo of the hunter and his prey.

* * *

In May, my father received word from Director Marks that, after serving USIA overseas for nearly a dozen years, he was being posted to Washington. "We had been overseas for more than eleven years," he later said, "and the Americanization was wearing thin, I suppose. A big job was opening at the State Department—public affairs advisor to the assistant secretary for Latin American Affairs—and USIA wanted me to 'get up here and take it.'"

My father needed to be in Washington within weeks, but the English School would not be over for another month. Mom insisted that we be allowed to complete the year.

When our parents told us of the coming move, Susie and I were thrilled with the novel idea of living in the United States. We wouldn't have to learn another language and living without household help sounded downright fun. We argued about who would get to do the dishes, or the cleaning, or the ironing. Mom listened with a bemused smile on her face.

My father had less than a month to prepare his PAO work in Bogotá for his replacement, get up to speed on the new assignment, and show up behind the desk in DC. He was quickly immersed in the routine chaos of embassy transitions, leaving Mom with the task of packing up our life. "Although all of my experience showed me that Washington cared about the total picture," she later wrote, "I had a feeling that the powers that be really did not treat families quite fairly."

She got on the phone with the embassy to begin the moving routine, but, this time, alone. Burly men arrived to strip our home away from the house. Susie and I watched as our books disappeared into cardboard boxes, our clothes into suitcases, and our toys into crates. The furniture was loaded into huge wooden boxes.

Dad flew to Washington ahead of us to start his new job and find us temporary housing. Before he left, my father gave our dog, Caesar, to Bonifacio, who had long admired the boxer and would provide him a good home. Susie and I hugged him tight one last time, but the big move to America quickly took over.

* * *

My sister and I took the English School final exams one more time, but our scores no longer mattered. The English School would vanish into the past as soon as the airplane left the runway, and we would be onto our next life.

The Friday school ended, I got my braces off and graduated to a retainer, just in time for my *despedida*, a boy-girl farewell party that included Peter. The night slogged along, ordinary and disappointing, until hostess Vicky took command.

"Okay, Jane and Peter!"

All the other kids grew quiet and moved aside to expose Peter on one side of the living room and me on the other, like in *West Side Story* when Tony and Maria see each other across the gym dance floor. I was glad for the dim lighting that hid my hot face, surely bright red. I stared at the floor.

"Time for you to say good-bye," Vicky said. "Come on. Into the bedroom." She opened the door to the guest bedroom, its twin beds piled high with our spring jackets. I hesitated.

"Go ahead, Jane!" The kids around me began to push me forward, their elbows poking into my ribs. I kept my head down as I slowly moved toward the door.

"Yeah, come on, Peter!" The approaching shuffling from the other side of the room told me that Peter was getting pushed my way. Our feet met at the open doorway.

Vicky gave us a shove across the threshold. "Be sure to kiss!" she commanded.

The crowd cheered. The door slammed behind us.

Everything got very quiet. I shot a glance at Peter and saw him do the same, and then looked away. We stood there long enough for my feet to get that tingly, falling-asleep feeling. Acting casual, I stepped toward the window, hoping that Peter would do the same. He did not. Of course not, there was nothing to see in nighttime Bogotá.

I refocused my gaze into the room and sidled over to sit on a corner of one of the twin beds. My jacket lay where I had tossed it ages ago. The springs creaked as Peter sat on the edge of the other bed.

I was no longer me. The words that came out of my mouth sounded like those of a character in *Cherry Ames: Girl Nurse*. "Do," I said. "I mean, don't. Oh, I don't know what I mean."

I burst into tears, grabbed my jacket, and ran out of the bedroom as Mom came in the front door. I flopped, weeping, into the back seat of the Mercedes.

The next day, the car was gone, sold on the Colombian market.

* * *

The week before we left Bogotá, Mom called Señora Cárdenas to invite her and the children over for tea. It would be their pleasure to attend, Señora Cárdenas replied.

So, the last time together with our friends was not atop the wall but in our living room. We looked like strangers, sipping tea and nibbling Mom's sugar cookies.

Astride the wall, conversation had always been easy. Now, it seemed that we were all tongue-tied. Luis and I smiled at each other over our teacups, kind of bashful. I told Andrés I liked his socks, realizing how idiotic that sounded even as it came out of my mouth. Tere's pretty ribbons and Isa's nice sweater were next—*bello*, I said, *lindo*.

Señora Cárdenas said some very nice things about *nuestros queridos vecinos*, our dear neighbors, and Mom said how happy we were to have real friends next door, how much they helped us to love Bogotá.

I handed Luis my autograph book. As he searched for a blank page, I gave Isabel our Beatles record.

"*Las Escobas Que Cantan*," Isa read from the cover. *The Singing Brooms*, a nod to the Beatles' mop haircuts on the cover of *Meet the Beatles*. Isabel added, "Wow."

I laughed. We taught them that word the first afternoon on the wall. "*Muy americana*," I said. Very American.

"*Bueno*," okay, Señora Cárdenas said. She stood. We all stood.

The mothers traded cheek kisses, and then Mai, Luis, Isa, Andrés, and Tere each shook Mom's hand. Susie and I shook hands with Señora Cárdenas, and I reached for Mai's hand next.

She extended her arms instead. "*Adiós*, Juanita."

One by one, each Cárdenas kid hugged each Amerson kid and walked out our door. That night in bed, I opened my autograph book. Los amigos de la pared, Luis had scrawled over his name: the friends of the wall.

We didn't know it then, but we would see each other again, five years later, in this very house.

* * *

Julia had been very quiet in the weeks since Mom had told her and Rosanna that we were leaving. It wasn't a surprise, of course. This was an embassy house. It had been home to the previous PAO family, and it would be home to the next PAO. The maids were part of the package. Before long, Rosanna would be cooking dinners for another American family, and Julia would be picking up other kids' bedrooms.

We were finishing breakfast on the day before we left when Julia stepped into the dining room a little ahead of schedule.

"*Señora*," she said with her head low, asking permission to interrupt us.

"*Sí*, Julia," Mom said with a smile, pushing her chair back a little. "*Ya terminamos.*" We're finished.

Julia pulled a brown paper package out from behind her back. "*Para las niñas*," for the girls, she said.

She handed the package to Mom. Their hands met on the exchange. Julia looked up, her eyes wet. Mom nodded a grownup thanks.

"Well, girls, how about opening your gift?"

The twine came off the bundle easily. Carefully folded inside were two sets of homemade Colombian folklore dance costumes—full black skirts with colored zig-zag tape at the hem, poofy white blouses, straw cowboy hats, even the special alpargatas, slippers, worn by farmers, *campesinos*.

"*¡Ay que lindo!*" Oh, how pretty, I said, holding the longer of the two skirts up to my waist. I twirled a little.

Susie hugged Julia's waist, and I layered my own hug around them both. Although she was a grownup, Julia was just our size.

Rosanna came in from the back hall. We hardly ever saw her away from the kitchen. She pulled a flat package from behind her back.

"*Y nuestra música*," and our music, she said as she handed the package to Mom.

It was the record of our favorite song from the radio—"*Espumas*," "Foam", by Garzon y Collazos.

"*Gracias*," I said. The record player was packed and gone but I had an idea. "Mommy, could we please ask Julia and Rosanna to play this for us in their room?"

"Well, you know how much we have honored their privacy, but maybe just this once."

"*¿Lo tocamos en su cuarto?*" Can we play it in your room? I asked.

Julia and Rosanna looked at Mom. "*La loza puede esperar*," the dishes can wait, she said.

The maids, giggling a little, accompanied Susie and me down the back hall, past the kitchen, and out to their room off the laundry patio.

We had never stepped inside. Two twin beds occupied most of the space, with a small table in between like in American motel rooms.

There was a crucifix over each bed, and another one above an altar made of a soap box covered with a scarf. Several images of the
Madonna were framed on the altar, and a couple of used votive
candles sat ready to be lit.

The record player was against the front wall.

"*Te lo pongo*," I'll put it on for you, Rosanna said, reaching for the
album.

Julia sat on her bed and motioned Susie and me to join her. "*Ven-
gan, mis niñas.*" Come, my girls.

Rosanna lowered the needle, releasing the first strains of the song.
I hadn't realized how sad the lyrics were: The river's waters flow
away like lost loves and broken promises, never to return, those
traveling waters. They will never return. This time will never return.

* * *

Once again, the future took hold. Next stop, the USA. Finally, a
place I could simply be myself, an American in America.

I had no idea that the months ahead would prove the most difficult transition yet and that our four-person family unit was about
to be smashed to pieces.

Part VI

Rockville

(1966-71)

I started eleventh grade in my Pommie uniform, my Sun-In lightened hair falling to my shoulders like a Glamour magazine cover girl. I had finally arrived.

1. ARRIVING

Mom, Susie, and I flew to Washington, DC, after school let out. Dad met us at the airport in a black Lincoln Continental that looked a lot like Bonifacio's limousine back in Bogotá.

It seemed normal to me, but not to Mom. "You didn't buy this." It was not a question. Dad smiled and patted the hood of this sleek machine that he had purchased as his replacement for the Mercedes. "Perfect transportation."

"Bob." Mom bit off the word, tightening her lips in disapproval of the splashy consumerism represented by the American luxury vehicle.

"This'll be my car," he assured her. "We'll get you something a little simpler when we get settled. And, meantime, we can travel in comfort out to see family."

Two days later, we began our routine pilgrimage to the Midwest, only this time, it wasn't home leave. We lived in America now.

Halfway across Indiana, the Lincoln Continental broke down. Mom bit her lip and sighed.

We were back on the road within a couple of hours and arrived in Winona on schedule.

We tapped all the touchstones: supper in the kitchen, lunch at the lake, a visit with our cousins at their big stone house beneath Sugar Loaf, and a stop at Grandpa's Robb Brothers Store. Grandpa was quiet, but that was normal. When we drove off to see the Amersons in the Twin Cities, I didn't know that it would be the last time I would see my grandfather. No one used the word "cancer."

When we got back to Washington, Dad drove off in the Lincoln and came back in a Buick Skylark. Mom didn't say a word.

We moved into a suburban Virginia residential hotel, the American version of a *pensione*. Across the Potomac River, the Washington Monument glistened in the sun and shone even brighter at night, a shard of light between Mr. Lincoln and the Capital's cathedral dome. It was odd to see such a white city. Bogotá was coated in gray diesel and shrouded in clouds, and Rome was all crumbling burnt sienna.

My father worked for the assistant secretary of state for Inter-American Affairs, Lincoln Gordon, a seasoned expert on Latin American economics who had advised Kennedy in the development of the Alliance for Progress. Gordon had served as the American ambassador to Brazil for five years before assuming his post at the State Department. I now understand why Dad began teaching himself Portuguese on his daily commute with language tapes on a small tape player. He must have loved the luxury of solitude in which to take on the challenge of adding a fifth language to his repertoire.

He was back in the public relations business. The daily media summaries, drafting speeches, and traveling were familiar work, but now his clients were senior staff plugged into the White House. He found it exhilarating to be so close to power.

My father and his staff of five hit the ground running every morning to track press coverage of the issues predominating the United States' interface with Latin America—the Alliance for Progress, Castro's communist Cuba, Betancourt's democratic Venezuela, the Dominican Republic's recovery from civil war—and to draft responses reflecting the position of the Johnson administration. The clock was ticking. The issues and the responses needed Assistant Secretary Gordon's review and approval prior to eleven o'clock, when the State Department spokesperson, Bob McCloskey, met with Dad and his counterparts covering other parts of the world. By noon, McCloskey was primed for his daily briefing to the press.

* * *

My parents went house-hunting for the first time in their married life. Unlike their peers, for whom home-ownership was old hat by 1966, my parents had never owned property. Now was the chance to buy a place close to Dad's work in DC, where Mom could continue to enjoy direct access to all that urban life offers.

However, foreign service friends in the DC area recommended Montgomery County in the Maryland suburbs for its school system. My third-grade friend from Rome, Camille, at whose house we watched television the day after President Kennedy was killed, was going into seventh grade at Herbert Hoover Junior High School. That sealed the decision. My parents bought a house in the same school district, a nearly new split-level home in a development called Potomac Woods.

The day after we moved into our house on Bartonshire Way, Susie and I ran down to the neighborhood park by ourselves and became just American kids. The teenage camp counselors organized arts and crafts projects far more interesting than what we invented at home, and a yellow school bus took us to a place in nearby Rockville where we did duckpin bowling.

I kept the fact that this was my first yellow school bus ride to myself. No one needed to know that we were different.

As camp wound down in mid-August, the counselors announced a kids' talent show. I knew immediately what Susie and I would do for the audition—"*Abierta Golpes,*" the Colombian song from our English School repertoire. We could wear the costumes Julia had made for us. Mom ironed our outfits the night before tryouts. It was very strange to see her doing a maid's job. There were no maids' quarters here, and the laundry room was in the basement next to what Americans called a rec room.

For the first time in our lives, we were living without what Americans called "the help."

Mom had dominion over the kitchen. No one would pick up after us. Mom was glad that Susie and I had the orange-painted basement for our games and art projects but still worried about all the mess. After all our talk about "getting to do" housework, Susie and I grudgingly emptied our waste baskets and changed our beds on Saturday mornings. For a while, having the freedom to do her own housework was liberating even for Mom.

The talent show auditions took place at a public high school in Rockville. Susie and I sat with camp friends on the bus ride to the school, changed our clothes in a bathroom, and found two seats in the back of the darkened auditorium. We watched some boys doing karate, a baton twirler, and a group of girls lip-synching and dancing to a Beach Boys song. The audience whooped their approval.

As the acts rolled along, I got a sick feeling in my stomach. This was an American show with American words, and American kids in shorts and t-shirts. After a month of blending in, we were going to be the weird kids wearing dumb costumes and singing words no one could understand.

We were next. The lady running the show stepped out from the wings and looked down at the list. "And here are sisters Jane and Susan Amerson singing . . ." she scrunched her eyebrows together. "Alberto Gulps."

I thought I would die, but a big sister has responsibilities. I squeezed Susie's hand as we walked up the steps to the stage. We hit the opening notes in harmony right on the nose and made it through the song a cappella perfectly. The auditorium was dead quiet, and then there was a little grownup clapping.

"How charming," said the lady running the show as we walked off stage.

I couldn't get that stupid costume off fast enough. We sat by ourselves on the way back to Potomac Woods. Susie found her friend Barbara to walk home with, but I ran home alone.

"Hi, honey," Mom called from the kitchen as I walked in the front door. "How'd it go?" I burst into tears and ran up to my room. I didn't want to explain, and my mother didn't push. When we got the call saying we had aced the audition, I asked Mom to make up some excuse. Susie didn't care one way or the other.

I was going to have to be way more careful. America was not the magic summer land of our overseas visits, but a universe apart from our real world. Blending in was going to be much harder than I thought.

* * *

It was still hot and humid on the first day of school as I joined a small parade of Potomac Woods kids walking to the junior and senior high school bus stop. Susie and Barbara, who was also going into fifth grade, were walking together to the nearby elementary school. It was the first time in our lives that we were in different schools.

My new dress glommed onto my sweaty legs as I took bigger steps to catch up with Linda, our high school neighbor. Her dress seemed to slip along her bottom, and I realized that she was wearing stockings like a grownup. Wow.

"Oh, hi, Jane," she said as I came up alongside her half a block before the bus stop. "First day at Hoover, huh?"

It is hard to act casual when you're out of breath. "Uh-huh."

"You're going to love it," Linda said, tossing her flipped hair off her sleeveless shoulders.

Her baby pink lips stuck together when she smiled.

"Thanks," I said. Oh, for goodness' sake. Thanks? "I mean, yes. Yes,

I am sure so." What language was I speaking?

The school bus pulled up, saving me from more embarrassment.

Herbert Hoover Junior High School was a sprawling two-story grid of locker-lined alleys connecting identical rooms. Somehow, the crinkled map from orientation got me through the morning's jumble of classes. With my lunch bag in hand and book bag over my shoulder, I walked toward the cafeteria. Mom's baloney and salty butter sandwiches on soft American bread made anything better.

I couldn't wait to find Camille. We had seen each other only a couple of times since arriving in Washington, but knowing one person in this enormous school was still something. I turned the corner and nearly ran into my old friend. Perfect. "Hi!" I said. "Let's eat together."

Camille took a step back and looked down at my legs. "You know that no one wears anklets in junior high," she said and continued down the hall.

I sat at an empty lunch table and watched girls parade by. Camille was right—I saw knee socks, tights, even some stockings like my neighbor Linda, but no stupid anklets. I tried to look casual as I slid my hands down my right calf, slipped off my church shoe, and rolled my sock off my foot. I stuffed it into my book bag, and then did the same with my left sock. My loose shoes clattered against the linoleum all the way to Spanish class.

I slunk into an empty desk in the corner and tucked my feet under my seat. I glanced at the kids in my row, wondering why they seemed so old. Then, I remembered. At orientation, the Hoover seventh-grade counselor had suggested that I take ninth-grade Spanish. The second bell rang. I shrank down and hoped for the best.

"*Buenos días, clase*," good afternoon, class, the teacher said. His accent was gringo, but at least I was on familiar territory.

"*Buenos días*," I said.

No one else had answered. The teacher smiled at me.

"*¿Tu nombre?*" Your name?

"Juanita Amerson," I said. It was a Bogotá reflex.

"Hey, how'd that new kid get so smart?" a girl behind me said.

"Whaddya, showin' off?" some boy said. Everyone laughed.

When the bell rang, I waited in my seat until after the big kids left and then beat a path to the door. I wasn't fast enough.

"Jane," the teacher called. I walked back to his desk. "Sounds like you really speak Spanish," he said.

"We just moved here from Colombia," I said. Please, don't ask me any questions.

"Great. You know, I really think you belong in another class," the teacher said. Relief flooded me. "Your level is being taught at the high school, just across the athletic fields. Here, take this paper to your counselor, and he'll see to it that you are enrolled there. *Buena suerte*, good luck!"

The distance between Hoover and the high school was about four times the length of the potato field behind the English School. I would die if I had to walk all the way over there, just this weird kid out on the big field heading toward a school filled with A-line shifts and stockings and flipped hairdos. No way I was going over there.

Instead, I dropped Spanish and joined beginning French. I didn't let on as I picked up the language quickly through its Latin connection to Spanish and Italian. I was determined to limp along like everyone else.

I had been wrong to think that moving to America would be easy. I thought all I had to be was myself. After all, weren't we professional

Americans? Maybe in Bogotá. Maybe in Rome. But here, I was just a little foreign girl wearing the wrong clothes, speaking the wrong language, and clueless about how to fit in.

Retired USIA foreign service officer Alvin Perlman, reacting to an early draft of this book, wondered if the sense of alienation experienced by embassy kids upon their return to the States might be one of the reasons few of us have chosen to pursue foreign service careers.

Mom wrote home: "Well, the girls got off to school with butterflies in their stomachs and not too much breakfast. Can well understand how they feel but by next week at this time it will be normal for them."

Not for me. And not for her.

2. SLEEPERS

S ara Mansfield Taber, who was also raised in the foreign service during the Cold War and who holds a doctorate in Human Development from Harvard, observes in her memoir *Born Under an Assumed Name*: "When you're new, one of two things happen: you're befriended by another marginal girl, or an in-crowd girl decides to adopt you as a sidekick." Camille and her friends had rejected me, but there was a true friend waiting in homeroom.

It was a happy accident of the alphabet that Alice Ammerman and I were assigned to sit together in homeroom first thing every morning, and we were assigned the same locker. Alice was as studious and earnest as I was, and as tall as I was shrimpy. We made the most of our obvious difference in size by giving ourselves the nicknames of Tall One and Small One. Batman and Robin. Alice-New-Shoes and Janie-New-Glasses. Yep, we flaunted our "marginal girl" status.

Alice and her family lived on a large tract of land in rural Potomac, where I became a frequent overnight visitor on the weekend. Despite our different dimensions, we fit together on the seat of their riding mower, a wonderfully exotic experience. It was a thrill to ride through that quintessential American scent of fresh-cut grass, driving a vehicle without adult supervision for hours at a time. Her mother's large fruit and vegetable garden produced fantastic Saturday night dinner salads and Sunday morning pancake toppings.

We remained close friends for two years, but Alice left Hoover— along with nearly half of the ninth-grade class—when a new junior high opened in Potomac. By the time the two halves came back together as the sophomore class at Winston Churchill Senior High, my attention had shifted to boys.

But, back at Hoover, Alice knew me. She really knew me.

* * *

My parents had adjustments of their own to grapple with. "Foreign service people have to make adjustments often, moving from pillar to post, but in some ways no posting requires more adaptation than Washington," my father wrote years later.

As I look back at the five years we spent in the Maryland suburbs, severed from the embassy community on which we had depended for my entire life, it was as if we were like the family of Soviet spies in the FX series, *The Americans*: assigned to blend anonymously into the American landscape, putting our real selves on hold pending instructions to return to active duty.

With the move to DC, my parents lost the American community of diplomats, expats, and businessmen who were each other's social network overseas. Although Dad's work environment expanded in new directions—encompassing the White House, the Department of State, USIA, and USIS offices in American embassies across Latin America—the diplomatic perks of overseas posts were absent in DC. Dad saw former ambassadors drive themselves into the State Department parking lot in ordinary cars. In a town of important people, nobody was special.

My mother felt the absence of General Services staff, people at the embassy that would help find a house to live in or a school for your kids, but it was the lack of a social network that made the biggest difference. She homed in on foreign service friends from Caracas, Rome, and Bogotá also on rotation through DC, like Camille's mother, and Macalester College friends like her roommate Mary Caldwell Mudge and Dot and Don Wortman. Don, already a seasoned federal government administrator, had graduated in the same class as Fritz Mondale, now a senator.

Being adrift in America was especially disorienting for my mother when it came to monitoring Susie and me. For a dozen years, she and Dad had been the intermediaries between their kids and a foreign world. Now, Susie and I jettisoned off in different directions to make our own friends at school and in the neighborhood, their identities—and those of their parents—largely unknown to our parents. Accustomed to hovering, Mom had to have faith we could handle ourselves. She gleaned what she could while driving us home from school whenever we had late activities. She discovered what American parents already knew—the carpool parent becomes invisible behind the wheel.

"I loved the foreign service for how strong it made our family. In Rockville, it seemed to break into fragments," Mom later wrote. "The girls had their own activities and friends we had never met, from families we knew nothing about. This surely was a change from the tight foursome who operated as a whole within a generally foreign situation."

Dad left home at seven to dive into a job filled with interesting issues and important people. Susie and I were out the door at eight, going to different schools, and we stayed behind closed bedroom doors in our private spheres until we had dinner watching television. Dad and Mom ate when he got home. Then it was bedtime.

"It was as if we all barely got a glimpse of each other," Mom would later write.

The greatest change of all in this post was that my mother was no longer required to participate in her husband's job. There were no "hearts and minds" to win at home. The USIS traditional after-hours workload of cocktail parties, receptions, and cultural activities simply vanished. Now and then, she drove into Washington to join Dad for a special event, but not very often. After a dozen years of being her husband's teammate, Mom was unemployed.

Had we purchased a home in a more familiar urban setting—Chevy Chase, for instance—Mom could have walked to museums, explored Georgetown antique stores and boutiques, shopped at grocery stands and made herself at home in another big city. Instead, she was in the deserted suburbs, with a used Ford Falcon under the carport and the Rockville Pike strip malls for amusement.

For a few months, the novelty of tending to her own house carried Mom forward. She put on jeans and scrubbed the walls. She rolled up her sleeves and planted chrysanthemums. She bought a sewing machine, fabric, and patterns at JCPenney and made us dresses. On her way home from grocery shopping, she discovered the pleasure of a peach ice cream cone at High's.

Mom found a few new friendships among women in the neighborhood—making a real connection with Barbara's mother, Doris Murray. Camille's mother introduced her to the free-for-all sales at Loehman's. An embassy friend got her involved with the American Association of University Women, a membership organization of college-educated women whose history was as long as my mother's American ancestral line. It must have felt empowering to have her college education be at last acknowledged.

It was college friend Dot Wortman who finally connected Mom with the perfect volunteer job—giving tours of the collection at the National Gallery of Art. Our four years in Italy and the Fodors guide had given Mom a private class in art history, and she was an eager student of the Gallery's protocol and collection. Occasionally, Susie and I would accompany Mom to the museum on the weekend, but we were mostly interested in the cafeteria's tangy blueberry pie.

Largely, however, Mom was home alone, blaming herself for Dad's long commute, feeling guilty about having chosen our suburban home. She unplugged the telephone and took long naps every afternoon to discard the blues. This time, they didn't go away.

Years later, she would admit that those five years in the Maryland suburbs were the loneliest of all. "I never got over feeling that I was waiting to get out of there. I'd never felt that way in any place we'd lived, so it was horrible to feel that way about your own country."

* * *

Mom barely held us together as a family by continuing our tradition of Sunday noon dinner—a practice that had made the most of the only day Mom had the kitchen to herself in our foreign service life. Now, our Rockville kitchen filled with the aroma of American pot roast, Italian rosemary roast chicken, Colombian *ajiaco* stew, and all kinds of vegetables Americans didn't really know—eggplant, artichokes, asparagus, yucca. No one from school or the neighborhood ever joined us at this meal, sparing us the embarrassment of having to explain pasta *primavera* to friends that thought spaghetti was Chef Boyardee.

Now and then, if Dad could free himself from office paperwork, the four of us would pile into the Buick Skylark for a Sunday drive south to Mount Vernon or north to the Peter Pan Inn for a meal of fried chicken and corn fritters hushpuppies, all the while speaking Spanish to each other.

Spanish was our private language, the code we instinctively used when we wanted to be especially understood by each other, much as some Italian words would always carry more than their weight in family conversations. A waitress smacking gum got Dad's raised eyebrows and a muttered *brutta figura,* while a just-average soup would pale in comparison to *mamma's minestrone.*

Spanish became a source of silliness during one Sunday outing to a Mexican restaurant in DC. A *mariachi* song was playing as we entered, and almost immediately, Dad began to hum. Susie and I exchanged looks over the menus—maybe no one would notice. Dad's humming turned into quiet yips along with the song, and he was beaming. It was impossible not to smile back.

This was the music he first heard in South Dakota on the radio at night when the signals from Texas stations drifted north across the prairie. His summers in Mexico as a college student had cemented his love of the passionate songs. Although we had never lived there,

Dad's guitar repertoire included several Mexican songs that Susie and I could sing in harmony.

Please God, don't let one of those songs come on next.

Mom looked up from the menu. "Isn't it a pleasure to read Spanish?"

Susie giggled. "It's more fun to read the English translation. 'Homemade crap dip.'"

"Susie!" Mom said.

"I'm just reading what it says," Susie said, all wide-eyed innocence.

"I may need to order 'tortillas from sweet porn,'" I said.

Dad laughed quietly, his mouth in an open upside-down smile and his eyes tearing, a messy trait that Susie and I had inherited. Mom hid her smile with her menu, failing to see that the Mexican waiter had approached the table to take our order.

"You have chosen tacos?" His English was heavily accented. "Beef? Cheeken?"

"Cheeken, heere," Mom instinctively responded, then nearly inhaled her lips in embarrassment.

We finished ordering, dabbing at our eyes and mouths to sop up the tears and drool. We surely failed to live up to the sophisticated image diplomats are supposed to have. "Cheeken, heere" became a family saying.

* * *

Although Dad's travel schedule was far less hectic than it had been in Bogotá, he accompanied Assistant Secretary Gordon on trips to speak with American audiences and with the international press in the Caribbean and in Central and South America.

In the spring of 1967, my father embarked on the longest and most prestigious trip yet. He got tapped to be the liaison with American reporters at a conference of foreign ministers in Buenos Aires, Argentina, and to do the lead work in setting up the press for the Pan-American summit of Johnson and other country leaders at Punta del Este, Uruguay. It was a three-week trip, and his first to these South American countries.

The conference of foreign ministers brought the United States, Canada, and the countries of the Caribbean and Central and South America together about once a decade to discuss economic, military, and political cooperation. The Alliance for Progress, which took such a commanding presence in Colombia during my father's tenure in Bogotá, had been forged in the 1961 Pan-American meeting.

President Kennedy had committed to the concept in his January 1961 inaugural address. "To our sister republics south of our border, we offer a special pledge—to convert our good words into good deeds in a new alliance for progress—to assist free men and free governments in casting off the chains of poverty." Now, at about the halfway mark of the Alliance's projected ten-year course, the countries would assess its success. Kennedy's eloquent words would be difficult to live up to.

Dad boarded Secretary of State Dean Rusk's Air Force Two—identical to the 707 called Air Force One when the president was on board—for the twelve-hour flight to Buenos Aires. Assistant Secretary Gordon and USIA Director Leonard Marks were also on the flight.

The meeting lasted about a week. Dad got his messages through to the American press—*The New York Times* reported that Secretary Rusk and the foreign ministers would be discussing a proposed Common Market for Latin America, mentioning that America favored the idea. The newspaper also reported that a presidential summit was to be held in April in neighboring Uruguay.

To help set up the subsequent summit's press operations, Dad booked passage on an overnight boat to Punta del Este with a group of newsmen who had been covering the Buenos Aires meeting. In general, the press and the government were supposed to maintain a kind of adversarial relationship, but my father found that the camaraderie created by the week-long event and the travel experience was pleasant and useful. During his work in Punta del Este, my father even shared a room with friend Jerry O'Leary, State Department correspondent for *The Washington Star*.

* * *

Meanwhile, back home, my mother got the news that she had been dreading. The cancer that prompted our summer visit to Winona from Bogotá had taken Jim Robb's life. Her father was gone, and her husband was five thousand miles away. Dad's staff at the State Department helped Mom reach my father by telephone.

Could Dad have dropped things to get home to his grieving wife? Surely someone else could finish up the press preparations in Uruguay, and the embassy could snag Dad a flight to DC. Maybe, but it didn't happen. Perhaps Mom didn't even ask—the job took priority, and she would deal with family matters. Our neighbors, the Murrays, took Susie and me in for the rest of the week while Mom flew into Minneapolis, rented a car, and drove down the Mississippi to Winona alone.

Laying in the Murray's guest room bed, I realized that I would never again hold the soft, creased hands of my Grandfather Robb, never again hear his voice reading my poetry back to me over the telephone, never again seek his counsel on a rhythm or rhyme. The void was as big as the night sky over the White House when we stood vigil for President Kennedy.

Her father's loss was devastating to my mother, but she held in her emotions. When she returned, her daily afternoon ritual gave her room to grieve privately—she unplugged the telephone, closed the drapes, and retreated into sleep.

She never did cry for her father, or for her mother, or for my father when he died in his sleep a week after being diagnosed with pancreatic cancer. She wandered the world for two long years, stunned to be alone and longing to be reunited with Dad before being felled by a swift stroke.

My version of heaven for Mom has them all together and laughing.

3. TURBULENCE

D ad had set up the press operations for the 1967 presidential summit in Punta Del Este, but there was no controlling what journalists wrote and who interpreted the results of President Johnson's attendance at the Pan-American summit.

The AP reported that the effort to represent inter-American unity was a losing battle given the lack of greater American aid. In an address on the anniversary of the failed Bay of Pigs invasion, Fidel Castro, who had been ejected from the Organization of American States earlier in the year, denounced the summit for failing to address the Yankee occupation of the Dominican Republic and the "barbarous genocide practiced by the Yankee imperialists in Vietnam."

The civil war between North Vietnam (Hanoi, backed by Russia and China) and South Vietnam (Saigon, supported by the United States and its allies) became a proxy for the Cold War. President Johnson pledged to stay in Vietnam until the communist threat was over. Large-scale anti-war protests broke out in Washington and other cities.

The war in Vietnam was an issue for our image overseas. Newsreels of antiwar demonstrations—long-haired students confronted by stoic armed police—stood at odds with the wholesome image of American democracy. Martin Luther King, Jr., stated that the war in Vietnam was the biggest obstacle to the civil rights movement. Race riots hit across the country—in Tampa, Buffalo, Detroit, Milwaukee.

Che Guevara, Fidel Castro's deputy, was captured and executed in Bolivia. Castro reframed it as a lucky accident that would not deter the people's solidarity with the revolutionary struggle, a fight that sided with the Vietcong against the Yankee imperialists.

"¡Hasta la victoria siempre!" Ever onward to victory, went the Guevara mantra.

USIA had begun sending young foreign service officers to Saigon, where the traditional "representational" duties to engage "hearts and minds" was called psychological warfare, PSYOP. It was a dangerous assignment that also split families, with the wife and children in Thailand and the officer in Vietnam.

"These were the years of heavy slogging in Vietnam, when USIS officers were being asked to serve there not only to handle information and culture in that war-distorted atmosphere, but also as public-information advisors out in the boonies where the Viet Cong often threatened danger," Dad would later write.

Being tapped for such a tough post accelerated careers. Turning down the assignment could mean second-rate jobs for a long time. Up to now, Mom and Dad had understood that an order from Washington was not negotiable. However, people were beginning to push back.

Mom was grateful that my father's new job was in Washington. Perhaps the value of the assignment would keep him away from the war.

* * *

Lincoln Gordon left the Department of State to direct Johns Hopkins University, in whose graduate program Dad had studied in Bologna. President Johnson replaced Gordon with Ambassador Covey Oliver, whom Dad had worked for in Bogotá.

However, they would not be working together in Washington. Dad was on his way back to USIA as the assistant director for Latin America, one of six area directors who pretty much ran operations in the field. It was a plum job about as high as any career foreign service officer could expect to rise.

Before Dad moved into his big corner office at 1776 Pennsylvania

Avenue, there was one more trip to handle for the State Department. President Johnson was attending a July 1968 summit in San Salvador to promote a Central American Common Market. Dad was to handle the local and international press.

The arrival of Johnson was a high-visibility event. As the cameras whirred, the six-foot-four Texan reached out his big paw to shake hands with fellow heads of state, a gesture designed to illustrate how we were all in this together. Dad was not convinced by the Latin American smiles. The image of their contrasting statures—with LBJ a good head taller than any other leader—seemed to symbolize the imbalanced relationship between the oversized United States and the tiny republics to the South.

Dad was eager to get home. Instead of waiting for the White House plane, he joined a handful of other staff hitching an early ride on the big C-130 hauling the two cars that always accompanied LBJ's trips. The plane took off and began a steep climb.

"Nobody smoke!"

The order was barked from the cockpit as the smell of gasoline filled the huge plane. Someone had forgotten to drain the cars' fuel tanks. For a few minutes, Dad thought he would be a headline, but the plane leveled off and the fumes dissipated.

He spent the rest of the flight peering over the pilots' shoulders as they worked the complicated controls, a long way from the Piper Club he soloed in as a teenager way back in South Dakota.

* * *

Vietnam cost Hubert Humphrey the 1968 presidential election. Selected as the party's candidate amidst the furor of anti-war protests and police brutality at the Democratic National Convention in Chicago, Humphrey could not outrun culpability.

The winner of the November election was Republican Richard

Nixon, who had escaped serious injury in Caracas as Eisenhower's vice president, and who had failed against Kennedy in his 1960 bid for president. Spiro Agnew, the Greek American who had been elected governor of Maryland as "Ted," was the new vice president.

A Republican administration prepared to move into the White House. Dean Rusk, secretary of state for Kennedy and Johnson, was out. William P. Rogers, who worked on the Alliance for Progress under Kennedy and Johnson, was the new head of the State Department. Nixon also appointed a new director for USIA, Frank Shakespeare, a television executive whose politics and policy preferences echoed those of the new president. He was a conservative ideologue who thought senior officers in the agency should see American operations in Vietnam for themselves to convince USIA staff to serve there willingly.

My father would soon find out what that meant.

4. MOONSTRUCK

It was the summer of 1969, and the neighborhood social scene migrated to the Potomac Woods Pool. Susie and I—along with anyone who wanted to participate—were on the swim team. We pickled our eyes practicing laps every morning, rode our bikes home to watch *Jeopardy* over lunch, and hung out at the pool again all afternoon.

The coveted desk job at the pool that summer fell to Rich, a neighborhood kid who'd already completed tenth grade at Winston Churchill Senior High School where I would begin my sophomore year in the fall. Rich was a townie in suburbia—a little rough around the edges, a little dangerous. As long as my flip flops were glommed onto the wet cement, I felt safe flirting just a bit. Then a bit more.

On the night of the annual after-hours swim party, Rich locked up the facility and walked me up the hill to the neighboring elementary school to wait for my ride home. We sat on the curb, Rich's arm slung across my shoulders. Dad's car pulled into the lot, its high beams sweeping across the front of the school. Right before the lights found us, Rich leaned over and gave me a kiss. I went breathless.

Dad barely stopped the car before I jumped up, swung myself into the passenger seat, and closed the door.

"New friend?" Dad said.

"Not really," I said in one brief exhalation.

I wondered if Dad could hear my heart beating in my ears. I tore upstairs and almost ran into Camille as she came out of the guest room. I had forgotten that she was staying with us for a couple of days while her mother arranged for their move back overseas. We were not friends, just kind of related through Rome and our parents.

"Hi." I wished she were Alice. I could have told Alice. No way I was opening up to Camille about my first kiss.

"Honey?" Mom was standing at the foot of the carpeted stairs holding the portable TV. "I thought you girls might want to take this up to the guest room to watch the moon landing. Dad and I are watching in the family room."

Right, Apollo 11—Mr. Armstrong and another guy—were on TV tonight. "Uh, yeah," I said, my brain running to catch up with my emotions. I padded down the five steps and took the set.

Mom gave my forehead a kiss. "Glad you're home." She looked up the stairs. "Nice to have you with us, Camille."

"Thanks, Mrs. Amerson."

Funny how Camille could sound just like a good kid when she wanted to. She and her intimidating friends still cleared a path when they came striding down the hall.

I carried the TV into the guest room and turned it on. The black and white image flickered into focus. I turned the dial a couple of stations and found Walter Cronkite.

I knocked on Susie's door on my way to the bathroom.

"What?"

"We got the TV," I said through the closed door. "Moon, remember?"

I closed the bathroom door behind me. My whole head felt puffy. I leaned over the sink to get close to the mirror, seeking the traces of Rich's braces on my lips. I splashed cold water on my cheeks and reached for my toothbrush. No, toothpaste would ruin this. I wiped my cheeks dry.

Susie and Camille were sprawled on the guest room floor. I grabbed the remaining bed pillow and joined them. We watched the men from NASA in short-sleeved white shirts, black ties, and headphones as they watched a big TV screen and listened to choppy dialogue.

Then, the moon surface filled the television screen. It looked like a huge gray vat of oatmeal, pockmarked with air pockets.

Someone at NASA said, "A mile from the moon."

Mr. Cronkite said, "Wow."

We watched as the oatmeal became sand and the air pockets became craters, and a man said, "Three feet down, two feet, one forward." The screen went blurry, then briefly all black, and the man said, "Light on."

Mr. Cronkite said, "Man on the moon," and laughed. People said later that they had never heard him laugh. The newsman wiped his eyes like Dad did when he was moved.

Mr. Armstrong said, "The Eagle has landed."

"Oh, boy," Mr. Cronkite said.

"Neat," Susie said. She stood up, tugging at her pjs.

"He's going to climb down," I said. "Wait."

Mr. Armstrong stepped on the moon. "One small step for man, one giant leap for mankind."

One big kiss from a boy.

"Night." Susie went down the hall to her room.

"Night," I said, standing up. "Guess I'll give you the guest room, guest," I said to Camille.

I lay in bed with my shades up so I could see the moon. There were two humans there right this minute. All I could think of was that a boy with braces had given me my first kiss.

Swooped in and bam.

I barely slept.

* * *

The Apollo 11 moon landing was a global event that generated enormous goodwill towards the United States, and USIA took full advantage of the publicity. Working with NASA, the agency put together six touring exhibits—one for each geographical area around the world—about the lunar landing program. The centerpiece of each exhibit was a moon rock about the size of a walnut mounted in a rotating jeweler's display case inside a large plastic globe, with a spotlight on the rock and a continuous loop tape recording explaining its origin.

The rocks were considered priceless artifacts that needed protection, so USIA tapped staff in the field to accompany each exhibit. As area director for Latin America, Dad asked Harry Haven Kendall—the USIS information officer in Santiago, Chile—to accompany the exhibit as it toured nineteen countries over six months.

The moon rocks were positive publicity, but the promotion did little to deflect the negative press of the Vietnam War. Communist editorials denounced the US-Vietnam policy as American imperialism, not only in Castro's Cuba but also in places like Chile where Communist radio programs and newspapers competed aggressively against those of the Christian Democrats.

With the election of Salvador Allende in 1970, Chile came under the rule of the only major Marxist government in South America. The matter became one of considerable concern to high-level people within the United States government who feared that Allende would create a communist government. USIA stuck with its public diplomacy mission—the moon exhibit was regime-neutral—in an increasingly delicate situation. Allende's overthrow in a 1973 coup d'état was followed by Augusto Pinochet's brutal military dictatorship. There was talk of the CIA's clandestine support of the regime change.

Things were more cordial in America's relationships elsewhere in Latin America. Venezuela had seen the historic completion of the first five-year term of a civilian government under Rómulo Betancourt. His 1963 elected successor, Raúl Leoni, an ally in the Democratic Action party, had maintained the country's equilibrium. The 1968 election of Rafael Caldera, from the opposing Social Christian party, represented the first time in the history of Venezuela that there had been a peaceful and democratic transfer of power. My father felt something like familial pride in the country's decade of political progress.

Ousted dictator Marcos Pérez Jiménez, who had settled in Miami, was extradited from the United States to Venezuela in 1963 to face embezzlement charges. Convicted of the charges, he was exiled to Spain.

Colombia continued alternating presidencies between the Conservative and the Liberal parties, maintaining a certain stability despite the undercurrent of violence. For USIA, the classic Colombian Spanish accent continue to make the country a rich resource for the production and recording of scripts and radio *novellas* broadcast by the Voice of America.

In Brazil, where Lincoln Gordon, my father's former boss at the State Department, had been ambassador during the coup of 1964, the military governed with a light hand. The new capital, Brasilia, was far from home for elected officials, so USIS mid-week programming had quite literally a captive audience. Binational centers all over the country taught English, shared American newspapers, books, and magazines, and showed American films.

It might not overcome the Vietnam War narrative, but in Latin America, anyway, USIA continued to demonstrate that America valued education, cultural expression, and individual freedom.

My father was about to get an opportunity to see Vietnam for himself.

5. Vietnam

The war in Vietnam seemed very distant to me. The older sister of my friend Beth spent the weekends painting "Stop the War" protest signs with her boyfriend. He wore a khaki green military field jacket, and his hair was long and parted in the middle. So was hers.

We didn't discuss the war over Sunday dinners. Questioning the government that Dad worked for would be *brutta figura*.

In the spring of 1970, USIA Director Shakespeare sent down the order—my father was going to Vietnam for a two-week visit. The purpose, my father later wrote, was "To absorb the rationale for our involvement there in order to persuade any doubtful subordinate that our purpose was noble and our spirits should be high."

Despite having matured in the World War II atmosphere, sure in the knowledge that sometimes nations had to go to war as a matter of principle, Dad was feeling ambivalent about Vietnam. Something was out of kilter, and here was an opportunity to see the situation for himself.

He finagled a one-month trip itinerary around the world with stops to confer with USIA officers in Greece, Lebanon, India, and Thailand on the way to Vietnam, and in Hong Kong and Japan on the way home. Hawaii and California were just for fun. Holding the approved travel plan—how my father must have tingled. He was going to circle the world.

I never spoke to my father about this trip, but his journal about that month was among his papers when he died. Here is the story he left behind. It continues to resonate with world events today.

* * *

It was five thousand miles to Athens. The country was still reeling from the military's 1967 political coup that had unraveled democracy in its very birthplace. Dad came away from his embassy meetings impressed with how the USIS post had used the United States' 1968 elections to promote democracy, setting up an election center with American television coverage. Vice President Spiro Agnew's Greek American heritage spoke volumes about the opportunities America offered.

On his way to the Athens airport, Dad picked me up a blousy Evzone soldier shirt that I had seen advertised in *The New Yorker*. The irony of assigning my father, an official representative of American democracy, the purchase of a Greek uniform from a country under military rule did not occur to me.

In Beirut, Dad gained an appreciation for the difficulties of representing the official US position amid the Middle Eastern passions stirred up by the 1967 Arab-Israeli War. As I write these words, those passions have exploded in the most horrific way—the murder of 1,200 Israeli men, women, and children in a surprise attack by the Hamas Palestinian terrorist group has resulted in a full-out war between Israel and Hamas in the Gaza Strip that has killed tens of thousands of Palestinians. Secretary of State Antony Blinken made this impassioned plea for peace at the United Nations Security Council: "Act as if the security and stability of the entire region and beyond is on the line, because it is." Both the Israel-Hamas war and the invasion of Ukraine by Russia make ever so clear the importance of American diplomacy and a White House committed to our allies abroad.

My father's next stop was Iran, the country that today supports Hamas. Back in 1970, Tehran seemed to be coming into modern times under the Shah Reza Pahlavi, the latest in a line of monarchs dating back over two thousand years, but the resentments against America for its part in bringing the Shah to power in 1953 were simmering. On his way to the Tehran airport, Dad bought Susie and me Iranian silver rings with a turquoise inlaid design.

In India, Dad took in some serious sightseeing—visiting the Raj Ghat, the memorial in Delhi dedicated to Mahatma Gandhi, and the breathtaking Taj Mahal in Agra.

Bangkok was hot, bustling, and awash in American dollars from the families of US military men on duty in Vietnam. Dad must have pictured Mom, Susie, and me here if he were sent to Saigon.

* * *

Finally, Dad arrived in Saigon for two weeks "in country," as the military said. "I had not been prepared," he wrote in his journal, "for the sheer beauty of the city itself, with its tree-lined boulevards reminiscent of Paris."

The visit kicked off with the expected briefings by diplomatic and military staff at the embassy. It was an odd role to be playing—instead of organizing meetings for a visiting American dignitary, Dad was now *playing* the dignitary. It was an uncomfortable fit. "I am getting, it is a little embarrassing to report, the VIP treatment here," he wrote to my mother. "At yesterday's military briefing, a major general and two colonels sat through the presentation to keep me, the only recipient, company and to answer questions. I did my best to nod wisely at the right places."

He could see that serving in Saigon was not an easy assignment for his embassy colleagues, but they seemed to accept the rationale that this work had to be done. It was duty, a matter of principle. "Most of us," he wrote, "were old enough to remember the personal sacrifices of WWII."

Air America—"owned and operated by the US government, probably specifically the CIA," my father wrote—flew my father to Danang, the northernmost port city free from Hanoi's control. USIS had a regional presence in Danang, and Dad was put up in the home of the public affairs officer there. Sandbags lined the house's outer walls to protect them from caving in from bombings. "During the night, I could hear the rumble of artillery in the distance, like thunder," my father wrote. "No easy job, this cultural programming assignment for my housemate."

Two hours to the north, my father saw the ancient and beautiful city of Hue reduced to rubble by savage conflict. A military escort took him to the front lines to meet American soldiers, the "grunts," during a lull in the fighting. "Looking into the faces of these guys, in person, was not the same as glancing at a flickering image on the evening news," my father wrote in his journal. "How many of them will be lost or damaged before this thing is over?"

Air America flew Dad south to the Mekong Delta, where hostilities seemed to ebb and flow, hamlet to hamlet. The US Army worked alongside South Vietnam military forces there, with USIS handling PSYOP propaganda about the valor of the fight. As he was being briefed by American and South Vietnamese military officers, Dad again felt the discomfort: "So many individuals spent time and effort to inform, to influence, this supposed VIP."

Things got more real when his trip ventured outside the military-controlled areas. The enemy could be anywhere. The sampan boat pilot kept to the center of the Mekong River, strategically maximizing the distance between this American target and hidden Viet Cong riflemen—"those people in black pajamas," my father wrote. "Here the conflict would be near at hand."

Enemy marksmen also posed a danger for chopper landings and takeoffs. As the group's helicopter prepared to leave one remote area, Dad was urged to go first, per protocol. He paused a moment, then scrambled up to give a hand to his USIS escort officer, a petite woman. "As I hesitated," he wrote, "a vision flashed into my mind of deferring to the lady or to others, gentlemanly 'Alphonse and Gaston' stuff, with the rest of the group bunched up behind us and vulnerable to an enemy marksman. I lamented a situation that obliged me to feel (and perhaps look) cowardly, ungracious. Anyway, I was first on board. No big deal. It was the right decision. I guess."

Dad's emotional discomfort increased throughout the afternoon, when the South Vietnamese commander at a training camp asked my father to join him in reviewing his troops. "Striding purposefully to martial music along the front ranks of soldiers stiffly at attention . . . something seemed out of whack. Maybe it was me."

At the end of his troop walk-by, the soldiers gave my father a captured North Vietnamese flag. "My role in this peculiar theater of war, seemed obligatory," he wrote. "Accept the token, mumble appropriate thanks."

Dad's USIS colleague had one more going-away gift—a paperweight awarding him honorary citizenship in the Mekong Delta; it was inscribed: "For having commendably proved by personal courage, stamina and visitation via canal sampans, helicopter airlift and hazardous road travel in enemy contested areas, a genuine interest in and empathy with the aspiration of the people to forge a free REPUBLIC OF VIETNAM." Dad recognized that it was psychological warrior-speak, designed "to convey to visitors from Washington what might make them feel ennobled for having taken part in the US presence in this benighted country." Dad did not believe that it would sway a struggling people in the midst of war.

The two weeks came to a close. His departing flight taxied away from the Saigon terminal, passing an astounding array of US official aircrafts around the busy airport and raising questions that had no easy answers. "If such American commitment of our military might had still not won after more than five years," my father wrote in his journal, "how much more would it take? For how much longer? And if a mid-level career diplomat such as myself could be obliged to play an unwanted role as VIP during a two-week visit, was it possible that the whole US government had somehow got snookered into an artificial, unnecessary VIP role trying to solve the problems of this far-off place?"

Dad had hoped that the two weeks would reassure him that America was on the right track in Vietnam, but his doubts were only reinforced. He would remain a loyal government employee. However, if he were directed to Saigon, he would decline—career be damned.

He flew east, stopping only briefly in Hong Kong, Tokyo, Honolulu, and Los Angeles, before taking the cross-country flight to Washington.

All I knew is that Dad was gone for a month, brought me the Evzone soldier shirt and a pretty ring, and landed in bed with such a bad cold that he stayed home for two days.

I wonder now if Mom kept the news off the whole time Dad was gone.

6. Making It

merican presidents had engaged playwrights, composers, and musicians as cultural ambassadors for years, in part to offset the images of American civil rights strife. Dancers were also in the mix.

Modern dance, a uniquely American art form that my mother had made a brief career of, was one of the first Cold War weapons employed by President Eisenhower as USIA was launched. Mexican-born and American-raised José Limón toured Latin America with his dance company in 1954. His fluency in Spanish allowed him to directly address his South American audiences.

"With all our crudities, we are Americans," Limón said. "We are not afraid to declare ourselves and have done so in our dance. Hemingway and Faulkner write in English, but they write like Americans. In the same way, we are trying to find a new language for American dance."

Here was a message that the United States was not steeped in the past but looking toward new ideas, with exports that had nothing to do with soldiers and guns.

* * *

I had been dancing for as long as I could move. We had pictures of me twirling in our Caracas living room. In Rome, Dad filmed me twisting and leaping through the apartment in Mom's too-big leotard. In Bogotá, my friend Barbara and I made up dances to *The Nutcracker* in her bedroom, and Mom walked Susie and me to a ballet class in the converted living room of a neighboring Teusaquillo house.

The American Ballet Theatre came to Bogotá on a USIA/State Department tour when I was in fifth grade. Several of the dancers let it be known that they would love to have a swim in the pool at the Bogotá Country Club, so Mom offered to take them the next day. Susie was playing with friends, but I was in the back seat when Mom pulled up to the hotel, and there were nine dancers ready for a swim. Somehow, everyone squeezed into the Mercedes—with me on the lap of a prima ballerina—and off we went. Swimming with them was delicious.

During my three years at Hoover Junior High, there were a couple of quasi-dance opportunities, like the time we were told to create a two-minute routine in gym class. Jumping around to Herb Alpert & the Tijuana Brass was fun, but hardly the stuff dreams are made of.

Now that I was a sophomore at Churchill, there was a real opportunity to do something with dance—the high school musical. I had heard rumors that it was going to be *South Pacific*, a movie we had seen several times at the binational intercultural centers in Rome and Bogotá. *South Pacific* was the type of export that USIA wanted to share with American friends overseas—Mitzi Gaynor's perky persona, Rossano Brazzi's smoldering romanticism, the beautiful and dangerous Pacific war theater, and songs about love, enchanted evenings, and overcoming racism. I knew the music, and years of singing harmony with Susie made me one of the strongest altos in the school choir. If I could show off my dancing, I might just have a shot at getting cast in the musical, but I hadn't taken a class since Bogotá.

Serendipity threw me a lifeline. A childhood friend of my mother's, Don Redlich, who had coincidentally also gone into modern dance, called to invite Mom to see him teach a master class at the University of Maryland. I took the afternoon off from school to tag along.

* * *

The class was underway as we stepped through the side entrance of the old gymnasium.

We sat on folding chairs lined up against the back wall near a pile of jackets and sweatpants. About twenty dancers, mostly women but not only, in leotards and footless tights were doing a routine.

They moved as one organism, now pushing through their hips to swing a leg around like a beautiful compass, now shifting the weight into the legs to stand, reach, collapse. Their bodies were like Chinese jump rope elastic, stretching and recoiling, stretching and recoiling. I found myself inhaling as the dancers reached up and exhaling as they surrendered to gravity. It was impossibly beautiful.

A lean man in a tank top leotard and tights rolled down to his hips held the dancers' full attention as he demonstrated the next exercise with his sinewy arms and long legs.

"Is that Don?" I whispered. The man looked up as he completed the movement.

Mom nodded. He smiled and raised a hand. Mom waved back.

Don motioned toward the pianist seated at an old upright on the far wall, and she picked up the tempo. The dancers swooped and swirled in unison like a flock of starlings, pulsating as one. Then, the music changed and, two-by-two, the dancers flew from corner to corner, seeming to skim the floor. I was breathless.

The piano crescendoed, and the class was over. The students clapped and crowded around Don.

I was hooked. By the time we got home, Mom had agreed to find me a modern dance class.

The next week, I began studying at the studio of Ethel Butler, a former company soloist and principal teaching assistant to Martha Graham. I struggled to master the technique, wilting under the criticism of the young instructor who taught the lower-level classes. There was one way to do a step, and one way only.

One day, Miss Butler herself taught us. She had us come away from the barre and into the center of the room, where we explored different ways of moving from sitting to standing. For that hour, every move was right.

It was my first exposure to improvisation, and I felt the lid come off my creative energy.

There was something I had glimpsed at the university gym, a spark that I had felt during Miss Butler's class. I wanted that. It was worth struggling through the demanding technique sessions to perhaps one day get hold of that feeling again.

* * *

When Churchill High School held tryouts for *South Pacific,* I failed to qualify for even the chorus. I attempted to be happy for friends who were chosen for the musical, but even I knew mine was a fake smile. I turned away, blaming my new contacts for the tears in my eyes.

I had tried contacts in eighth grade, but my eyes could not tolerate more than a couple of minutes of the torture of the hard, plastic discs. The ophthalmologist had suggested letting my eyes mature a bit while the technology advanced. Now, I felt ready to try again. It didn't hurt that the doctor looked just like Glen Campbell.

Wichita Lineman played in my head as tears streamed down my cheeks, Mom timing me. Five minutes with these pieces of plastic on my eyeballs led to ten, and ten to thirty. I slowly worked my way up to half a day, and finally wore contacts for a full school day. I was sure they would change my life.

They did.

I nailed the audition for a pick-up modern dance troupe at the local Jewish Community Center, and I felt fantastic in the body-hugging tangerine leotard and peach tights. The performance was over all too quickly.

I set my sights on getting on the pompon team.

The Pommies were the Churchill drill team. I had watched them march in angular formations during halftime at the school football games on Saturdays in the fall and at the basketball games on weekday evenings in the winter. Pommies were school spirit personified in their short green skirts, bulky white sweaters sporting the Churchill bulldog patch, and saddle shoes. There were a lot of pompon girls, maybe twenty, and unlike the unattainable rank of cheerleader—which Susie had achieved at Hoover—being a Pommie seemed like a possibility. I had become proficient at picking up choreography at the Butler dance studio, though lifting my knees seemed like the most important skill to demonstrate at tryouts one afternoon.

The heavens opened. The week before school let out for the summer, I made the team.

Swim practices and Drivers Ed took up the next six weeks, and then Pommie training began. The final weeks of summer were brutally hot and humid. Gnats drowned on my sweaty face as I marched in line with the team on Churchill's crunchy dry grass. Bits of pompon flew into my gasping mouth, and my thighs itched with effort. Glamorous this was not.

But the shared suffering bonded us as a team, and new friendships sprung up as I hitched rides to practice with a couple of the older girls on the squad. Freddie, our captain—a great girl with a quirky name—promised that our new white-green-and-blue uniforms would be in by the end of August. For the first time in four years, I knew that I would be wearing the right clothes on the first day of school, finally in step with the cool crowd.

I even met a boy at an August party. Glenn was blond, his eyes crinkled when he smiled, and he had a car.

I started eleventh grade in my Pommie uniform, my Sun-In lightened hair falling to my shoulders like a Glamour magazine cover girl, with a lanky, equally blond boyfriend at my side. With my blue contacts enhancing my eyes, I had shed the four-eyes Poindexterette look that I was sure had confined me since Hoover. I had also shed most of my old friends.

No matter. I had finally arrived. In the words of another foreign service kid, author Sara Mansfield Taber: "Through sheer, pioneer determination, [America] had become my home. I had kneaded and pressed myself into the mold and achieved my goal: I had become ordinary."

7. Leaving

It was the spring of 1971. The five-year mark of my father's Washington assignment was approaching. Mom and Dad were both ready to get back to our normal life. "We were getting itchy again to go overseas," Dad wrote years later. However, Vietnam threatened to be the next assignment.

The USIA deputy director called Dad into his office to say he was a potential candidate for one of the top jobs at the Saigon Embassy. It was a real career advancement opportunity. Of course, Mom, Susie, and I would go to Bangkok with the other foreign service, military, and expat families.

My father knew that officers who refused to go to Vietnam had been required to resign. Still, Dad's position on the war had only grown more negative since his trip to the war-weary country. He shook his head, knowing that this might be where the road ended, and said that his personal views would not permit him to assume any position of leadership in Vietnam.

After a quiet moment, the deputy director nodded. As Dad was dismissed, he must have felt uncertain at best. Worried, even.

* * *

As he waited for next shoe to fall, my father got his first opportunity to have a look behind the Iron Curtain.

The Treaty on the Non-Proliferation of Nuclear Weapons was in its second year, but Cold War tensions were still high as the small group of USIA officers flew from New York to Moscow. The Kremlin impressed, but the city was drab and forlorn.

A side trip from Moscow to Yerevan, capital of Soviet Armenia, added a view of a distinct ethnic population obliged to form part of the USSR. The roundtrip Russian Aeroflot flight was classless in every sense and deadly dull, from the dour stewardesses to the inedible rubber chicken.

The following day's flight from Moscow to Warsaw on LOT Polish Airlines was quite a contrast. It seemed that the savvy Poles took delight in furnishing their flight with the best any airline had to offer, from sparkling interiors to attentive service by good-looking attendants.

The dissident flavor continued as the group toured Warsaw and then Krakow before flying on to beautiful, historic Prague and Belgrade. The Yugoslavs had long since declared their own independence from Moscow, and Dad could feel that the signs of strain, perhaps even early cracks, were beginning to show in the USSR.

All was not unified behind the Iron Curtain.

* * *

My father got his next post orders mid-way through the trip—not Saigon, but instead the noble city of Madrid—where my father was to head up USIS in Spain. I can imagine that, for once, the conversation with my mother about "Guess where we're going now" was upbeat on both their parts. Dad had ducked Vietnam and Mom had been ready to leave Rockville for years.

My father detoured through Madrid on his way home to acquaint himself with his new embassy colleagues and to take some snapshots of the house that came with the job. He flushed with excitement at the idea of returning to Europe, this time to the land of the conquistadors and the birthplace of the classical guitar. Dad longed to take his Ramirez out of the dusty guitar case, where it had remained largely untouched during our Maryland years.

While our parents were primed for the return to business as usual, Susie and I were not. We had so fully taken to the American suburbs that we had discarded the vestiges of our previous life. Few, if any, of our school friends had traveled, and none knew a thing about where we'd grown up. Although we used a little Spanish among ourselves, my sister and I had no Spanish-speaking friends, and a layer of Montgomery County Schools French had largely buried our first language.

I was looking forward to being a senior and maybe even leading the pompon team, and Susie and her friends were ready to move up to Winston Churchill as sophomores.

We had forgotten that this American life was only temporary.

* * *

The family conversation about the upcoming change was postponed for a few days after Dad's return by his usual post-travel cold.

I did not pick up on the cues that something was about to happen—Mom making pot roast and baked potatoes on a school night, Dad arriving home early, the four of us eating in the little formal dining room.

"So, girls, how about Spain?" Dad said as we finished off our first servings.

"What do you mean?" Susie said.

"What?" I asked.

"Dad's been assigned to the embassy in Madrid," Mom said.

"When?"

"After school lets out," Mom said. "Dad will go ahead of us."

"But what about Pommies?" I asked. "I'm in line to be captain next year." At least that's what I thought might happen.

"And I'm going to Churchill," Susie said.

"We can't leave," I said. "No."

"No," Susie said.

We sat back and glared at our parents. There wasn't much that we did together as sisters, just the two of us, but we were completely on the same page now. We had plans. We had friends. We especially had boyfriends. No way, not this time.

Mom and Dad exchanged a look across the table.

"Now, girls," Dad said, sitting back on his chair. "You know that we've been here five years, and that's way longer than any of us could have expected."

"I know this comes as a surprise no matter what," Mom added, extending a hand to each of us. "But we expect you. . . ."

I pushed away from the table and was on my feet before she could complete the sentence.

"You expect us to do what? We live here. This is our house. This is our life."

It felt like steam was coming off my cheeks, and tears were beginning to choke my words.

"Forget it." Susie stood up.

We were up the stairs before I could take another breath. Susie's door slammed. I threw mine closed, too.

Our reaction to being pulled away from our suburban life was exactly like that of the kids on the FX spy drama, *The Americans,* when their Soviet spy parents announce that it is time to go home to Moscow.

Home was America.

I sat on my bed, snorting through clenched teeth. I let a tear drop off my cheek and watched it be absorbed into my lime green shorts. There was an appealing level of drama in this, like when Glenn had taken me to see *Love Story* and the movie theater armrests were already damp with tears.

It still surprises me that I made the transition to acceptance so quickly that evening. Sara Mansfield Taber's memoir gives me the language to explain the switch. "Out of pure reflex," she writes, "the foreign service girl clicked into departure mode."

Rockville was over. I gave in to the pull of the inevitable future. I was going to Spain.

* * *

Our parents cleverly ensured my sister's and my cooperation—and jump started our Spanish—by including us in an Easter break business trip to Panama City, Bogotá, and Caracas.

As the date of our departure approached, the cities that had once been home shimmered in my imagination like a mirage. I barely believed it was possible to go back.

On Maundy Thursday, we flew to Miami International Airport, where a USIA man whisked us to meet the day's second flight of the Cuban airlift. These Freedom Flights, an immigration program initially supported by both Castro and the White House, had been transporting Cubans to Miami twice a day, five days a week, since late 1965. The USIA man told us that the passengers on that afternoon's plane waited five years to leave Cuba, during which they were treated as outcasts and called *gusanos*, worms. The men, women, and children who exited the small propeller plane wore dated clothing that was surely their best, and their few suitcases appeared to have been handmade from cloth and plastic.

I remembered the Cuban propaganda materials that Dad brought home from the embassy in Bogotá. They were cartoons in which children were told to pray to God for ice cream, and of course, none materialized. Then, they prayed to Castro, and "*voilà*," ice cream. I guessed that magic trick had worn off for these poor souls.

I hoped the children we saw that day would have American ice cream immediately.

* * *

We flew from Miami to tropical Panama City on the Pacific side of the isthmus. We were picked up at the airport by Mom's college roommate, Mary Caldwell Mudge, and her husband, Art, who Susie and I first met in New Hampshire on our way to Milan twelve years earlier and with whom our family shared several Thanksgivings while we were all in the DC area. Art now was engaged in some of Dad's Latin America relations portfolio in his work for the Agency for International Development (AID).

Over dinner, the adults talked about the 1964 "flag incident," when American students took down a Panamanian flag and a mob retaliated by burning American flags. Dad said that the riots had delayed the boat carrying our belongings from Rome to Colombia, and Art said that diplomatic relations were still delicate. Although the work AID was doing—building schools, roads, and hospitals—formed an important part of America's support of the Panamanian government, there were strong differences of opinion among American officials working at the embassy and in the Canal Zone about the proper role of the United States with respect to the Canal.

Embassy friends from Caracas, the Niswanders, invited our families to lunch the next day. Mel Niswander was the public affairs officer for Panama, so all the USIS staff was on hand to see Mom and Dad. I hadn't shaken that many adult hands in half a decade.

Sitting around the family pool with the Niswander and Mudge daughters that afternoon was the first time in five years that Susie and I had been around other embassy kids. They took it upon themselves to educate us on their town, telling us that The Zone, a US colony of military and business families, was good for shopping and seeing American movies in English—instead of dubbed Spanish—but not "real Panama," like where we were sitting. It was

227

a little like I felt about El Chico, the Americanized neighborhood in Bogotá.

The next day, Susie and I put on our tropical best for an afternoon cruise down the Panama Canal. The sun shone and the water rose and fell. The adults marveled at the mechanics of the locks. We girls watched boys.

On our way to the airport that afternoon, we stopped at Ambassador Robert M. Sayre's residence to see Mrs. Sayre, whom my parents knew from when the ambassador had been at the State Department with Dad. The house was very grand, with an enormous main foyer loaded with marble. I was beginning to remember why we liked the foreign service.

As we boarded the plane for Bogotá that evening, I told Mom that I had never enjoyed a visit so much. My sister was enthusiastic about resuming life in Spanish, venturing that perhaps she might stay in Madrid for college.

My mother must have breathed a sigh of relief, knowing that her daughters were back on her side. But I, who should have been thinking about college, didn't pick up on Susie's comment.

I was happy to simply be back on the job. The Embassy Kid had reemerged.

* * *

Going back to Colombia felt like time travel. As the plane touched down, Bogotá became real again. Who should be at the gate to greet us but Julia, along with the current public affairs officer, now her employer at our old house. Susie and I found ourselves chatting in basic Spanish with Julia on the drive to the Tequendama Hotel as if she had picked us up at the bus stop. Our "friends of the wall," the Cárdenas family, were invited to a big party for us the following night in our old house.

Señora Cárdenas greeted my mother with a warm embrace. I extended my hand to show I hadn't forgotten how people in the foreign service do things. Señora Cárdenas hugged me instead. "*Dios mío, como han crecido,*" she said. My God, how you two girls have grown.

She looked the same. Mai, now twenty, was a more mature version of the teenager to whom we had said our goodbyes. They retreated into a corner with Mom.

The tall young man who next extended his hand wasn't familiar, then he smiled, and I recognized Luis. We laughed as Isa reached for Susie's hand. The eighteen-year-old twins now looked more than a year my seniors. Andrés at fifteen and baby Tere, thirteen, were also enhanced versions of their younger selves.

"*Los amigos de la pared,*" I said.

"The friends to the wall," Luis ventured in careful English.

It seemed mean to correct the preposition, and so the six of us squeezed into the long couch in the study to try out our languages and to rekindle the friendship. It came easily.

Luis and Andrés showed up at the Tequendama Hotel two days later with a huge bouquet of orchids and an invitation to Susie and me for lunch downstairs. While Mom packed us up, the two American sisters and the two Colombian brothers feasted on *ajiaco,* the traditional Colombian chicken-potato stew that glimmered golden under the hotel restaurant's lights.

Too soon, Mom whisked us away, but the boys got themselves to the airport to wave goodbye from the outdoor balcony. I followed those raised arms until we left them behind as our plane taxied down the runway.

The airplane's wheels lifted off the tarmac, and Bogotá and our friends evaporated again into the past.

* * *

Returning to Caracas was coming full circle to our first overseas home. We were met at the gate by friends from Rome, Ed and Gerda Schechter. In the musical chairs' world of embassy people, Ed was now the Caracas public affairs officer.

The office limousine was waiting at the curb, the driver standing guard over the open trunk.

"My word! Ernie?" Mom said.

"*Señora* Amerson, *Señor* Amerson, *cuanto gusto.*" How nice to see you, the driver said. The adults shook hands.

"Jane, you were six months old when Ernie first met us at this airport," Mom said as we got into the back seat. "And you girls were five and three when Ernie took us to the *Santa Rosa*. Amazing."

So it continued for two days as we visited places and people that had caused my parents to fall in love with the foreign service—a Caracas teeming with people, traffic, and new tall buildings; many long-time Venezuelan staff at the embassy; the Méndez Gimón clinic where Susie was born; the beach near where we boarded the *Santa Rosa* boat. The only vaguely familiar spot to Susie and me was our little ground-floor apartment in Zucatarate, now a shabby-faced print shop surrounded by high-rises. Dad took a picture of us girls to send to Fina, who was now retired and back home in Spain, with our annual Christmas card. Mom had not missed one year in keeping in touch with our dear Josefina.

Our four-person, embassy family unit sprang to life during our trip, like those shrunken figurines that expand when submerged in water. Susie and I were ready to go back to our real world.

* * *

Seven weeks later, school was done, our home was rented out, and the Skylark was with Grandma Amerson in South Dakota. Dad was in Madrid, with Mom, Susie, and I to follow. First, Susie and I had to say our goodbyes.

My boyfriend took it hard. On my last night in America, Glenn presented me with a hanging pendant in the shape of a heart. "Today, tomorrow, forever," read the inscription.

"That's how I feel," he said as he fastened it around my neck.

"Yeah, me too," I said.

It had not occurred to me to buy him anything. I was already an ocean away.

Part VII

Madrid

(1971-73)

*Susie and I approached Fina, and her strong
arms pulled us to her dark padded bosom. At that
moment, we were Fina's babies once again.*

1. ARRIVING

From where we sat in the Biergarten, all the boys in Zurich looked like movie director Franco Zeffirelli's Romeo. It was hard to keep my head from swiveling.

Europe was going to be great. Feather beds at the hotel, ruby-red geraniums in every window box, these gorgeous men. I looked at the neighboring tables, where families sat eating and talking together on this Sunday afternoon, the children at ease in adult company. I could get used to this. I *was* used to this.

Dad caught my eye as I finished scanning the restaurant. "So, girls, what do you think?"

"Pretty good," I said.

"*Really* good," Susie said.

"*Amazingly* good," I said, reaching for her shin with my sandaled foot.

"Hey," she started.

Mom intervened right on schedule. "Okay, girls, let's not get carried away in a public place."

"Oh, no!" I said, my voice that little bit hysterical.

"Good grief, Jane," Susie said.

It was fun to be pushing the behavior envelope again. With just the four of us.

Dad held up his hand, one finger raised to signal for our bill. He lifted his chin in a way that made him look down his nose. It appeared a lot less rude here than it had at the Rockville Hot Shoppes.

The waiter presented a handwritten tab, which Dad scanned before counting out a small set of pink, green, and blue franc bills. "*Ach, danke!*" thank you, he said with a flourish as he handed the money to the waiter.

"Oh, Dad," Susie and I said in unison.

Mom hooked her arm through mine as we walked into the afternoon sunlight, following a path along the river. Behind us, I could hear Susie and Dad debating the best light meter to use on her new camera. We were just another family on a Sunday stroll.

"Boy-oh-boy," Susie laughed, catching up to Mom and me. "If our friends back home could see us now, out with our parents!"

It was great to be back in the roles we had stored away upon arrival in suburban America.

* * *

Dad had arrived in Europe before us to take on the job of public affairs officer at the US Embassy in Madrid without the usual handoff. His predecessor experienced run-ins with the strong-minded ambassador, Robert C. Hill, and had moved on to his next post, leaving the critical position vacant just as a Washington VIP was due to arrive.

"My need to get to the post had to do with the scheduled July visit to Madrid of Vice President Spiro Agnew," Dad later wrote, adding that he needed to make a good impression on Ambassador Hill. "Our ambassador was a Nixon appointee with a reputation as hard-boiled, egotistical, and demanding, and ready to ride roughshod over anyone who disagreed with him."

The skeptical ambassador, who served Eisenhower as ambassador to El Salvador, Costa Rica, and Mexico, viewed my father as insufficient to the job, given Dad's relative youth—just forty-six in 1971—and his rank, a level two foreign service officer. The ambassador believed he deserved a level one PAO.

Vice President Agnew and Ambassador Hill called on General Franco at the Palacio Real, with Dad actively working the reporters covering the event. As he and the vice president exited Franco's office, the ambassador's eyes paused to focus on his new PAO. Dad read his new boss's expression as triumphant. It was a win.

My father flew to Zurich the next morning to pick up two prized things—a new silver Mercedes Benz sedan, and, Mom, Susie, and me. After giving us a day to catch up on our sleep, Dad began the drive to Madrid.

We motored southwest through Switzerland toward Geneva, by kilometers of alpine meadows against the backdrop of the towering Alps. The scenery meant less to me than the warm and cozy feeling in that car. We were in our family seats—Dad driving, Mom reading out loud from the Fodors guide, and Susie and me in the back seat. Mom's voice washed over me as the green countryside blurred past. All was well in the family cocoon.

We stayed in Geneva that evening in a hotel overlooking the huge lake of the same name that dominated the city. The guides on the small tour boat were the cutest yet, and Susie and I were able to exchange greetings this time—Geneva was just four kilometers from the French border, and our American school language, French, was getting its first real test.

We crossed the border that afternoon. Dad pulled up in front of a small French village hotel in time for dinner. A congenial hum rose up from the dining room. The head waiter came over to us, his proprietary demeanor—and the cummerbund at his waist—distinguishing him from the two other men working the room.

Dad beat him to the conversation. *"Est-ce qu'on mange bien ici ce soir?"* Does one eat well here this evening?

The waiter gave a short nod of assent mixed with pride. *"Mais, oui!"* But of course! Would we do him the courtesy of allowing him to suggest our dinner?

Both annoyed at Dad for showing off and pleased to have understood the entire conversation, I followed Mom and Susie to our table. Dad lingered behind to make drink arrangements before sitting down.

"A little gas in the water will have us all good as new," he said, shaking out his cloth napkin.

"Yes," Mom said, "Fizzy water sounds exactly like what we need. And a bit of wine at the end of a long day?"

"Ah, well, when in France . . . ." Dad added a bottle of the house red to our order.

The waiter returned with a tall green bottle of Perrier. He released the cap with a little whoosh before pouring each of us half a goblet, then reappeared with a carafe of wine and a loaf of bread. I tore off one end, dipped my knife into the small bowl of salt, and sprinkled the crystals onto the warm crust.

Dad lifted his wine glass. "*Bon appetit!*"

Sipping wine with our parents sealed the deal—the embassy family was back. Our dinner arrived in courses—a light consommé, followed by a fresh spinach omelet, and a breaded pork cutlet with oven-browned new potatoes and buttery beans. Dessert was fresh fruit and cheese. I cut into my apple and stabbed at the cheese before carrying the combination to my mouth on the back of my fork.

I realized that my family had eaten every meal together since landing in Zurich three days before. I couldn't remember us doing that even for one day in Rockville.

* * *

"*¡España!*" Dad announced as we descended the rocky Pyrenees into Spain. He reached for Mom's hand, which she lifted for the moment from the Michelin Guide. "Home."

"It will be," Mom said.

I couldn't wait. I bet the boys were even prettier here than in Switzerland. Spain must be where that expression came from—tall, dark, and handsome.

The road flattened out as we entered Castilla. "So-called for the castles that can still be seen dominating the countryside," Mom read from the guidebook.

Tall, dark, handsome, and a prince.

It was mid-afternoon when Dad came up behind a motorcycle. The rider's regimental green uniform, including a black-strapped firearm, signaled his status as law enforcement. Just ahead of the motorcycle cop was another one. Dad eased up on the gas pedal.

"The Guardia Civil," he said. "Franco's men."

Like Pérez Jiménez' Seguridad Nacional back in Venezuela, the national police were the feared force behind the dictator Francisco Franco's regime. The Guardia Civil represented the worst of Franco's forty-year totalitarian regime and were answerable only to El Generalissimo, the highest of all generals, himself.

Dad hung back until the Guardia riding in the rear waved him by, then moved the Mercedes into the passing lane. We passed the motorcycle and were nearing the second cop as the dotted center line became solid. Mom reached for the dashboard as Dad gunned the car and moved past the second policeman, crossing the solid line as he moved back into the right lane. Mom's red nails disappeared into the Mercedes leather.

"Damn!" His eyes were on the rearview mirror. "Damn, damn!"

I looked back. The Guardia in front was waving us over. Dad eased his foot off the gas and slowed to a stop on the shoulder. Mom didn't say a word. I sat as far back in my seat as I could.

"We don't have diplomatic plates yet, right?" Susie ventured.

"Nope." Dad's voice was tight. "German. And I'm not going to play the embassy card."

Out of the corner of my eye, I saw the shape of the policeman coming up alongside the Mercedes, his goggles lifted onto his helmet. Dad rolled his window down.

"*¿No vió la linea sólida?*" You didn't see the solid line?

"*Ach,*" Dad said. Good grief, he was playing a German. He continued in halting German-tinged Spanish. "Your partner, *su colega,* waved me by, and I assumed, of course, that he meant I should pass you both. As a pair, you know."

The Guardia took a step toward the Mercedes and looked in, his eyes flashing in anger at this German driver with his two blond children and the brunette wife. He drew himself up in his boots.

"*Aquí,*" he said, practically spitting the words and standing tall in his boots, "*Somos individuos.*" Here, you order-following scum, we are individuals.

With a flick of his leather glove, the Guardia dismissed us. He stalked back to his motorcycle, where the other cop had been keeping watch all this while. Mom's hand reached into the back seat, but Dad's fixed stare kept us quiet as he put the Mercedes in gear and eased back onto the highway. His eyes glanced up at the rear view more than once as he distanced himself from the Guardia Civil.

How dare that fascist tell this boy from the prairies about individualism? Rugged individualism landed his Norwegian grandfather a stake in the New World and brought forth the next generation of Amersons—including this diplomat in his new Mercedes.

We drove on in silence. I looked out at the buff-colored Castilian countryside and contemplated what had just happened. The cop looked incredibly handsome when he stepped up to the car, and the fire in his eyes told of something more. There was a dark and proud character here in Spain, way more interesting than what Switzerland offered. Those were pretty boys.

These Spanish men, they were something else.

This was going to be fun.

* * *

Hotel Los Delfines took its name from the fountain of dolphins on the roundabout it faced. The PAO's house was a few blocks in one direction from the hotel, and the embassy was a few blocks in the other. Los Delfines was home while the house was being cleaned and painted in advance of our furniture arriving.

Compared with the muggy Maryland summer, Madrid's dry heat was fantastic, and our hotel rooms opened on a terrace made for sunbathing. Baby oil in hand, Susie and I made a beeline for the lounge chairs to bake under the cloudless blue sky. The terra cotta tiles shimmered in the heat. Six floors down, city traffic hummed around the circular fountain. If I lifted my head a little, I could see the outer spatter of spray from the stone dolphins toss in the breeze.

The phone rang. Mom called out through the double doors. "Girls, that was your dad. Our *bienvenida* is this evening. Can you find something nice to wear?"

"Okay," I called back. The embassy welcome party had just been added to our schedule.

Susie and I looked at each other through our sunglasses. Meeting a bunch of people seemed like way too much work. She took a sip from her glass of fresh-squeezed OJ and rolled over. I checked my bikini bottom tan line and poured on another coat of oil.

It was back to work this evening. First, we enjoyed the perks of this foreign service life a while longer.

* * *

Dad pulled up in front of the hotel. "A pair of tanned *madrileñas*, I see," he said as Susie and I climbed into the back of the Mercedes. He gave Mom a kiss as she slid into the front seat.

"Hmm," Mom said. "A little too tan maybe. That sun is awfully strong."

Susie and I rolled our eyes at each other. Dad pulled into traffic and began the briefing. "Okay, so these are the McNearys. He's a colleague at the embassy."

"You met Mrs. McNeary when she took me calling," Mom said.

Dad continued, "Their daughter goes to the American School."

"But, Dad, I don't want to go there," Susie said. "It's too small."

"I thought we were going to the air base school," I said.

"Yes, yes," Dad said. "But you might want to keep an open mind."

Torrejón Air Base, ten miles outside Madrid, was the American-run base of operations for the US Air Force. It was part of the agreement the United States worked out with Franco in the 1950s. Like the bases in Italy which provided Mom with Thanksgiving ingredients back in Bologna, the American presence in Spain was consistent with Washington's communist containment policy. The US-Spain military agreement was renewed periodically without much controversy. Spain provided an important strategic and logistical piece of geography of Western defense strategy. Just as Torrejón was home to our Air Force—fighters, bombers, cargo craft—an American Navy base in Rota, on Spain's southern shore, housed a fleet of submarines that patrolled the Mediterranean.

Like other American military bases, Torrejón provided servicemen's families with schools, a large hospital with the full range of health care, an enormous Post Exchange—the PX—and a movie theater, all of them open to embassy and expat American families, as well. Compared with the small, private American School of Madrid, Torrejón High School sounded much more like Winston Churchill. Susie and I could just drop our American selves into place.

Mrs. McNeary greeted us with the two-cheek air kiss that we had become familiar with over the past month. Mom steered Susie and me by the shoulders into the living room, where clumps of adults began to gravitate toward us. I held onto Susie's elbow, a smile on my face. We nodded and shook hands with people whose names we immediately forgot. Someone led Mom toward the bar.

Mrs. McNeary appeared at my side. "Will you have one?" She held out a plate of golden onion rings pierced with toothpicks. I lifted a morsel.

"It's squid!" she said.

The toothpick and its catch were suspended before my lips, my teeth already parted to begin the bite. My mouth stretched into an uncomfortable smile.

"Oh," I said without moving my lips.

There was nothing to do but proceed. My teeth closed over the squid. An unexpected warm crunch was followed by a tender, savory chew.

"It's wonderful!" I said.

"It's Spain!" Mrs. Neary said as she moved on.

Susie had escaped during the squid encounter. I spotted her in the far corner of the room, talking with a girl about her age. "Jane, this is Tamara," she said.

I saw the McNeary family resemblance. "Hi," I said, shaking her hand almost without thinking about it. "Thanks for having us over."

"Hey, it comes with the territory," Tamara said with a small nod. "So, how do you guys like Madrid?"

"What we've seen of it, we love," I said, holding out my tan arms.

Tamara laughed. "Yeah, pretty great sun, huh? I go to the pool over by the soccer stadium. You guys should come with me sometime."

Susie said, "You go to the American School, right?"

"Sure," Tamara said, twirling her dark hair around a finger. "It's the only place to go."

"Why? What about the air base school?" Susie said.

"Torrejón?" Tamara laughed. "Well, that's okay if you're a redneck." She shrugged. "Plus, it's way too big."

"So, how big is your school?" Susie said.

"We're twenty in ninth grade," she said.

"Gosh, that's tiny compared to our school. I mean, where we were in the States," I said.

Well, that sounded rude. I switched gears. "So, how about sports or that kind of thing?"

"Last year, some of the boys put together a soccer team, and they were pretty good. They looked cute in those small shorts, too."

She sounded like she had sidelines experience. "So, you're a cheerleader?" Susie said.

Tamara clutched at her chest in mock drama. "Cheerleader? Please. Yuck. No, no, we're way more evolved. That's sort of, you know, Torrejón level."

"The base, huh?" Susie said.

"Oh, sure. They have all that, you know, *American* stuff," Tamara said, rolling her eyes. "Like football and jocks and rednecks." She laughed.

"Tamara!" Mrs. McNeary called from across the room.

"Oops, time to get back to work," Tamara said, pushing off the wall with her foot. She brushed her bangs away from her eyes. "Listen, give me a call anytime you want to go swimming. There are tons of really cute Spanish guys at the pool over by the stadium."

Susie looked at Tamara's receding back. "I won't go to that American School."

"Look, we're going to Torrejón," I said. "I'll be on the drill team, you'll be a cheerleader, and that'll be that."

I didn't stop to consider how much like the Panama Canal Zone the base would be like, the difference between military kids and diplomats' kids, or how good it already felt being in real Spain.

* * *

Like in Bogotá, the Madrid home we moved into was leased by the embassy for its public affairs officer. It was a free-standing house in the quiet, residential neighborhood of El Viso, where people like us—the families of diplomats, politicians, and businessmen—lived.

It was a four-level home. The kitchen, maids' quarters, and storage areas were in the basement; a dumbwaiter connected with the first-floor butler's pantry. A large dining room, two small living rooms, and a half-bath completed the first floor. Our three bedrooms were on the second floor, each with its own bath—after sharing the small bathroom in Rockville with Mom and Susie, this was like moving into a posh hotel. A full guest suite was on the third floor, along with a roof-top terrace. A formal garden maintained by the embassy surrounded the home, and a six-foot wall separated the property from the street. The adjoining single-car garage led directly onto the street.

Two maids—sisters Mari Cruz, the housekeeper, and Brigi, the cook—had served the previous PAO and his family and were ready to stay. During his stop in Madrid that spring, Dad assured them that we would keep them on, but I imagine the deal wasn't sealed until Mom, the new *señora de la casa*—the lady of the house — shook their hands.

We added to our family before school began—a white and tan English cocker spaniel we named Tori. Although Susie and I picked her out, we really didn't have much interest in taking care of her. Dad still thought dogs should be outdoor animals, but Tori found a nice overnight home in the basement with the maids and became Mom's daytime pet. She was the only one who walked the dog.

School started. Susie tried out for the sophomore cheering squad and made it. I, too, was successful in my venture and joined the Torrejón drill team. I felt sure that the camaraderie of the Churchill pompon girls would transfer to this new situation. We took the early Air Force bus to the before-school practices.

* * *

It was toward the end of the second week of school, and drill team practice was nearly over. Lori Mae, the captain, yelled at me from across the football field. "Hey, Jane, you don't need to get your knees up that high, you know. Just do it like the rest of us!"

The other girls laughed. "Yeah, like the rest of us brats!" said a girl in the next row. Her blue eyelids glinted in the early morning sun as she squinted at me through gummy lashes. I smiled with my lips pressed together. The routine started up again, thirty girls straggling down the field in a ragged formation. Someone near me snapped her gum in time to the beat. I dragged my feet. Screwing up was becoming less and less of an effort as practice went along.

The morning bell rang.

"Okay, girls, that's it." Lori Mae walked in from the sidelines. "Now, don't forget, you have tomorrow off but it's back to practice on Monday, and the first game is a week from Saturday."

"Oh, Johnny's gonna kill those guys from Turkey!" squealed the girl who might be called Jackie. The Torrejón football team played teams from other American military bases, like the Navy base in Rota, but also in Turkey, Italy, and West Germany. They traveled by military plane.

"Yeah, yeah, Johnny, Johnny," her friends chorused, slapping at each other as they walked across the grass toward school.

The rumble of jets shook the ground as a squadron rose one by one into the sky from the runway just behind the brick school building. A car honked twice and a couple of men in uniform called out to us as they drove by, leaving a chorus of giggling in their wake. The girl in front of me reached back to tug her hot pants down unsuccessfully over her round cheeks.

Churchill's pompon team—and my place in it—seemed a long, long way away. I had been dead wrong about my Churchill persona fitting into this new place. Every day I showed up at practice confirmed that, here, I was an outsider, and I cared less and less. Susie seemed to have found her crowd, but I needed to get out.

On the bus ride home that night, I realized I had the excuse. The month before we left Rockville, a cold-hearted gynecologist diagnosed me with ovarian cysts. "Cancel Madrid!" she said. A subsequent test revealed no such thing, but I had a plan for getting off the team.

Friday morning, I tracked Lori Mae down in the hall. "Hey, I'm so sorry, but I must quit the drill team. My doctor says I can't exert myself. Cysts in my ovaries. You understand, right?" I prayed she didn't ask for a note.

"Okay," she said.

247

I fled before she could say anything more.

My new friend Kelsey found me later that morning. Her huge teeth glinted inside the goofy Cheshire cat smile that was her trademark.

"Hi!" She arched her open palm through the air, the rainbow completing the greeting. She had smiley faces plastered all over her school folders. "Howareya?" She clamped her lips together for a moment to emphasize the down-home greeting. Kelsey was Southern.

"Hi, Kelsey," I said, smiling in spite of myself.

"Did Megan talk to you about getting together after school? Daddy's working late again."

Kelsey's father was the military attaché at the embassy.

"That's pretty usual. . ." I began.

"So, Momma's gonna take me shopping. Again." She rolled her big eyes. "Wanna come?"

Someone ran into me. "Hey, watch it!" I said.

It was Megan. "Watch it yourself," she said with a friendly sneer.

If Kelsey was light effervescence, Megan, another Torrejón newcomer, was dark smolder, her brown eyes already radiating a Castilian-like *hauteur*. I had met Megan and Kelsey at the Eurobuilding Hotel before school began, and the three of us formed an unlikely but sturdy "new girl" alliance.

Megan raked her long hair away from her eyes. "What's up?"

"Shopping, that's what," Kelsey said. The class bell rang. "Oh, my God," Kelsey said, walking backward down the hall. "He is gonna kill me for being late again. Look, call me if you're coming. Otherwise," she turned, calling back over her shoulder, "have a nice day!" Her head bobbed side to side in time with her bouncy step.

"Geez, I really hate cheerful people," Megan said, "especially when I like them." She strode down the hall.

I hurried toward History; the teacher didn't show up until five minutes after the bell, but you never knew. Playing it safe had its advantages. I felt strong, happy, and alone.

* * *

That afternoon, the embassy car took Susie and me to the train station. We were meeting our parents in Jerez de la Frontera, an Andalucian town about six hours southwest of Madrid in the heart of Spain's sherry-producing vineyards. The town's name and that of the fortified wine came from the city's Arabic name, *Sherish*. *Frontera* referred to the thirteenth-century border between the Moorish and Christian regions on the Iberian Peninsula.

Already playing a key role as a duo, Mom and Dad had flown down with Ambassador and Mrs. Hill a few days earlier for a presentation to the ambassador at the annual Jerez Sherry Festival, a three-week party involving wine, horses, and flamenco. The final week was dedicated to the United States of America, a very big part of the sherry market.

"We went with the official embassy group to the sherry festival in the south of Spain," Mom wrote her mother. "Each night there was a black-tie dinner starting at 11:30 in one of the big sherry warehouses, fantastically large, pillared places with huge barrels. Wonderful food and flamenco."

Mom and Dad's work was over by the time Susie and I arrived in Jerez de la Frontera. We spent the weekend strolling the picturesque cobblestone streets of the white-walled town, wandering in and out of the bodegas maintained by each vineyard, sniffing and sampling the varieties of sherry drawn from huge casks with long-handled, ceremonial dippers.

My sister and I quickly discovered that the pale sherry was sharp and dry, not much to our liking. Laughing with each other about how weird it was to drink in public with our parents—we were going on seventeen and fifteen—we stuck with the dark, sweet sherry.

The Jerez Sherry Festival's final evening featured a flamenco performance by the majestic Antonio Gades and his fiery company. The women's haughty bearing and impossibly lithe torsos made me sit up straighter, and I could see Mom twitching unconsciously as she followed the rise and fall of the choreography. Gades completely blew up the place with wild staccato footwork that seemed ready to light a spark under his heels. Even as I watched, however, I knew that I would feel about flamenco heel-tapping the way Mom had felt about tap-dancing—it was way too much work to be fun. There would have to be another way for me to continue dancing in Madrid.

Dad drove us back home in one of the embassy cars. We had absorbed a huge amount of this country's culture—Arabian, Mediterranean, Spanish—in the two days. It was hard not to feel that we were leaving Spain that Monday morning as Susie and I boarded the bus to the base.

2. Coffee Cake

"**M**y time in Spain fell in what were expected to be 'the last years of Franco,'" Dad said in his oral interview for the Association of Diplomatic Studies and Training. "And, of course, these were interesting times because you'd never know from one day to the next how much longer the old man would last and what would happen when he disappeared."

General Francisco Franco—El Generalissimo—had been running Spain for more than thirty years as winner of the country's awful civil war, an atrocious struggle that took more than half a million lives. His dictatorship—conservative and Church-supported—had presided over a wounded, impoverished country with no political parties, no anti-government meetings, and no press criticism. Now, signs of a growing prosperity were beginning to show, and the regime's repression had eased some. The embassy cultivated many solid, anti-Franco leaders, obliged to bide their time until the old man passed from the scene.

There was an entire cottage industry of jokes about the aging dictator, something that would have been unthinkable in his prime. One had Franco on his deathbed, listening to a crowd of supporters calling "*Adiós*, Franco." Goodbye, Franco. He shakily raises his head from his pillow to ask, "Where are they going, these young people?"

El Caudillo, the political and military leader designation Franco had given himself, was nearing eighty. In his infrequent public appearances, he appeared weak and unwell, and he spent most of his time in his personal palace, El Pardo, on the edge of the city. Prince Juan Carlos, grandson of the last king of Spain, was being groomed to eventually take over as head of state. His wife, Princess Sophia, wore the serene look of a Spanish Grace Kelly.

Though Franco was weak, his government kept a tight rein on Spanish life. People remembered the rule of terror in the decade after the war, when the fascists purged society of "enemies of the state"—leftists, Protestants, liberals, intellectuals—in what was called the White Terror. Fear of the ubiquitous Guardia Civil kept the lid on trouble. The government cracked down hard on any drug traffic.

A centuries-old Madrid tradition, the neighborhood watchman, kept the night vigil. These men were the descendants of the lamplighters of yore, whose hourly call was followed by "all is well," translated into Castilian Spanish as *sereno*, a word that had become synonymous with the job. Many of these *serenos* were old civil war veterans rewarded for their loyalty to El Caudillo.

There was a huge upside to a harsh dictatorship. Repression made Madrid a very safe city, and the nightlife was amazing. Restaurants began serving dinner no earlier than ten. The evening session at the many discotheques on the Via José Antonio began at eleven, and the night session didn't begin until the wee hours of the morning. Tapas bars abounded, offering small plates of finger food along with the house wine. Students dressed like medieval troubadours—called *tunas*—strolled the alleyways around Plaza Mayor, serenading.

It was a perfect place to ring in the new year.

* * *

Our Christmas traditions sailed us through December. For the first time in five years, we updated our manger scene, picking up new figurines, mini olive trees, and fresh moss at the stalls that popped up on Plaza Mayor. Mom produced our traditional Christmas Eve tacos and Christmas Day breakfast with the leftover shredded cheese in scrambled eggs, and then the end of the year was upon us.

On New Year's Eve, my parents—Dad in his tux and Mom in a gown she hadn't worn since Bogotá—prepared to go to the traditional New Year's Ball organized annually by the Marines assigned to guard the embassy. Susie and I caught the downtown bus to meet up with her boyfriend, Craig, and my date, an expat Southern kid named Roger, along with pals Kelsey and Megan. We were to rendezvous at Puerta del Sol—"the door of the sun" named for the original east-facing medieval city gate—where a small stone slab in front of the clock tower marked the geographic center of Spain.

It was early yet, not quite eight, and we easily spotted Craig near the bus stop. Roger was just across the street, with Kelsey and Megan in tow. The plaza would be a completely different scene by midnight when revelers gathered to ring in the new year.

We had our first glasses of wine and potato omelet *tapas* in a bar just off the plaza, the Spanish tortilla a satisfying bite of dense potato, egg, and olive oil. We stopped next at Calle Limón for barnacles, the crunchy little hooves releasing a gush of seawater into the mouth, flushing away the velvety coating of red wine until the next bite. The boys and Megan tossed down tumblers of amber brandy and anise on Plaza de San Antonio between bites of bread topped with Manchego cheese.

We wound our way through the network of white-walled bar caves off Plaza Mayor, downing pitchers of sangria and singing along with the *tunas*, minstrels in tights and beribboned capes. Spanish flew from my mouth as I defended Susie from the fierce attendant of the bar bathroom in which my poor sister threw up.

We were having an excellent time.

We finished off another round of Cuba Libres and were halfway across Plaza Mayor when Roger had a suggestion. "Hey, Jane, close your eyes, put your head back, and open your arms."

The next moment, I found myself sprawled on the cobblestones. Roger and Craig doubled over in laughter. Kelsey and Megan stood me up.

"Jane, you're drunk," Susie said.

"Well, you're the one that got sick back there," I said.

She shrugged and walked on across the plaza with Craig. It was time to ring in the new year.

Puerta del Sol was now wall-to-wall people. The watchtower clock read 11:55. We squeezed into the small vestibule of an old building, and Kelsey passed around the packets of grapes that her mother had made us, a dozen in each bundle. It was Spanish tradition to eat one grape for each toll of the midnight hour.

The first chime sounded as I pulled my packet apart, and I popped a grape into my mouth. The next chime was right on top of the first, and the next one just as quick. I chewed and jammed grape after grape into my mouth, finally giving up with a mouthful of mush and several grapes still in my hand. Roger simply tossed his grapes into the air, a sort of Spanish fireworks.

I tossed mine up as well as the final chime sounded. "Happy 1972!"

It was time to go home to complete the planned celebration with my sister's pancake breakfast celebrating her fifteenth birthday. Susie and Craig managed to snag a cab, but the rest of us waved them off.

"It's so nice out," I said. "We'll walk home."

It was three miles, and we had never done it on foot. Susie gave me a withering look and took off.

An hour and a half later, I rang the front doorbell. Dad opened the door, still in his tux.

"Dad, you look wonderful!" I said, throwing my arms around him.

"Why, ah, thank you, dear," he said.

"You too, Mom," I said as my mother came into the entryway. She had replaced her gown with casual clothes. She nodded at me and looked at the platter of pancakes in her hands.

Susie and Craig were in the dining room, staring at plates sticky with syrup.

"Oh, right," I said. "Happy birthday, Susie."

Some party. I scarfed down a pancake or two. Craig and Roger shared a cab home, and an embassy car picked up Kelsey and Megan.

I went to bed.

Four hours later, daylight burned its way through the slits in my blinds and picked at my eyelids. My stomach burned and twisted. My skin felt thin and tender, and my belly felt bruised.

A mist of nausea rose up at the slightest movement. My head ached.

So, this was a hangover. I hauled myself out of bed and stepped gingerly down the stairs.

"Good morning!" Mom was standing at the foot of the stairs, smiling brightly up at me.

"Good morning," I said through gritted teeth.

"Say, would you run down to the kitchen and make us a coffee cake for this beautiful New Year's morning?"

She had to be kidding. "Coffee cake?"

"Sure. Doesn't that sound like the perfect breakfast?"

"Yeah. Sure. Okay."

I descended the basement stairs slowly, carefully lowering my body weight onto each step. At least it was darker down there and quiet. Mari Cruz and Brigi had the holiday off and wouldn't be back until evening.

The buzz of the fluorescent lights in the kitchen beat hot in my ears as I tore open the box of Betty Crocker cake mix from the Torrejón PX. I cracked open an egg, watching the yellow gob slide off the shell and plop into the tan powder, slowly oozing into the mix. The milk slid in more easily, but adding the oil brought back the stench of old tapas. The mixer churned at the gluey mass, turning it into a yellow goo that dripped off the beaters like mucus. Somehow, I got the thing in the oven. Eventually, it and I appeared at the breakfast table.

"Oh, thank you, honey, this is delicious, don't you think?" Mom said.

Dad and Susie nodded. She looked like I felt.

I somehow got down a slice. "May I be excused?"

I disappeared upstairs into heavy, troubled sleep for the rest of the morning.

A knock at my door pulled me to the surface. It was Mom. "So, how you feeling?"

I sighed. "Well, not great."

"Long night."

"Yeah."

"And lots to drink."

I nodded. "Yeah."

A small smile appeared at the corners of her mouth. "How about that coffee cake?"

"Umm . . ."

Mom's smile got broader.

"Oh, boy," I said, realizing I had fallen for an obvious lesson.

"Pretty bad, huh?" my mother said.

I smiled in spite of myself. "Really bad."

She gave me a long hug. "Now, you get some rest."

Mom shut the door behind her. I resolved to increase my alcohol tolerance.

3. Decision

Nixon had won re-election in November. Even before he took his oath of office for a second time in January, he was making staffing changes. Ambassador Hill was among those Nixon re-assigned. Hill went to Washington as assistant secretary of defense, and the second-in-command, Deputy Chief of Mission Joseph Montllor, became the *chargé d'affaires*, the acting chief of mission. The ambassadorial residence—attached to the embassy but with its own entry on a parallel street—stayed vacant while Hill's replacement was identified, and the engine of diplomacy soldiered on.

The embassy was housed in an eight-story building on the well-traveled artery, Calle Serrano. USIS, staffed by fifteen Americans and some thirty Spaniards, occupied one full floor. The local employees were highly educated people with impressive backgrounds and competencies. As in other posts, local USIS employees provided a consistent underpinning to the effort as Americans cycled in and out, contributing greatly to the office's effectiveness and to my parents' social network.

As public affairs officer, Dad planned and carried out the traditional public diplomacy programs across Spain—working with the media and projecting American culture into Spain's major institutions through visiting authors, musicians, and other artists, and educational exchanges like the Fulbright program.

After five years of being on the sidelines, Mom was again an integral part of Dad's "representation" responsibilities. She was a frequent hostess of cocktail parties which spilled out into our garden, kept well-manicured by a surly gardener.

With the new year came talk of college. Kelsey had a legacy acceptance to Sweetbriar.

Megan was opting for the Spanish university system. The school bus buzzed with updates. I had no idea. We were an ocean away from the United States, and the potential landing spots were just mirages. My grades were nearly impeccable—straight As in all subjects but math —and my SAT scores were fine. A college counselor in Rockville had suggested a half-dozen small liberal arts colleges in the Midwest, several of which we visited on our last drive to Minnesota. My parents' alma mater, Macalester, had accepted me at birth—the legacy notice lies in my baby scrapbook.

However, my thinking had not advanced one bit since we left the States. Faced with the challenge of going somewhere alone, I decided not to engage in the conversation at all. I didn't complete a single college application.

The solution presented itself when Mom and I met an American college student at church. The Community Church of Madrid was a new, interdenominational English-speaking congregation that met in the Eurobuilding Hotel. Kathy was a senior at Hiram College in Ohio enrolled at the University of Madrid through a study-abroad program.

Kathy became a regular at our Sunday dinner table, and suddenly I had an American college friend. She was very enthusiastic about Hiram, a small liberal arts school, and I soon felt like I knew the place. Mid-winter, Hiram's president visited Madrid, and the deal was made. I would do a "study abroad" year in Madrid—the same coursework that Kathy was now taking—and transfer a full year of college credits to Hiram as a sophomore.

I would go to Hiram College without ever having visited, without having family or any experience in Ohio, and with only two college acquaintances—a student who would graduate before I arrived and the college president. I don't remember looking at pictures or asking much about its location in the hills between Youngstown, Akron, and Cleveland. Later, I would hear the area described as "the armpit of the nation."

None of this made one bit of difference to me. I turned away from the decision, ignoring the cognitive dissonance tolling in my head. Throughout my childhood, I had dealt with difficult challenges by procrastinating, crying, and sucking my thumb. Stalling the real work—figuring out what I wanted out of college, out of life—suited me just fine.

I drank a little more and put it all out of my mind.

* * *

I also turned away from Roger. A fight broke out between Black and White students at school one Monday, triggered by a film on civil rights shown at the base that weekend. Someone pulled the fire alarm. As I followed Kelsey outside, we passed Roger going the other way, his belt wrapped around his fist. That charming Elvis sneer was suddenly sinister. We did not date again.

There had been a handful of Black students at our Montgomery County schools. The kids at Torrejón High School reflected the racial make-up of the military, with many more students of color. It all felt foreign to me.

Other boys nosed their way in. Puerto Rican El Viso neighbor David—well-spoken, studious, and way too much of a gentleman—was the best conversationalist on the school bus, but I had a crush on the football captain, Greg, whose good looks and hunky body made him the natural choice for the lead in the school musical *Li'l Abner* that spring. I lost the role of Daisy Mae to a long-term Torrejón student but was given the job of choreographer. I took some tips from the contemporary dance teacher whose studio I attended each week. There was decidedly some satisfaction in directing Greg's hips.

Susie and I both went to the senior prom—she with Craig, and me with a boy I barely knew. He and I left the prom before it was over and drank our way through three discos. I had improved my alcohol tolerance since New Year's and avoided Mom's hangover remedy this time.

My Churchill High School boyfriend had written me just twice, most recently to tell me he was coming to my graduation. I was both annoyed and flattered. Glenn appeared on the redeye morning flight, sporting his familiar jeans, loafers, and golden golfer tan. As we walked down to luggage claim, I felt the return of the blond, good-looking American twosome. The skirt of my tank-top dress swung to the sway of my hips.

As Glenn and my family took their seats on the football field the next morning, I stood at the head of the line of graduating girls, where either God or the Devil had decided to pair me with my *L'il Abner* crush, Greg.

I crammed the days after graduation with outings designed to show Glenn my new home—the amusement park, the royal gardens of El Retiro, *tapas* bars around Puerta del Sol, the ancient hilltop city of Toledo. Glenn's jet lag morphed into exhaustion. We had barely really talked when he got back on the plane to go home. The letters between us died away.

I felt myself leaving the tracks that had guided me for nearly eighteen years.

My American peers were on their way back to the States to begin their new lives, experimenting with independence. My Spanish counterparts, however, were living at home through college, into employment and even engagement, moving out only when they got married.

I was attempting a hybrid experience—staying home in Madrid while taking classes with emancipated Americans two years older than me, for whom Spain was a novelty.

As I prepared to leap into a structure of my own making, I knew it was a mistake.

4. NOVIA

The embassy welcomed President Nixon's new ambassador to
Spain, Admiral Horacio Rivero, Jr.

He had an impressive resume. As vice-admiral in 1962, Rivero commanded the United States Atlantic Fleet's amphibious force during
the Cuban Missile Crisis. The first Puerto Rican four-star admiral
and the second Hispanic to hold that rank in the modern Navy,
Rivero was vice chief of naval operations and NATO command-
er-in-chief in southern Europe before retiring. Now, as ambassador
extraordinary and plenipotentiary, he was given the full power of
independent action on behalf of the United States.

Diplomatic protocol required new ambassadors to present their
credentials to the head of state. My father was among the American
dignitaries who accompanied Ambassador Rivero to this event at
the Palacio Real. "You should have seen your boy today all dressed
up in tails when our new ambassador presented his credentials to
General Franco," Mom wrote to Grandma Amerson.

The traditional ceremony was a formal event hundreds of years old,
with costumes harkening back to the monarchy of yore. The Palace
dispatched a liveried coach drawn by fancy horses in shiny harnesses to pick up the ambassador, resplendent in his medal-adorned
Navy uniform. My father and the deputy chief of mission, both
in white tie and tails, as well as several military attachés in bedazzled uniforms, met Ambassador Rivero at the Palace entrance. The
Americans walked up the broad stairway, lined on both sides with
color guards, and then proceeded through the Palace past military
and protocol officers in still more dazzling uniforms to the majestic throne room. They reached the inner sanctum and the awaiting
Generalissimo.

It was like being in a play, Dad said later. In a photograph of the moment, Dad is grasping a pair of white gloves in his left hand, and his right holds the ancient hand of Francisco Franco, dressed in his own theatrical costume sporting sashes and epaulets. Dad's six-foot frame towers over both the diminutive Franco and Ambassador Rivero, who was reported to have said: "The only reason the president picked me is because I'm the only guy they could find who's shorter than Franco."

In a conversation on Cape Cod years later, my long-retired parents offered these personal perspectives on ambassadors.

"Every president has the prerogative of filling embassies with whoever he wishes," my father said. "This is a sore point with most of the professionals. Many of the ambassadors who are chosen for political reasons are disastrous as ambassadorial material. The career people would like to see more people rising through the ranks to become ambassadors."

My mother offered a practical point as to why political appointments of ambassadors might hold sway. "One of the factors is that, especially in the big posts, you've got to have money, because foreign service officers are not given funds to entertain each other," she said. "In Rome, I remember, the budget we were given was $2.50 a person for a cocktail party, but only for Italian guests—we would host an equal number of Americans, but we paid for those people ourselves."

Dad added, "The apparent stinginess of 'representational funds' goes back to some abusers or jealousies on the part of Congress, which, after all, approves the line budget item limiting how much the Foreign Service will have to spend." My father parodied imagined politicos: "'These cookie pushers, ya know, those striped pants boys, they're gonna spend money like water if you give 'em the chance.' So, if you want to do the job right, you have to pay it out of your own pocket."

* * *

My mother and her peers subscribed to the view that foreign service couples were, together, integral to the mission. Like my parents, most of their embassy colleagues were extremely close and good friends. Now and then, there was a wife who seemed less than enthusiastic about some of the group's efforts, but this was rare, and the void was usually filled by the collective without making a major fuss.

Mom knew that her work helped contribute that spring to Dad's promotion to grade one, the credential that the outgoing ambassador had desired in his PAO. Dad was now at the top of the USIA career ladder. My mother was justifiably proud of their achievement and did not take it lightly. "Each year when the list comes out there are many sad people, so our fingers were crossed," she wrote to Grandma Amerson.

However, there began to be inklings of some wives feeling they were being taken advantage of. A 1971 State Department task force reported: "Wives in the foreign service are individuals, with their own value systems and their own priorities. Some find the two-for-one expectations a happy opportunity to share in the professional interests of their husbands, which promote the interests of their country abroad. Others find the same expectations exploitative of their time and talents." A State Department directive in 1972—the *Pink Paper*—threw cold water over the mutual support that had defined my parents' foreign service life.

"No one was to be asked to do anything," Mom said. "If you heard about something going on, you might volunteer. But it put a pall over all the women."

Now, Mom was getting pushback when she reached out to embassy wives. A case in point was the wife of a new USIS staffer, Cesar Beltrán, a child of the sixties who wore his hair long and shaggy as a sign of independence and his Filipino heritage as a badge of honor. Dad had observed Cesar's feisty style during a visit from a Chicago congressman. Spying Cesar's name tag when the USIS officer arrived at his hotel, Congressman Lapinski was taken aback.

"Beltrán," he said. "Is that an American name?"

"As American as Lapinski, sir," replied the young officer with a sweet smile.

Cesar's wife was fresh from being briefed on the *Pink Paper*. She was determined to be seen as an individual, separate from her husband. When Mom offered to take the young woman on some calls, continuing the traditional protocol that helped acquaint new arrivals to the embassy team, Ms. Beltran would have none of it. Nor would she host gatherings at their home for her husband's business contacts. She would not be seen as a servant.

The jettisoning of the helpmate tradition that had given my mother purpose felt like a personal loss.

* * *

At the end of the summer, the four of us drove south to Málaga to take the overnight ferry across the Mediterranean to Italy for a family vacation. The night before we sailed, Dad and I went to the hotel bar, where he bought me a mixed drink for the first time. It was a Tom Collins, gin tingling in Andalucia lemons. After a year of rum and Cokes, Brandy Alexanders, and sangria, it was almost touching to be introduced to a new drink by my father. We were not often just the two of us.

"*Salud, amor, y pesetas*," I toasted Dad: health, love, and money. It was one of the first drinking phrases I learned in the alleyways around Plaza Mayor.

"*Cin cin!*" Dad said. Cheers. "Time to get some Italian practice." He sipped from his drink. "Have I told you how proud I am of you?"

"Sure," I said. "The Olivetti says it all." The portable typewriter was his graduation gift, kind of a technical upgrade from India ink and dip pens.

"Your words will take you far." He took another sip. "But, first, it's good to look back, eh?"

The ferry dropped us in Genoa. We shot down to Pisa—avoiding the terrible roads and tourist traffic around Cinqueterre—to take corny pictures of Susie and me holding up the Leaning Tower. Lunch at a small trattoria took a delicious two hours, from first course—*prosciutto e melone*, ham and melon—to dessert—*frutta e formaggio*, fruit and cheese. Equally luscious was letting Italian cascade around us. We had been away for nearly a decade.

We spent the afternoon in Florence's Uffizi Gallery on the top floor of the Renaissance palace of the ruling Medici family, strolling past iconic images like Botticelli's Venus rising from a scallop shell. We had a copy of the painting on a tile in our first-floor bath, along with other masterpieces reproduced by EDART Roma. It was odd seeing something so personally familiar on a museum wall. We overnighted near the Piazzale Michelangelo, from which the medieval city shimmered ochre and tan across the Arno.

Lunch the next day was in Bologna, where Dad was quick to show the waiter that we were no strangers to the Fat City. "*Si mangia bene a Bologna la grassa,*" he said. One eats very well in Bologna the Fat.

The waiter lifted his chest with pride, "*Sempre.*" Always. He recommended the traditional tortellini in the eponymous meat sauce. The pasta pockets relinquished their dollop of cheese as gently as a dandelion releases its fairy seeds.

After lunch, we went looking for our past. My first-grade Italian school was not in session, but the villa looked as forbidding as ever. The whir of the Mercedes' tires over the pebble driveway evoked the memory of being driven to school in its station wagon on the day that a black blood blister blossomed on my thumb when it got slammed in the car door. We drove past our old house with the snail-track rose garden. It was smaller than I remembered.

The next day, we traveled north to lake country, retracing the routes of weekend trips from our long-ago life in Milan. In the romantic walled-in town of Sirmione, we took a motorboat out on Lake Garda and had lunch on the water. Susie and I were more or less patient as Dad had us pose, lifting wine glasses to recreate the black and white photo of ourselves doing the same thing a dozen years before.

We wound our way home along the French Riviera, where hot pink bougainvillea bloomed against the white-walled houses overlooking the pebbled beaches and azure waters. We lingered over a few more lunches under grape arbors and a few more sublime dinners by candlelight. We spent the final night of our family vacation in the Principality of Andorra, a tiny autonomous microstate nestled into the Pyrenees between France and Spain. Over mid-morning coffee, Susie and I flicked dead flies at each other across the white tablecloth.

It was time to go home.

* * *

The school year once again got underway. With her boyfriend gone to college in Florida and ready for more challenging academics, Susie had transferred from Torrejón to the American School for her junior year. She was quickly enthused and among new friends. "Sue says her school is 100 percent better than last year," my mother wrote home.

My college choice that seemed so wonderfully simple a few months earlier was a little more complicated up close.

For starters, like traditional American college students, I expected to move out of my parents' home and into a university dorm. However, the American norm was not replicated in the Spanish experience. Only students who were far from home were forced into the dormitory system, where things were glum and uncomfortable, not fun and sociable. The other Americans enrolled in my

University of Madrid program were embedded with local *familias,* so I kept living at home, like other *madrileñas.*

I also wasn't an American college student like the others in my study abroad program. They were two and three years older than me with college and dorm life under their belts, and most of them were first-time travelers. The orientation trip to the seaside town of Sitges, south of Barcelona, revealed our differences—the group's collective Spanish was awful, their fascination with drinking and bars was old hat, and I completely missed the gist of their jokes.

The coursework for the American students also came easily to me, and classes were over by one.

I had way too much time on my hands.

* * *

My new Spanish boyfriend took up some of the slack.

I met Enrique while vacationing with a high school friend, Kay, at her family's beachside home south of Valencia. Kay was going to college in the United States in August, and her father, also with the embassy, was being transferred, so this was her last stay in a place that had grown dear to her.

The "dear to her" part picked us up on the single-lane road where the bus dropped us off.

"*Hola,*" he said, shaking my hand, "Rogelio."

Rogelio's fraternal twin brother Enrique, who ran the art gallery in town, joined us for lunch. He didn't have Rogelio's intelligent eyes and social ease, but he was tall, dark, and not ugly, and he drove a red Morris Mini. The twins' best friend, Jesús, tagged along, and his witty repartee from the back seat was all the conversation I needed.

Cuba Libres and Brandy Alexanders, slow dancing to loud music, and fast drives in the dark on the winding coastal road didn't require one word. Kay and I slept until noon, breakfasted on *café con leche*, warm crusty bread, and fresh melon, and worked on our tan lines.

It had been great fun, but I was ready to say good-bye to the boys at the end of the week when they drove us to Madrid. While Rogelio and Kay engaged in a long farewell, Enrique announced that he was staying in Madrid for a while and that he would see me Friday.

So, I had a full-time Spanish *novio*, and it didn't take long after Kay's departure for Rogelio to take up with my pretty blond classmate Jeanie. Like me, Jeanie was right out of high school, although hers had been in Indonesia. She was the daughter of Dutch parents who had repatriated to a town just outside Amsterdam. Jeanie was as odd as I was, and we fit perfectly together.

The four of us, and sometimes Jesús, got coffee downtown, ate late dinners on the Avenida El Generalissimo, and discoed on the Avenida José Antonio. I attended the twins' twenty-first birthday party at the family *finca*, a farm about forty miles outside Madrid, where the boys played at toreador in the town's small bullring. I even got behind the wheel of Enrique's Morris Mini, but only in the village.

While we were moving or kissing, it was fun. Enrique gave me his ID bracelet and a silver half-coin on a chain, the companion of which he wore around his neck. Then came the day in November just before my eighteenth birthday when Enrique showed up at the university with a buzz cut for his compulsory military deployment. Shorn of his hair, he lost his appeal. That weekend, with the Mini parked under the short oak trees in the Casa de Campo, I told Enrique that I couldn't be his *novia* anymore. I cried. He cried.

And then, far too quickly, he took back the ID bracelet and the coin necklace.

* * *

The semester ended, and Christmas came. Susie and I placed the figurines on the mossy tabletop. The four of us ate tacos on Christmas Eve and opened presents on Christmas Day. On New Year's Eve, Susie turned sixteen and celebrated downtown with new friends from the American School. Mom and Dad went to the Marine Ball.

I stayed home and ate. Food binges had moved into the space that thumb sucking had once occupied, rescuing me from feelings of inadequacy while also serving as a twisted personal revenge on the powers that pushed me toward perfection.

Mari Cruz and Brigi had the night off. The basement was mine. I started with the ice cream-stuffed orange shells in the extra freezer, scraping slivers off one, and then another, and then all of them, pushing the shell tops down hard to hide my theft. Not enough.

I went down the hall to the pantry and dipped my hand into the dark brown sugar box, seeking a hard nugget to suck on but losing it to saliva and shoving my hand in again and again until my fingers were gooey and grainy. Not enough.

I moved into the kitchen and found the fresh loaves of bread Brigi had bought for our holiday. I pulled out wads of dough and pushed them into my mouth with my sugary fingers. When all I had was a crusty shell, I found some American butter in the refrigerator and slathered it on the carbohydrate exoskeleton, barely chewing as I downed it. My stomach started to hurt. I was tired. I went to bed.

Food anchored me, weighing me down both literally and figuratively. Floundering in a life with little structure and few friends and trying to pull away from home while living in the heart of it, I was drowning.

What I needed was a life raft.

5. FIRE

In January 1973, Richard Nixon began his second term as president with the announcement that the Vietnam War was over. Nixon's groundbreaking trip to China in February 1972—what the president referred to as "the week that changed the world"—and his visit to Russia later that same year laid the foundation for the Paris Peace Accords by relaxing those countries' support of the Hanoi government. Nixon overcame his anti-communist instincts to create a great moment in American foreign policy.

However, the Watergate scandal would drive Nixon from office in August 1974 as my father and mother, by then in Rome, listened on the radio. Richard Nixon had been high in Dad's esteem in 1958 Caracas for his graciousness under pressure, but my parents had not voted for Nixon. His resignation was a reminder that American democracy operated under the rule of law.

* * *

Dad found a new hobby—partridge hunting on Sundays.

A group from the embassy drove an hour out from Madrid, where local organizers carted the Americans off, two to a blind. A dozen local boys drove the quail-like birds toward the hidden hunters.

Drawing on his years of hunting pheasants in South Dakota, Dad peered around and over the blind, calculating which of the speeding dots might materialize into a shot, when to aim, and how soon to pull. There was something primal about feeling the kick at the shoulder and the exultation when he did everything right, and the bird dropped.

Dad brought home a couple of garbage bags full of quails. Although he handled the plucking and cleaning out in the garage, the stench of death followed those birds down to the kitchen, and the random metal shot left an unpleasant tang on the tongue as you chewed.

* * *

That spring, Washington cabled Dad to say he was to head a USIA inspection team in Iran, where Shah Reza Pahlavi was still firmly in power. The United States supported the Shah's repressive regime as a bulwark against the USSR, just across Iran's northern border.

Dad's first brief visit to Tehran was on his way to Vietnam in 1970. Now, with two weeks in which to observe the American-Iranian relationship, my father perceived that beneath the surface simmered strong emotions against the Shah and inevitable resentment of America for its support. His report praised the USIS binational center—a vibrant complex where young people could learn English, read uncensored American books, and participate in candid discussions—for continuing to shine the light of democracy, nonetheless.

Six years later, Iran would explode into revolution, banishing the Shah, and installing religious extremists. The embassy in Tehran was captured, and fifty-two American diplomats were held as hostages for 444 days.

* * *

I grew fat on private food binges. I dropped the modern dance class I began in high school and was miserable when we went to see Mom's old dance company—now called Nikolais Dance Theater—when they came through Madrid on a State Department tour. Winter slowly morphed into spring.

I armed my exterior with an exaggerated lisp-y Castilian Spanish, honing my language in conversations with my Art History professor Tuesdays and Thursdays at the Prado. Her boy-cut short hair and lean body reflected an aesthetic I couldn't imagine for myself, but I was consumed by her passion for Velásquez.

My former bus-buddy, David, who was finishing his senior year at

Torrejón, sought me out now and then to listen to jazz near the embassy or to hang out with his DJ friend at a disco down the street. His hissy Puerto Rican Spanish grated on my ears, and he said my lisped language made me "*más papista que el Papa*," more papist than the Pope. I was pleased to show off but didn't warm much to David's courting. He was too young, too formal, and too interested in me.

Instead, I went to a wedding and grabbed another Spaniard for one final embassy kid acting gig.

We knew the Susos through Winona family friends, and it didn't hurt for Suso Wine Products to have an *amigo* in the US Embassy. Mr. Suso enveloped Dad—"*Bohb!*"—in a hearty embrace when we were their guests for lunch and bullfighting at the family's *hacienda* in the fall. The invitation to the wedding of one of their sons arrived at winter's end.

I teased and sprayed my hair so my face didn't look so fat, and I wore one of Mom's dresses, which covered my hips better than what I had in my closet. Black stockings kept my thighs and calves under wraps, and Mom's dark Spanish shawl completed the camouflage. As we moved through the room at the reception, I noticed a swarthy, chiseled man in a cluster of Susos. We approached to congratulate the happy couple, and the stranger's heavy-lidded dark eyes sought mine.

"*Hola*," hi, he said. "*Soy* José Mi," I'm Jose Mi, using the nickname for José Miguel.

"Juanita." I hoped my chins didn't squish together as I smiled.

José Mi smiled back. "*Lo sé.*" I know. His teeth glowed white.

The happy couple, his cousins, were inviting us young people out for dinner, he said. If I would do him the honor, he said, "Geni." He held my hand up to his lips, and called me by my American name, as Fina had all those years ago. *Geni.*

"José Mi," I said. I loved how that very Spanish name put stars in my eyes.

So, Geni and José Mi became an item, but our affair was primarily conducted long-distance. He was usually on the road in northern Spain for Susa Wines, traveling from town to town by car. One week, I got three postcards, each with a sentence or so about how I was in his heart. It was great stuff. When he was in town a couple of times a month, we hung out at restaurants with the Suso cousins and then retreated to my living room couch for long, exciting clinches.

One Friday afternoon, I got a telephone call from Zaragoza, about three hours northeast of Madrid. José Mi had been in a very bad car accident and was in the hospital. He was in a body cast from his neck to his hips but was expected to make a full recovery.

In an instant, I decided to rush to his side. The timing was perfect—I could go on Saturday, spend a few hours at the hospital, and then return home well before Monday morning classes.

My mother tried to talk me out of it. "Honey," she said, "Spaniards don't do this. Unless you want him to take you more seriously."

"Mom, I have to go."

I knew she was right. He had been talking about all this long-term stuff. After all, I was his *novia*, a word that translated as "fiancée." In conservative 1973 Spain, you were either *amigos*, friends, or you were engaged.

I had deflected his comments with vague responses like, "Well, we'll see." Now, I didn't care if I appeared too serious. It was just too romantic of an opportunity to pass up.

My eight-hour round trip train ride resulted in a fifteen-minute visit with a woozy patient, a three-hour conversation with his best friend, and sleeping in a berth across from two Spanish soldiers in uniform. Conservative mores and Franco's grip on Spanish society protected this impulsive American during her foolhardy errand.

José Mi's accident limited his trips to Madrid. Telephone calls couldn't compete with clinches on the couch, and our lust diminished as the summer heat rose. The rest of his romantic allure evaporated when he decided he wanted to be called just José.

Plain Joe, there was no sexiness in that.

* * *

As the final quarter of the university year droned on, an unlikely venture collided with a potentially deadly event.

Susie and I had helped a local record producer cut two songs the previous summer. It had been a fun, short project involving singing bubblegum pop lyrics into a microphone just like in the movies. It seemed highly unlikely that anything would come of it.

However, the producer called one morning in early spring to announce that the record was coming out. We had a publicity shoot in the morning, and radio and television events were in the offing. I went to bed early to get a pop star's beauty sleep.

I was startled out of my sleep by the sound of thudding. My waking thought was that clumsy robbers were in the house, but when I opened my bedroom door, I smelled smoke. Orange flickers lit the stairwell. I dashed to Mom and Dad's room and then to Susie's. "Fire! There's a fire downstairs!"

I followed Dad to the first floor through a cloud of acrid smoke. Flames were licking at the drapes in the smaller of the two living rooms. I ran to the basement to alert Brigi and Mari Cruz and to get our cocker spaniel outside to the walled-in garden, where Dad was assembling several lengths of garden hose.

"*¡Fuego! ¡Fuego!*" he yelled. Fire, fire! In his journal, my father the linguist later recognized that the word he should have used was "*incendio.*"

Wrong vocabulary notwithstanding, there was no reaction from the neighboring apartment buildings. Mom brought Susie through the smoke into the garden and ran back inside to call the fire department. She rejoined us as Dad dragged the hose into the house and sprayed at the base of the flames. Steam and smoke filled the first floor. By the time the firemen showed up, Dad had put out the fire.

The cause of the blaze was an overheated transformer, standard equipment used to convert the standard European 220-volt power to 110 volts in homes with American-made electronic equipment like our stereo and tape recorder. The only permanent damage was to the curtains, a few furniture pieces, and Dad's painting of Lorenzo de'Medici, after the Macchietti portrait in the Uffizi. Lorenzo was the only loss we mourned. But the entire house stank of burned plastic, a cloying, fishy smell that hung in the air for weeks.

The stench was heavy in the air when the record producer showed up a couple of hours after dawn to ferry us to the Sierra Nevada mountains for the photo shoot. Though we knew our hair smelled of smoke, we reveled in the fresh air. Two weeks later, we lip-synched the record on national television, and I did an interview on a local radio station.

On her way home alone one evening, Susie was robbed of her shoulder bag by a group of boys. She was not hurt, but the psychological and physical shock of being attacked in our safe Madrid had a lasting effect. When Dad opened the front door and saw her girlish face with tears welling up in her eyes, it broke his heart.

Franco's grip was loosening, and our Spain was changing.

6. FINA

B y the early summer of our second year in Spain, the immediate
future seemed secure. I was packed up to continue my studies
as a transferring sophomore at Hiram College in Ohio, which we
would visit as part of a scheduled home leave. When my family returned to Madrid, Susie would be a senior at the American School,
and Mom and Dad would continue working as the PAO team for
two more years.

Then, Washington called. President Nixon and Henry Kissinger,
the new secretary of state, had tapped Nixon's secretary of transportation, John Volpe, to be the new ambassador to Italy. James
Keogh, a former Nixon campaign aide and speechwriter who was
now the director of USIA, needed a man of Dad's experience—fluency in Italian and knowledge of the country—as PAO in Rome.
This was not a request. It was an order.

Years later, in a conversation with other retirees on Cape Cod, my
mother recalled how my father delivered the news. "Bob took me
to an Italian movie. On the way home, he asked me, 'How would
you like to live in Rome again?' And I said, 'Well, love to visit, but
no.' And he said, 'We're going.'"

Dad, a master of public diplomacy, could never finesse a smooth
approach when breaking the news to my homebody mother.

Mom was aghast. Leaving our lovely Spain? And with Susie finally
settled in school? In the end, Mom had to accept—we all had to
accept—that our family was leaving Spain. Dad emphasized the
positive—how great it had been to see Italy the prior summer, and
how returning was a privilege few ever got.

He had even secured a spot for Susie in the incoming senior class at
the Overseas School of Rome. Lucky her, and how strange in this

ever-forward lifestyle, to be able to graduate from the same school she began in kindergarten all those years ago.

I was already halfway gone. I accepted a parting gift from a forlorn José, a set of *jota* music tapes from his part of Spain. "Perhaps you will return," he said, "and we can listen to these together."

"Well, we'll see." It had become my everything-answer.

* * *

My family had a final visit to make before leaving Spain: a reunion with our dear Josefina. Fina was retired from Venezuelan domestic work as a relatively rich woman, and she was living on the family farm in La Coruña, a village in the region of Galicia about six hours northwest of Madrid.

The flat beige landscape of Castilla gave way to the lush hills of Galicia, and soon we were in the region's capital—and pilgrimage holy ground—Santiago de Compostela. The five-star Parador Santiago de Compostela, a thirteenth-century edifice providing lodging and shelter to religious pilgrims, was part of Spain's national network of convents, castles, and other landmark buildings across the country that the government maintained in stellar shape to encourage regional tourism. Our four-course Galician seafood dinner confirmed Mom's wisdom in making the reservation. We slept deeply in our four-poster double beds.

The next morning, we drove through the city of La Coruña and into the countryside toward Fina's family farm. Mom and Dad had their windows cracked open, and the summer air flowed in, warm and green.

The Mercedes pulled off the hardtop and onto the rutted dirt drive, sending chickens and dry corn cobs flying. A couple of skinny dogs slowly padded away. From the back seat, I could see several stone buildings bobbing in and out of sight, their thatched roofs shaded by a small grove of trees. We hit another pothole. Dad muttered.

Mom reached for the dashboard.

The road widened as we approached the largest of the rustic buildings. Hay tumbled from a covered stable adjoining the house, what in Maryland would have been a carport. Dad pulled to a stop where a steep stone stoop jutted out of the dirt, and we clambered out.

The front door opened. A stocky woman started down the steps. She wore a button-down jumper over a sweater and the sturdy stockings and footwear of country folk. Her hair was dyed black and recently styled, her brows revealing the grey, her mouth held self-consciously over an uneven set of teeth.

"Geni . . . Susi . . . *Señor y Señora* . . ." It was Fina. Thirteen years stood awkwardly between us. Mom pushed the years aside. "*Querida* Fina," dear Fina, she said, hugging our long-ago friend.

Dad had his hand extended as Mom disengaged Fina. "*Hola,* Josefina."

"*Bienvenido, Señor* Amerson," welcome, Fina said as she pumped my father's hand. She dipped her head in a noble nod. "*Mi casa es su casa.*" My home is your home.

How long she had waited for this moment. Our house in Caracas had been her house, and now she could finally return the kindness.

She looked over at Susie and me. "*Mis niñas,*" my girls, she said, hiding her teeth behind one hand as she smiled.

We approached Fina, and her strong arms pulled us to her dark padded bosom. At that moment, we were Fina's babies once again. It was hard to know how much I remembered and how much I absorbed through the black and white photos, home movies, and reel-to-reel tapes from the years in Caracas. Fina holding me as I waved at Mommy. Fina hugging us both by the front door. Fina counting with us to ten and singing *Feliz Cumpleaños,* Happy Birthday. One thing was for sure—she had filled our home with loads of love.

Fina released Susie and me and led the way up the stone steps and into the house. The morning sun glanced off the rough beige walls of the kitchen, where a tiny old woman swathed in black stood hunched over a bubbling vat.

"*Mi tía* Maria," Fina said, introducing Aunt Maria.

Tía Maria gave us a shy, gummy smile and kept stirring. "*Conejo,*" rabbit, she said.

I hoped that it was true that the meat tasted like chicken. We took our places at a large wooden table as Fina retrieved small glasses from the shelf above the sink.

A man came through the front door carrying a couple of jugs. "*Muy buenos días.*" Good morning.

"*Mi hermano* Manuel," Fina said, her hand on her brother Manuel's shoulder.

This was the brother who wrote us on Fina's behalf, saying that she was back in La Coruña to care for her elders. He didn't have to say that Fina was illiterate. Mom did not expect an answer to her annual Christmas card—she updated Josefina's address, and here we all were. Manuel put the jugs on the counter and shook hands with Dad and Mom. He uncorked one of the jugs and filled the small glasses with an amber liquid.

"*Vino para celebrar,*" wine for celebrating, he said as he sat a full glass down in front of each of us.

"*A familia,*" to family, Dad said, raising a glass toward Fina.

"*A familia,*" Fina echoed as she lifted her glass toward us.

We sipped as Fina brought two long baguettes to the table and cut each into chunks. The bread tempered the acidity of the local wine, and each chewy mouthful went down smoothly. Tía Maria ladled steaming golden spoonfuls of meat onto plates, the juices shiny with oil and tinged saffron orange.

Fina brought the first plate to Dad. "*Gracias,* Fina." Thank you, he said.

I watched Mom and Dad as the rest of us were served. How they had matured in this foreign service life. It had been fifteen years since the three of them—Mom, Dad, and Fina—listened for the roar of Pérez Jiménez' airplane overhead as the dictator left Venezuela. Milan tempered my parents' newbie optimism, Bologna gave them scholarly perspective, and, in Rome, they rose to the White House's expectations. Bogotá connected with their hearts. Mom's unexpected banishment in Rockville was coupled with huge steps forward in Dad's career. And Madrid? Madrid had been like falling in love with their chosen work all over again.

"*¿Te gusta,* Geni?" Do you like it, Fina asked me, as she put another loaf of bread on the table.

"*Oh, sí,*" oh, yes, I said, putting a forkful of meat into my mouth. It did taste like chicken. I soaked a chunk of bread in the amber juices and packed my fork. More wine. More bread. More rabbit.

As I watched Fina bustle around the table, I thought back to the women who had stepped into Fina's shoes as our custodian. The vain Maria Pia in Milan; canny Angela in Bologna; Giovanna of the lofty dreams in Rome; humble and kind Julia and Rosanna in Bogotá; the sisters, Brigi and Mari Cruz, for whom we had become family these past two years. Eight women in all had been part of my upbringing, part of our story.

Mom tried to help clear the table.

Fina protested. "*Ay, no.*" She moved the dishes to the sink and retrieved a small bundle from a drawer in a nearby cabinet. "*Sus cartas,*" your letters, she said, laying all of Mom's Christmas cards on the table.

Mom and Fina sorted through the envelopes, pulling out the photographs. Here were little Susie and me on the terrace in Milan; on the beach in Capri; in the backyard in Bogotá. Two girls blooming from novice Americans to practiced teenagers in America, me in my pompon outfit, Susie in her cheerleading uniform.

"*Mucho tiempo*," a long time, Mom said at last.

We stood to go. A round of handshakes. Manuel took the photograph of Fina and the Amersons—her *niñas* on one side of her, the *señores* on the other—that inspired the illustration that opens this chapter.

Fina stood in the dusty farmyard as we drove off, waving until we rounded the curve and hit the blacktop.

What I didn't know then is that Marcos Pérez Jiménez, the dictator who Fina, Mom, and Dad had heard flying over our Caracas house into exile, was at that minute living just outside of Madrid, where he would die in 2001.

The circles kept closing.

7. Leaving

Our household effects were packed into a truck bound for Rome, while my Olivetti typewriter, rhyming dictionary, and thesaurus were in a steamer trunk labeled "Hiram, Ohio."

 It was time to go. The embassy needed the house empty to clean and paint in advance of the next PAO's arrival, and Brigi and Mari Cruz were ready for a vacation before getting rolling with the next family. Our goodbyes were sincere, but tearless. Mom added their home addresses to her Christmas card list.

Dad pushed Washington to allow for a week's vacation before his required Washington briefings.

We spent the week in Scotland and England.

My great-great-grandfather Robb had traveled to America from Paisley, Scotland. Our Scottish, Norwegian, and German ancestors formed part of the wave of northern Europeans who would populate the center of our country in the latter part of the eighteenth century. The Robbs were letter writers, poets, readers, and thinkers.

My Grandpa Robb's creative musings were baked into his chemistry long before he ever took pen to pad. Maybe mine, too.

We flew into Edinburgh, where we spent the night in a small B&B in the shadow of the looming medieval castle that dominates the city. Exploring the town after our morning tea and scones, we heard bagpipes—like those in Piazza Navona all those Christmases ago—and followed the sound into a tartan gift shop. Mom soon found the red plaid belonging to the Robb clan and picked some up as gifts for Grandma and Uncle Jim.

Dad braved the left-driving traffic—while Mom gripped the glove box—and we motored west to Paisley. Another small hotel there served us shandies, a beer and lemonade combination that should have tasted awful but was quenchingly fresh. There wasn't much of anything to see or do. After all the years of wondering about Paisley, from where her ancestor had traveled to America, Mom must have been disappointed.

I didn't care one way or the other. I was in full teenager mode, heavy through my thighs and clipped in speech. I couldn't wait to get away from this. From them.

Another long day in the back of the car and we got to the Cotswolds, managing to argue ourselves out of lunch in Stratford-Up-on-Avon by waiting until we were famished, and the restaurants were full. The charm of the fairytale thatched roofs was lost on a hungry family. The next day's shopping on London's Carnaby Street was a much better experience.

I wore my new mod overalls onto the plane to the States.

Part VIII

America

(1973-74)

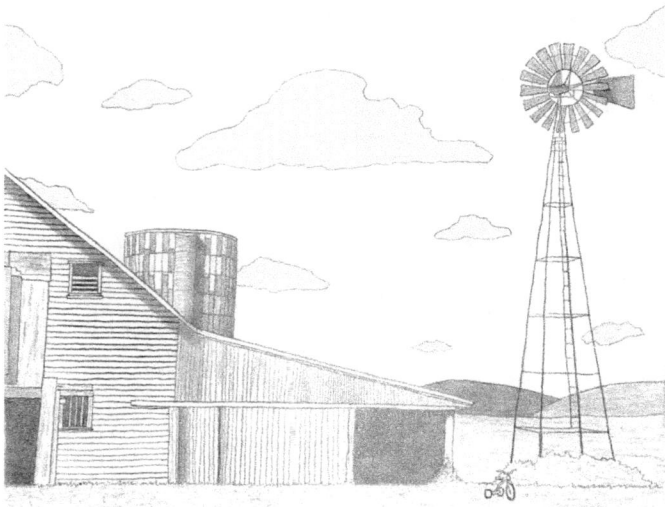

*Home Leave Territory and the family
that inhabit it are still sacred.*

1. AMERICA

After two summers in Spain's dry heat, Washington in July was like walking face-first into a steaming washcloth. We stayed indoors. Although we weren't far from the sights of the city—a foreign service friend had loaned us his apartment on Dupont Circle—the heat and humidity made for heavy going, and there were no sidewalk cafés to stop at for *refrescos*, refreshments.

While Dad was in meetings at USIA, Mom called family, and Susie and I hunted down old friends. My sister's pals were still right where she left them, ready for their senior year at Churchill. I called Alice, probably for the first time since eighth grade, but she was working in Appalachia, her mother said. I tried a few of the girls I hadn't alienated during my year of being a girlfriend, but they, too, were scattered by college and work. Just one, Ruth, picked up when I called. Our conversation was enthusiastic but superficial. I wished I had stayed in closer touch. I had very little practice in returning to a place.

I spent the afternoon with my old boyfriend drinking beer on the shores of the Potomac, the heat and the alcohol adding to my feelings of regret. The intimacy was disappointingly mechanical. I was lonelier than ever.

We did not drive out to Potomac Woods, where renters were in our house. We weren't really back.

It had never been home.

* * *

We drove west in our familiar positions—Susie and I each on our sides of the back seat, Mom riding shotgun with the map open on her lap, and Dad behind the wheel of the rental car. As we left the Beltway, we crossed the border between Washington and the rest of America.

About noon, Dad pulled into a Pennsylvania rest stop. We joined the herd walking into the main building. I held the swinging glass door open for the people behind us, keeping a polite smile on my face. As they barged through without making eye contact or saying a word, I noticed how the seams of one mother's stretch pants made her bulging stomach look like buttocks.

I caught Dad's eye. "Ass backwards," I said, in Spanish.

He smiled his approval of my wit and tilted his head in the family's receding wake.

"Whom we represent," he said, in Italian.

Susie and I joined Mom in the ladies' room line. The teenager ahead of us was spilling out of her cutoffs, and her mother's hair was in curlers. Both were sucking from liter-sized plastic cups with huge orange straws, the insides of their lips dyed Maori blue. A woman passed us on her way out of the toilets, dragging paper from her heel like a sorry train.

When we got back in the car, Mom sighed. "Not quite Spain, is it?"

"*Brutta figura*," Dad said. No Italian would have left the house wearing those clothes.

I felt a tugging at my mind—these are your people. I ignored the voice.

* * *

Mid-afternoon, Dad exited the interstate in Ohio. "Time to check this Hiram College out, *non è vero?*"

"Right," I said. A now-familiar panic tightened my chest.

We drove through a few miles of farmland, all rolling hills like southern Minnesota. As we rounded a curve, we came up behind a black horse-drawn buggy.

"Cool," Susie said. "Where are we, Little-House-on-the-Prairi-eland?"

"Amish," I said.

"Pretty weird," she said.

I thought so myself. What century were we in? The speed limit dropped to thirty as we passed the sign announcing the hamlet of Hiram. Hamlet? Had the college literature used that word? Surely, I would have noticed.

Downtown was a convenience store and a post office. No traffic light, just a four-way stop. A short brick wall proclaimed Hiram College. Dad turned onto the deserted campus.

Three connected brick buildings bordered a small plaza to our right; on the left, a quaint, steeple-topped auditorium announced, "Commencement 1973." Further down the block, a white carved eagle and columns presented the entrance to a two-story building.

"Centennial," I said. "That's my dorm."

"Bob, why don't you park, and we can do a proper tour," Mom said.

Dad pulled over.

"No," I said. "I'll be here for orientation in a couple weeks."

There was that old ache to have something that was mine alone. A path I created myself to a place where no one knew who I was.

"You sure?" Mom said.

"Yeah."

"*Va bene?*" Dad said.

"*Andiamo,*" I said.

Let's get outta here.

2. Home Leave Territory

Home Leave Territory materialized with the first A&W just outside Chicago.

We wound our way up the beige Mississippi to Lake Winona's rocky sentinel, Sugar Loaf. Around the lake and up Huff Street, past the ice cream store like the one in Bogotá, past 478 Wilson Street where Grandma used to live before she moved to California with her sister, to the Robb Brothers Store that Uncle Jimmy now ran. We had dinner with our girl cousins.

We followed the Mississippi north to the Twin Cities, land of Aunt Snooky and Uncle Bob, Aunt Jeanie and Uncle Carl, cousins, laughter, potlucks, and singing. They joined us in an Amerson caravan to trek west across the South Dakota border to the rural Hidewood neighborhood of Dad's childhood for fresh sweet corn, hayrides, and laughter at our boy cousins' farm.

We returned to Aunt Snooky's home in South Minneapolis, where my parents and sister changed into fresh clothes for their flight to Europe. I put on the Alpini chorale album Dad had sent his sister when we first lived in Italy. The familiar strains of the close male harmonies awoke a nostalgia I quickly pushed aside. Rome was going to be home again, after all.

It wasn't until Mom, Dad, and Susie drove down the street, took a left, and disappeared that I realized that they were traveling back into the foreign service, and I was not. Home had just left me.

Just like Fina way back in Caracas, I stood on the curb as my family disappeared.

Alone in that big house in South Minneapolis, I turned up the Alpini album and let my heart break.

* * *

Stranded in America (1973)

The four of them
—the two parents, the two daughters, a single package—
arrived from abroad three weeks ago,
causing this American Midwest summer to appear.
As it has in random years since forever,
this familiar Brigadoon materialized just for them:
the sand-barred Mississippi, floating houseboats;
kitchenfuls of family, casseroles, and music;
cornfields and silos slipping away under blue-and-white skies;
harmonies and laughter floating deep into the night.
Every other time, the eldest daughter
has gone away again with them,
as the four return to their splendid isolation
across the universe.
But now, she has outgrown her role.
She watches the three drive away,
and by the time the car turns left and disappears,
Brigadoon has also vanished, and the girl cannot understand
how she will know
what to do next.

* * *

I don't know how long I stood weeping in that South Minneapolis
living room letting waves of Alpini harmony overwhelm me. Many
years later, as I sat with my husband in the Italian Cultural Institute
on Park Avenue at a live performance of the Alpini men's chorus,
the tears came unbidden. This time, they were sweet.

Aunt Snooky's key in the back door snapped the spell. "Yoo-hoo,
Jane!"

I made a dash for the upstairs bathroom. "Be right down!"

I slapped cold water on my face, blew my nose, and took a couple of swipes at my hair.

Alright. The ready-to-be-independent American college student looked back at me.

My aunt was in the kitchen unpacking a farmer's market haul. "Ready for ratatouille?" Uncle Bob carried in boxes brimming with tasseled sweet corn, long snap beans, baseball-sized juicy tomatoes, and zucchini as big as a swaddled newborn.

I pulled out an eggplant, its taut rubbery skin familiar on my fingers. "I guess it was Milan when Mom announced that we were going to be eating something called an eggplant." I smiled. "And I thought, yuck!"

"And then your amazing mother cooked it, and you were hooked," Snooky said. "She was way ahead of us around here with all those different veggies."

"Yeah, Italy," I said. "Eggplants, artichokes, asparagus. Susie and I called arugula 'poison grass.'"

Home might have left, but I was still with people who knew me. I was with family.

I pushed away the comforting thought. This was going to be my year to strike out on my own.

August passed quickly. Laughter with family eased the separation from my parents and sister. Walks around nearby Lake Harriet began pulling off some of my avoidance-eating weight.

Then, I was off to become a real American college kid.

3. ARRIVING

Kathy, the Hiram College student who my family had adopted in Madrid, met me at the Cleveland Airport.

"Jane! You're finally here!" She wrapped her arms around me, smooshing my head into her chest.

I'd forgotten how tall Kathy was. Her gangly enthusiasm seemed even more pronounced that it had in Spain.

"I can't wait to introduce you to your roomie!"

Kathy had brokered this whole thing: Hiram College, my dorm assignment, even my roommate. Her loves were now supposed to be my loves. Never mind that Kathy was a local Ohio girl who I'd only known for a few months.

I sighed as the Ohio farmland slid by the window. This would be just one more post, I decided, another brand-new setting to discover, to master, and to leave. Only, this time, I was on my own.

Things began to fall apart almost immediately. Kathy's choice for the person with whom I would share a tiny dorm room, was reserved, distant, and disinterested. Laura was a Black junior from Youngstown with zero curiosity about where I was from, and there was nothing in her background for me to latch onto.

For the first time in my life, I failed to charm a stranger into being a friend. Laura played her Barry White albums in our little room, while I took my cassette player to the empty football bleachers and listened to João Manuel Serrat while scribbling poems of unhappiness in my journal.

I declared my major as Comparative Literature, hoping to continue living a life of variety with a little Spanish and a little Italian and a little French. In my Latin American authors class, I tried hard to mask my Castilian lisp and to hide my disappointment in the language of my classmates and the unsophistication of my professors. For about a week, I asked people to call me Nita. As in Jua-nita.

I gravitated toward the theater people, the ones who were good at faking it. I was cast as the vamp in the fall production of a Noel Coward play. By the time I flew home for the Christmas break, I had already left behind a couple of boys. Commitment was the last thing I was interested in.

This was all pretend.

* * *

Home also felt unreal. The posh Roman penthouse apartment that came with my father's new PAO job was unfamiliar territory, and Susie had morphed from little sister to independent young woman in the four months of being an only child. It was all darn unsettling.

Two weeks in the guest room barely gave my ears time to tune into Italian before I flew back to the icy fields of rural Ohio and a tiny college I was quickly outgrowing, while disappearing inside myself.

This whole thing was a failure. As the snow melted into sloppy spring puddles around Hiram's little post office, I packed my footlocker and prepared to retreat to Rome, defeated. They would take me in, even if the fit no longer made much sense.

4. LEAVING

Then, in early May, I found traction in a one-time movement class sponsored by the Hiram theater department. Bending and stretching in my old red leotard, I felt more like myself than I had all year. More confident. Almost centered.

The yearning to dance was still there, and, this time, my life stretched ahead, unencumbered by other responsibilities.

I would become a dancer.

Hiram didn't have a dance program, but I discovered that Mom's first mentor, the modern dance pioneer and Broadway choreographer Hanya Holm, was still teaching the summer course Mom had attended in Colorado College. With barely a thought, I signed up, relabeled my footlocker, and hitched a ride to Colorado with a Hiram couple who were headed west to release coyote pups into the wild. They had really sharp teeth—the pups, not the couple.

Halfway there, lying under the stars at a KOA campground in Lawrence, Kansas, I felt sure I was on the right path. The big night sky was oddly comforting to this big city girl.

The Colorado College classes felt like home from the first beat of the floor exercises to the last flying leap across the gym, and the afternoon breakout groups reinforced that, although I was just learning the craft, there was something in me that responded to the challenge of dance in a way more satisfying than anything I'd done before.

This would be the new me.

There was just one problem—people kept calling me June. My dancer roommate and I were similar in size and shape, but June was over-the-top enthusiastic in a way that allowed her voice to carry across the campus. It was inevitable that people confused me for her. "Hi, June!" "I'm Jane." "Oh, right."

It happened once too many times, and then I answered, "Call me Kelly."

It was my middle name, my maternal grandmother's family name. Jane Kelly Amerson. My mother told me that she beat out the rhythm—one, one-two, one-two-three—on the drum she used to teach dance classes at Macalester before I was born. The drum sits in a corner of my family room today.

Jane—Janie, Giovanna, Juanita—had seen me through twenty birthdays. Kelly would take me into the future.

"Call me Kelly."

I leapt into my next life, one more time.

EPILOGUE

R ome was my parents' final overseas post.

Of the enchanting city, my father later said, "Every day was a privilege because of that fabulous place. And the work was interesting, though not without risks. The Red Brigade terrorists—the ones that kidnapped American military people—had our apartment on a list of targets."

My mother was particularly disturbed by the impact of terrorism on one of the symbols of American democracy, the USIS library. Speaking at the Brewster Ladies Library in 2000, she said, "There'd been a bomb at the Rome library some time before and security was on high alert. When I went in for the first time—without introducing myself as the boss' wife—every eye was on me as I walked through the shelves. It was such a saddening experience." She appealed to her audience. "We treasure the freedom of our libraries, and they are such showcases. Anytime you have foreign visitors, bring them here."

Susie graduated from the Overseas School of Rome, then moved to Minnesota to attend our parents' alma mater, Macalester College.

Dad's assignment as Rome PAO came to an end after four years, and America called.

"We'd been overseas for nearly six years," my father later said. "Our daughters were in the States, our mothers too, and we were ready for something else."

* * *

My father's final USIA appointment was as the Edward R. Murrow Fellow in Public Diplomacy at the Fletcher School of Law and Diplomacy at Tufts University in Boston. Boston held a quasi-European charm in its history and architecture and being able to walk everywhere made it feel like home to my mother.

Dad served as the Murrow Fellow for two years. "At that point," he said in his 1988 ADST oral history interview, "although the agency was offering posts in the field, we had done just about everything that was to do in USIA. So, we decided—with a certain amount of regret—to cut the cord and go out into the wide world."

Looking back, he concluded, "I can't imagine a better choice for anyone with my own makeup than a career with USIA in ideas, operations, and communications directly with people overseas. I have never had anything but positive feelings about the agency and the rewards of foreign service."

My parents moved to Cape Cod to what they—and their embassy friends—laughingly called their "terminal home." When a neighbor casually inquired what Mom had done while Dad was in the foreign service, Mom wanted give Ginger Rogers' answer when asked about dancing with Fred Astaire: "I did everything he did, but backwards and in heels." Instead, ever the diplomat, she just smiled and left the room.

In retirement, my father devoted his time to the expression of ideas through language, music, and art, and he played tennis through his eightieth year. My mother dove into community service, and she became a master gardener.

Dad's death in 2006 caught us flat-footed, but he had no regrets. Susie and I sang our Colombian songs at his memorial in South Dakota. Mom died in 2008. Hearing their voices through the words they left behind as my *Embassy Kid* roadmap has been an exquisite pleasure.

And me, Jane Kelly? Dancing helped me find my way to New York City, where the man who would become my husband was waiting in a John Travolta-worthy three-piece white suit to take me on the rest of the adventure. *Saturday Night Fever* was our first movie date.

But perhaps that's a story for another time.

Acknowledgments

I am so very grateful that my parents took the time to document our foreign service life.

My mother was a life-long letter writer, a trait she inherited from her literary Scottish ancestors. Six binders of weekly letters to her parents (1955–1975) allowed me access to her real-time thoughts about the experiences captured in this book.

My father's book about the 1958 revolution that overthrew a Venezuelan dictator and the subsequent attack on Richard Nixon (*How Democracy Triumphed Over Dictatorship: Public Diplomacy in Venezuela*, University Publishing Association, Public University Press, 1994) is woven throughout this book's opening section. My father's journal of his 1970 trip to Vietnam allowed me to write the chapter about that experience.

My parents also created two journals of recollections—*Amersons on the Record* and *The USIA Years*—and spoke about their experiences in a 2000 talk, "Officer and Spouse: The Foreign Service Partnership" at the Brewster Ladies Library on Cape Cod, which I transcribed. My father's 1988 interview by the Association for Diplomatic Studies and Training (ADST) is one of the many ADST oral histories of American diplomats that I have also drawn on in writing this book.

I am grateful to retired USIA foreign service officer Alvin Perlman for his review of an early draft of this book.

Thank you to fellow Embassy Kid and ADST President Susan R. Johnson, and to ADST Deputy Executive Director Lisa Terry for their support and guidance of this project, the first book by the child of an American diplomat in ADST's *Memoirs and Occasional Papers* series. I am also indebted to the ADST peer reviewer who suggested I read Sara Mansfield Taber's memoir, *Born Under an Assumed Name: The Memoir of a Cold War Spy's Daughter,* which showed me it's possible to weave a child's memories and an adult's perspective into one story.

Thank you to editor, poet, and memoirist Margaret Diehl for her thoughtful and thorough early edits and for encouraging me to share the inner life of the child narrator.

To Camila Acosta, *gracias* for finding the heart of this story in your beautiful drawings of places and people which were part of my journey.

My Hudson Valley Writers Guild critique group helped birth the stories that became this book. Thank you to the Florida Writers Association for connecting me with authors, agents, and publishers who helped me tell this story. Thank you to the West Boynton/ Wellington Writers Group for your encouragement, and to Terry Garrity for believing in this book. To the Squirrel Critique Group, a special shout out.

I am deeply indebted to my aunts Jean Brookins, who died in 2021, and Mavis (Snooky) Voigt, who both dug into an early draft of this book when I was sure it was finished. It was not. Home Leave Territory and the family that inhabit it are still sacred.

To my husband Ray—my devoted first reader—and our daughter Victoria, thank you for your steadfast love.

Thank you to my sister, Susan Robb Amerson Hartnett, for being the sweetest soprano to my alto. You are my rock.

Bob and Nancy, true patriots, live on in us.

Related Titles from Westphalia Press

The Limits of Moderation: Jimmy Carter and the Ironies of American Liberalism

The Limits of Moderation: Jimmy Carter and the Ironies of American Liberalism is not a finished product. And yet, even in this unfinished stage, this book is a close and careful history of a short yet transformative period in American political history, when big changes were afoot.

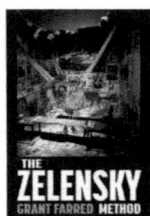

The Zelensky Method
by Grant Farred

Locating Russian's war within a global context, The Zelensky Method is unsparing in its critique of those nations, who have refused to condemn Russia's invasion and are doing everything they can to prevent economic sanctions from being imposed on the Kremlin.

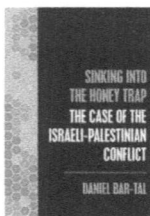

Sinking into the Honey Trap: The Case of the Israeli-Palestinian Conflict
by Daniel Bar-Tal, Barbara Doron, Translator

Sinking into the Honey Trap by Daniel Bar-Tal discusses how politics led Israel to advancing the occupation, and of the deterioration of democracy and morality that accelerates the growth of an authoritarian regime with nationalism and religiosity.

Essay on The Mysteries and the True Object of The Brotherhood of Freemasons
by Jason Williams

The third edition of Essai sur les mystères discusses Freemasonry's role as a society of symbolic philosophers who cultivate their minds, practice virtues, and engage in charity, and underscores the importance of brotherhood, morality, and goodwill.

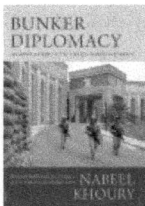

Bunker Diplomacy: An Arab-American in the U.S. Foreign Service
by Nabeel Khoury

After twenty-five years in the Foreign Service, Dr. Nabeel A. Khoury retired from the U.S. Department of State in 2013 with the rank of Minister Counselor. In his last overseas posting, Khoury served as deputy chief of mission at the U.S. embassy in Yemen (2004-2007).

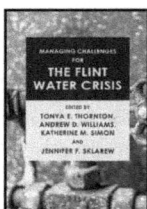

Managing Challenges for the Flint Water Crisis
Edited by Toyna E. Thornton, Andrew D. Williams, Katherine M. Simon, Jennifer F. Sklarew

This edited volume examines several public management and intergovernmental failures, with particular attention on social, political, and financial impacts. Understanding disaster meaning, even causality, is essential to the problem-solving process.

User-Centric Design
by Dr. Diane Stottlemyer

User-centric strategy can improve by using tools to manage performance using specific techniques. User-centric design is based on and centered around the users. They are an essential part of the design process and should have a say in what they want and need from the application based on behavior and performance.

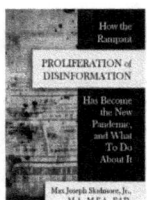

How the Rampant Proliferation of Disinformation Has Become the New Pandemic, and What To Do About It by Max Joseph Skidmore Jr.

This work examines the causes of the overwhelming tidal wave of fake news, misinformation, disinformation, and propaganda, and the increase in information illiteracy and mistrust in higher education and traditional, vetted news outlets that make fact-checking a priority.

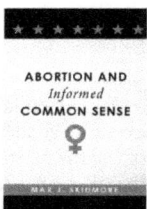

Abortion and Informed Common Sense
by Max J. Skidmore

The controversy over a woman's "right to choose," as opposed to the numerous "rights" that abortion opponents decide should be assumed to exist for "unborn children," has always struck me as incomplete. Two missing elements of the argument seems obvious, yet they remain almost completely overlooked.

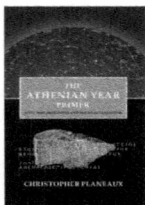

The Athenian Year Primer: Attic Time-Reckoning and the Julian Calendar
by Christopher Planeaux

The ability to translate ancient Athenian calendar references into precise Julian-Gregorian dates will not only assist Ancient Historians and Classicists to date numerous historical events with much greater accuracy but also aid epigraphists in the restorations of numerous Attic inscriptions.

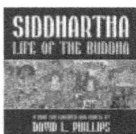

Siddhartha: Life of the Buddha
by David L. Phillips,
contributions by Venerable Sitagu Sayadaw

Siddhartha: Life of the Buddha is an illustrated story for adults and children about the Buddha's birth, enlightenment and work for social justice. It includes illustrations from Pagan, Burma which are provided by Rev. Sitagu Sayadaw.

Growing Inequality: Bridging Complex Systems, Population Health, and Health Disparities
Editors: George A. Kaplan, Ana V. Diez Roux, Carl P. Simon, and Sandro Galea

Why is America's health is poorer than the health of other wealthy countries and why health inequities persist despite our efforts? In this book, researchers report on groundbreaking insights to simulate how these determinants come together to produce levels of population health and disparities and test new solutions.

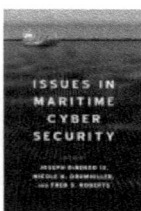

Issues in Maritime Cyber Security
Edited by Dr. Joe DiRenzo III, Dr. Nicole K. Drumhiller, and Dr. Fred S. Roberts

The complexity of making MTS safe from cyber attack is daunting and the need for all stakeholders in both government (at all levels) and private industry to be involved in cyber security is more significant than ever as the use of the MTS continues to grow.

Female Emancipation and Masonic Membership: An Essential Collection
By Guillermo De Los Reyes Heredia

Female Emancipation and Masonic Membership: An Essential Combination is a collection of essays on Freemasonry and gender that promotes a transatlantic discussion of the study of the history of women and Freemasonry and their contribution in different countries.

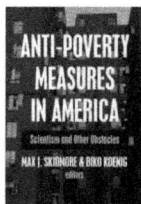

Anti-Poverty Measures in America: Scientism and Other Obstacles
Editors, Max J. Skidmore and Biko Koenig

Anti-Poverty Measures in America brings together a remarkable collection of essays dealing with the inhibiting effects of scientism, an over-dependence on scientific methodology that is prevalent in the social sciences, and other obstacles to anti-poverty legislation.

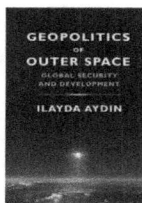

Geopolitics of Outer Space: Global Security and Development
by Ilayda Aydin

A desire for increased security and rapid development is driving nation-states to engage in an intensifying competition for the unique assets of space. This book analyses the Chinese-American space discourse from the lenses of international relations theory, history and political psychology to explore these questions.

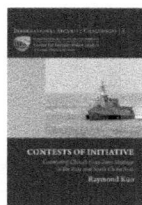

Contests of Initiative: Countering China's Gray Zone Strategy in the East and South China Seas
by Dr. Raymond Kuo

China is engaged in a widespread assertion of sovereignty in the South and East China Seas. It employs a "gray zone" strategy: using coercive but sub-conventional military power to drive off challengers and prevent escalation, while simultaneously seizing territory and asserting maritime control.

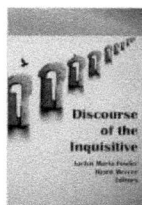

Discourse of the Inquisitive
Editors: Jaclyn Maria Fowler and Bjorn Mercer

Good communication skills are necessary for articulating learning, especially in online classrooms. It is often through writing that learners demonstrate their ability to analyze and synthesize the new concepts presented in the classroom.

westphaliapress.org

Policy Studies Organization

The Policy Studies Organization (PSO) is a publisher of academic journals and book series, sponsor of conferences, and producer of programs.

Policy Studies Organization publishes dozens of journals on a range of topics, such as European Policy Analysis, Journal of Elder Studies, Indian Politics & Polity, Journal of Critical Infrastructure Policy, and Popular Culture Review.

Additionally, Policy Studies Organization hosts numerous conferences. These conferences include the Middle East Dialogue, Space Education and Strategic Applications Conference, International Criminology Conference, Dupont Summit on Science, Technology and Environmental Policy, World Conference on Fraternalism, Freemasonry and History, and the Internet Policy & Politics Conference.

For more information on these projects, access videos of past events, and upcoming events, please visit us at:

www.ipsonet.org